W9-DDV-933

Charles Carroll of Carrollton:

The Making of a Revolutionary Gentleman

by

THOMAS O'BRIEN HANLEY

THE CATHOLIC UNIVERSITY OF AMERICA PRESS

Washington, D.C. 20017

1970

DEDICATION

To my brothers, James and John, with esteem and affection.

TABLE OF CONTENTS

v

Portrait of Charles Carroll of Carrollton
by Sir Joshua Reynolds, London, 1763

PREFACE

Curiosity, idealism, and even envy continue to lead men into the eighteenth century, where the passage of time has left monumental events. Even more striking are the heroic figures who produced these landmarks. The obligation of a professional historian is perhaps the most justifiable reason for going beyond the usual humane need of studying the past to writing about it. Apart from this, I would still have the desire to write about what I have studied of men and events in the eighteenth century.

A call of the spirit, so to speak, brought Carl Sandburg to his moving portrayal of Abraham Lincoln, although he did not call himself a technical historian. My aspiration, I suppose, is also to have some very modest share of this kind of author fellowship. The rich collections of Charles Carroll of Carrollton's writings and not my own presumptions led me to the desire. I have been at pains to see that a great young American in his own words and thoughts comes into communication with any person who is curious about man.

Without troubling this authentic inspiration to biography, the writings of Carroll carried me into what historians would call cultural biography. I found two central themes here, that were very much the focus of his intellectual and social vision: revolutionary thought and a special concept of gentility. This discovery makes clear the direction of his life and its historical significance. There is an overwhelming multiplicity in a great man's life, but cultural biography tells of the simplicity of its thrust. Greatness by historical accident is possible, but not a sustained greatness that is progressive in this unity of moral force. The greatness of Charles Carroll of Carrollton, last living signer of the Declaration of Independence, is seen in such terms.

To pursue the whole life of the man in the manner employed here would have been unsatisfactory and less useful. I therefore have seen Carroll as a young man attaining the age of thirty-seven. In this way, a single volume makes clear the nature of the man and the forces that brought about this particular kind of leader. I take a similar view of the period which follows when he is involved in statesmanship of the War for Independence and formation of the new republic. His later life in terms of historical importance is equal at best to only one of these phases and the quantity of the Carroll collections reflects this proportion.

Out of respect for the literature of the field and contributions to it I have also confined myself to Carroll's earliest period. For the present, Dr. Ellen Hart Smith's one volume biography continues to serve its purpose admirably in its style and scholarship. With somewhat fuller collections now available, and the purpose of extensive detail, I have been able to enlarge what she has written of the period up to 1773. In doing so, I have revised certain topics as treated by her and established many new areas of knowledge regarding Carroll's cultural life. The study accomplished in this fashion suggests exploration of the general topic of how revolutionary leaders tended to emerge and from what background.

Far more than a pedestal has been provided me by the many authors to whom I have turned in moulding the figure of this revolutionary gentleman. Scholars will have to pursue my stated differences with them in the many Carroll manuscripts, in order to get any comprehensive satisfaction. In some more important instances, however, this kind of critical discussion has been briefly done in the documentary notes for the chapters. In the same place is also noted any light which Carroll's experience of the eighteenth century might throw on the current problems of historians. Only in this way can the story of the man progress with the greatest possible clarity. The more important studies related to matters of the various chapters are found in these notes. The traditional bibliography of other works did not seem necessary.

The Maryland Historical Society has been my special patron. Its staff has always been hospitable amid the tedious demands I have made on their excellent library services. Miss Bayly Ellen Marks, until recently Manuscripts Curator, especially has been helpful and Miss Eugenia Calvert Holland, Assistant Curator, who provided materials and suggestions on genealogy. Reverend Redmond A. Burke, C.S.V., former Associate Director of the Catholic University of America Press, was a continual source of encouragement. I am indebted to Mrs. Mary A. Durham for her reading and notations, Mrs. Dianne Francesconi Lyon for assistance with working notes, and Mrs. Kathleen Hanley McGahey for typing parts of the manuscript. To others, who helped so much at the early stages of the study, I wish to express my thanks. I gratefully acknowledge financial grants in aid from Marquette University and the American Philosophical Society. To the Loyola College and Loyola Academy communities I owe a very special debt of gratitude for their very Ignatian spirit of hospitality shown during my residence with them. Mrs. Mary Lee Carroll Muth, a descendant of Charles Carroll of Carrollton, has shown me much kindness in helping my work along. I wish also to thank Mr. Charles Bancroft Carroll for permission to use a reproduction of the painting by Sir Joshua Reynolds of Carroll. The Frick Museum Art Reference Service provided the photographic print. I would like to thank Reverend Edward Gannon, S.J., for proof-reading the galleys and making several helpful suggestions.

August 15, 1970
Washington, D.C.

GENEALOGICAL CHART
Origins of
CHARLES CARROLL OF CARROLLTON
and his
Contemporary Relations

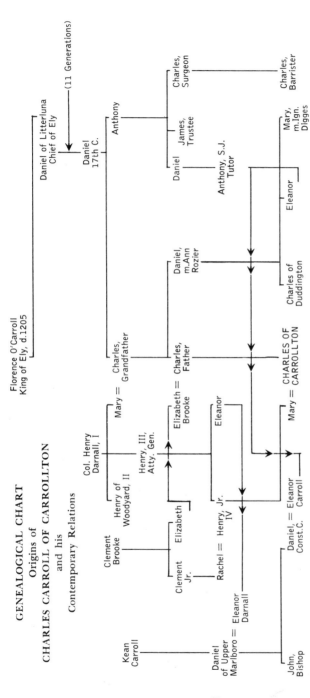

Legend: Only pertinent offspring are noted. Parallel grouping of generations is approximate, terminating more exactly in the last line of names. Marriages are indicated by symbol = ; lines with arrows indicate marriages by female or one branch with another branch of the related families.

Abbreviated or Short References: Grandfather—referred to as the Founder in this study; elsewhere as Carroll the Settler, or Immigrant. **Father**—often known as Carroll of Annapolis, or Doughoregan; but as Charles' father throughout this study. Henry Darnall, III, Atty. Gen. is often confused with Henry, Jr., father-in-law of Charles; the former was the province custom official. James [Carroll], Trustee [of the estate of Charles' grandfather]. Daniel [Member of the Federal Const[itutional] C[onvention] is also known as the Commissioner [of the District of Columbia Commission].

Sources: Carroll Collections—See footnotes for first references of name; Rowland, I, 401 and II, 433-48; Johnson, MHM, I, 66, 184, 294, 376; Bowie, pp. 242-43; MHS Genealogical Files, "Darnall."

x

Chapter 1

REBEL FATHER

Charles Carroll of Carrollton's father had a great influence on the future signer of the Declaration of Independence.* His life also reveals the environment and times in which Charles developed as a Catholic revolutionary gentleman. The year 1720 especially proved critical in this respect and serves as a starting point for the story of Charles' family background. The family traditions and legends which Charles would inherit took root in these troubled times.

Born April 2, 1702, his father, who was also named Charles, had gone to St. Omers College in France at about the age of twelve. His brother Henry was already there, and in a few years his younger brother Daniel joined him to be educated under the Jesuits. The young Carrolls brought the childhood story of their family's origin with them to Europe. As they studied English history, they began to understand how important their father, known as Charles Carroll the Founder, was and took pride in him. He had been born the year of the Stuart Restoration with Charles II, 1660. With the wealth of a landed estate in Ireland in his family, the Founder had obtained an excellent education, culminating in enrollment at Inner Temple, London, for legal studies. With such training, he won a position with William Herbert, Lord Powis, through which he became known to King Charles II, and the king's brother the future James II. As the oppression of English rule fell upon Catholics in Irish estates such as Carroll's, the Founder sought landed wealth in the New World. The Stuarts made generous promises to him, but it was ultimately the ruling proprietary family of the Maryland colony, the Calverts, who rescued the family fortunes and the Founder's career.[1]

Charles Calvert, the Third Lord Baltimore, appointed the Founder his Attorney General of Maryland in 1688, a position which promised handsome emoluments. As it turned out, however, the family fortunes were not to be inaugurated in the New World with Maryland as a sanctuary. Upon his arrival, he found a revolution in progress, which was aimed at overturning Lord Baltimore's proprietary government and removing appointed officials such as Carroll would be. The Carroll children were given to understand the religious character of this revolution in Maryland, which was a counterpart of the Glorious Revolution in England. Catholics often called these events the *Protestant Revolution,* since James II's leniency toward his fellow Catholic

---

* Throughout the book this form of reference to Carroll's father will be used. They both had the same Christian name. Writers have attempted other distinguishing references, but without uniformity and clarity.

dissenters had ignited the flames of rebellion. John Coode led the revolt in Maryland with the particular religious emphasis, which his recently formed Protestant Association gave to it. Yet it was all very complicated, even to mature minds in Maryland. Did not the Revolution place the Crown under the authority of the people's Parliament? On the other hand, was not the people's Assembly in Maryland now subservient to the laws of Parliament for the first time? Protestant dissenters were freed from much oppression by William and Mary with the passage of the English Bill of Rights and Toleration Act; but what of Catholics who were now under disabilities contrary to the Maryland Charter of 1632 and Toleration Acts of 1639 and 1649 which had provided general religious freedom? Rebels are considered on the side of freedom, but was not the Founder, rather than Coode, the rebel in the new era as a royally supervised colony, directly restricted as it was by the power of both Crown and Parliament?[2]

The Founder surely played the role of rebel and his sons at St. Omers relished certain romantic episodes in his career. The English Catholic aristocracy with whom they studied had a propensity for celebrating imprisonments in their life beyond the law, which went back to the penal codes of Queen Elizabeth (the bloody queen in their view). The Marylanders had fellowship with them when their New World haven was suddenly engulfed by the revolutionary storm of 1688. A sturdy fiber of their personalities was being woven of chapters from the life of the Carroll Founder. Imprisoned in 1693 for opposition to the new regime, the Founder threatened in true aristocratic fashion to appeal to high stations in London for redress. He mocked his jailers with the wager that he could secure a bond for a bottle of cider for an imprisoned Catholic of lower status than his own. It was between stays in jail that he married the woman who bore him the three sons who were at St. Omers. He was confused, he wrote to Lord Baltimore, by this "strange rebellion your ungrateful people of this your Lordship's Province have involved themselves in." Lord Baltimore, all the same, found ways within the hostile laws to reward the Founder. By 1707, the Founder had been endowed, or enriched by his own industry with more than six Maryland manors, including Doughoregan which Charles' father and Charles himself would one day possess.[3]

Charles' father had been in college only a few years, when the Founder paid him a visit. This was in 1715, when the Calvert family was reaching a great religious and political crisis. Old Charles Calvert, Third Lord Baltimore, had come to rely on the Founder as his legal adviser and called for him in his last days. He was sorely tried by his son, Benedict Leonard Calvert, who had conformed to the Church of England and was pressing for a restoration of the colony with himself as proprietor. His wish was accomplished in 1715 following the death of his father, but Benedict lived less than a year to enjoy his title of Fourth Lord Baltimore. Benedict's children had been taken from St. Omers College to secure their own conformity to their father's religious decision. Benedict's eldest son Charles did not at first share his father's view of conforming to the Church of England, but under the guardianship of Francis North (Lord Guilford) he acquiesced and became the Fifth Lord Baltimore, upon the death of his father. The Founder was very busy settling the estate of Old Lord Charles as best he could to the advantage of the widow. Since he was a long-suffering servant of the family, he was not resented by the new Protestant line of proprietors. Future trouble would be found not in London but in Maryland, where Carroll benefices through the hands of Old Lord Charles were envied by ambitious gentlemen intent upon rivaling his impressive fortune.[4]

As the Founder recounted the state of his affairs to his sons at St. Omers, they did not feel that the future was without hope. In 1712 their father had been made the proprietor's agent and receiver general. There were indications that Lord Guilford would recommend him for other offices of trust and profit, in a way compensating him for the prestige he once claimed as attorney general, an office he could no longer hold as a Catholic because of the Revolution and related Maryland legislation. Charles' father felt assured by the landed wealth of his future inheritance, which now stood at nearly sixty thousand acres. With such topics to discuss the Founder visited with his sons at St. Omers. He enjoyed the little community at the college— the "good family," as he referred to it. No doubt he found old acquaintances among the faculty, who years before had been with him at the Jesuit English College at Douai. Even Henry who would be returning to America following his study of law in London might again receive a visit from the Founder. Certainly, Charles' father and Daniel could expect another visit soon.[5]

By the spring of 1719, however, the Founder had not returned to Europe for a visit. Charles' father suspected that all was not as well with the colonial government as it had appeared at the time of his visit. Henry had left for London a couple of years before and would now be on his way back to Maryland. As for himself, he was soon to begin his final year at St. Omers, which was marked by a public defense of philosophical views. It was likely that at least one of his parents would use this occasion to visit him in the spring of 1720. Since his two sisters Mary and Eleanor were to enter a convent school in France at this time, an immediate member of the family, a parent if possible, would have to accompany them on the voyage.[6]

In July, Charles' father was stunned by the letter which he received from the Founder. Henry had indeed left for America, but he had died in a shipwreck off the American coast. The Founder sought some consolations in remembrances for his lost son. Henry had made a satisfactory public defense of his philosophy, but a transcript had not as yet arrived in Maryland. Charles' father was to see to it that a copy was secured. The Founder used the occasion to urge his son to the same success which Henry had attained in his studies. The style of family pride was clearly indicated by the Founder's injunction that "Marylando-Hibernus" should be affixed to his name in the written record of Charles' forthcoming defense. He must get the opinion of the rector and his professors on his prospects for the defense. "If they do not think that you can go through it with applause," he cautioned, "it is better let alone, for a dunce in a pulpit makes but a very awkward appearance." His mother was taking his sisters either to Graveling or Dunkirk. Their visit to him should not be allowed to impede his preparation for the public defense. Charles' father was thus made more fully aware of the established intellectual traditions of the Carroll family.[7]

All of these exciting plans for 1720 were shattered at the time of the philosophical defense; the great founder died on July 20, 1720. Not only would his widow be absent from the defense, but the contemplated journey of son and mother to England for his enrollment in the inns of laws was cancelled, and Charles' father was called home to take up the burden of the Founder's role in the family. His uncle James Carroll would see to the establishment of his sisters in the proper school. Charles' father presumably met them in France and learned the details of the Founder's death. As he proceeded homeward, his sadness grew heavier. He was on the sea that had claimed Henry and soon he would embrace his mother, who had recently lost both husband and son. He could not stop in England, where he had once hoped to study law, and this thought further distressed him. The unhappy family misfortunes had struck a blow at his own ambition and pride. Study at the inns of law in London would have secured him an inestimable advantage as a young man entering upon life at Annapolis. It was a long voyage; the pitching and tossing of the vessel was but a reflection of the anxiety and resentment that disturbed his mind. He knew full well how the harassed latter days of the Founder's life had shortened it, and a vindictive mood came over the young heir to the family's traditions and fortunes. He would take his place among the gentry society in this dissenter frame of mind, for he was as a Catholic, a member of a harassed minority group within that society and subject to its disabilities. Had he not possessed the foundations for success in the wealth which he had inherited and could turn to good account in his lifetime, Charles' father may well have proved a paranoic burden to his own aristocracy as well as to his son in the future. As it was, he would be aggressive but touchy, highly intelligent but emotional, affable but with an unpredictably cutting edge to his wit. He was cast in the rebel's role.[8]

When Charles' father disembarked at the foot of Duke of Gloucester Street, the scene was not changed much from what it had been more than eight years earlier. The family mansion was there; so were those of his wealthy uncle James Carroll, of Daniel Dulany, the future attorney general, and of other men of importance in the provincial society. The state house and the governor's mansion stood on the hill far up the street surveying Annapolis harbor.

Most important of all for Charles' father upon his return, was the time spent with his widowed mother, Mary Darnall Carroll. She too became part of the family legend. She married the Founder between his jail sentences, finding him a young widower of Martha Underwood of St. Mary's County. Her father, Colonel Henry Darnall I, stood high in proprietary favor. In 1712 he had died during his tenure of the office as Proprietor's Agent in Land Affairs, an office which was then conferred on the Founder. The Darnall family lineage was composed of the English Catholic gentry originating in Hertfordshire, England; but this ancestry would always be overshadowed by the intense Irish pride of the Founder and in Charles' father, whose son would take the same satisfaction in *Marylando-Hibernus* as a proud ethnic designation. Raised amid affairs of state in the family household, Mary Darnall Carroll was observant and retentive of the political experiences of her husband, especially during his last five years. Charles' father was aware of these episodes only in the vagueness of letters. His first months in Annapolis led him to seek from his mother, other family members, and friends, the details of the Founder's conflicts with Governor John Hart. These events were pivotal to the development of the family fortunes, the Catholic aristocracy, and the Carroll legends and traditions.[10]

Charles' father knew from the St. Omers visit of the Founder that the situation at the beginning of Hart's governorship in 1714 had been favorable enough. The Founder functioned as the Proprietor's Agent and Receiver General, and Hart made no difficulty as a royal governor directly accountable to the king and his privy council. Having arranged the estate of the deceased Third Lord Baltimore in England, the Founder returned to find a restored proprietary government in Maryland. Hart was now under Benedict Leonard Calvert, Fourth Lord Baltimore, and within a year under Charles, the Fifth Lord Baltimore, then in his minority. The Founder was in good standing even though he was no longer so closely tied to the proprietary family. The Protestant proprietor confirmed this impression, when in 1716, the Founder was given the commission of Naval Officer. By 1717, he was in addition Keeper of the Great Seal, and Register of the Land Office. He functioned as a lawyer, and his right to vote and hold office seemed technically restored. The assembly in these respects chose to follow the decrees of Queen Anne in favor of Catholics, as opposed to those of King William which restricted them.

In 1717, the Founder did not hesitate to defend the clergy and the private worship which they conducted on their estates, even though this did not help in his own defense against Hart's attacks from another quarter. He made the very important constitutional argument that the original Conditions of Plantations from the days of the colony's founding legitimized their possessions and the private use they chose to make of them. As Receiver General under the now restored proprietary government, the Founder proceeded to collect revenues, out of which the governor's salary would be paid. It was in this matter that Hart challenged the validity of the Founder to hold the office. It was difficult for Hart to do so in the simple way of outright exclusion of a Catholic from office because of the legislation of Queen Anne and previous acts of the Maryland Assembly. He therefore resorted to an old device, a demand for the oath of allegiance of the Catholic officeholder. Catholics would not accept such an oath, which dealt with questions of belief (the nature of the Sacrament of the Eucharist) as much as with civil loyalty. Hart put himself to the task of winning coercive legislation from the assembly in order to apply it against the Founder.[11]

He met with success in 1718 due to complex conditions of which he made capital. The governor was playing a precarious game starting in 1715. He was trying to retain a manner of exercising his office which he had as a royal governor; before that date he did not have to give account to the deposed proprietor. In the re-established proprietary government he hoped to keep his former power, at least insofar as the Founder, as powerful Receiver General and Keeper of the Seal, was concerned. He strove to make the veiled charge of coddling papists hold up against the proprietor and his colonial sympathizers. Favorable treatment of Catholics, he pointed out, was a grave danger to the state in 1715, the year when James III, Stuart pretender to the throne of England, led an uprising in Europe. Hart smelled the smoke of sedition among the Catholic gentry. On September 10, 1716, he found a chance to make his case with the nephew of the Founder, William FitzRedmond, a Catholic, but business associate of Protestant gentlemen. Witnesses declared that they had seen and heard FitzRedmond drink to the Pretender's health. The Founder as well as Dulany defended FitzRedmond. Such an accusation was all that was needed to strengthen support for hostile anti-Catholic legislation. The previous year a cannon had been fired on the Pretender's birthday, but the quest for the pockets of sedition verged on the comic. The present case was more effective, and Hart did not fail to get a penalty against the Founder's client.[12]

Amid this atmosphere, the Founder continued to press his claim to the office of receiver general for the lord proprietor, to whom he intended to appeal against the governor. Hart now turned to another device to mobilize opposition to Carroll and his co-religionists. He claimed that such a maneuver by the Founder was contrary to the Maryland Constitution and then made a play by appealing to the self-conscious assembly to assert its rights. When the assembly finished the business to which Hart led them in 1718, Catholics would never again sit there, nor would they have the right to vote for those who did. A Catholic was forbidden to practice law in Maryland courts. It was a bitter blow to the Founder. Was his assertion of legal right only an imprudent and needless precipitation of antagonism? Did not English judicial right, on the other hand, fundamentally depend upon persistent assertion to the point of establishing custom and precedent? Charles' father pondered the problem and came to the Founder's affirmative conclusion. In applying it to Maryland politics he would be no different from the Founder. His would be a role of rebel without using violence.[13]

Charles' father was approaching only twenty years of age when he took his place in the deceased Founder's household. His mother, Mary Darnall Carroll, would abide here and at the mansion which he would later build at Annapolis for more than two decades, a reminder and counselor in the traditions of the Founder. The legal guardian of Charles' father, James Carroll, bachelor son of the Founder's brother Anthony, gave him further support and attachment to the Carroll traditions. James had distinguished himself in the service of the proprietor and had attained landed wealth, particularly in Anne Arundel County. When James III, the Stuart pretender to England's throne, carried out his uprising in Europe, he found James a captain in Lord Dongan's regiment of dragoons, at the Battle of the Boyne, where the Stuarts went down to defeat. James had a mansion in the neighborhood, which he left at this time to reside in the deceased Founder's household. With such support, Charles' father was equal to the rebel's role.[14]

This period of quasi-minority for Charles' father was not without excitement. Outspoken like the Founder against even those in the highest station, he soon had a major political encounter with James Hollyday, a member of the lower house of the assembly. In their exchange of words, he challenged Hollyday to a duel. The assembly-man found a way out which satisfied revenge without resort to the duel: Hollyday took advantage of the law against challenging an assemblyman to a duel. When faced with a fine, Charles' father chose a short time in prison, in the tradition of the Founder. There were less dramatic duties which he met during his first decade at Annapolis. He went to Europe in order to escort his sisters Mary and Eleanor back to America. In 1728 James Carroll named Charles' father a trustee of his estate and died the following year.[15]

The will was a source of endless litigation by the very natural pro-vision which James had made for his nephew Anthony, who had become a Jesuit. That circumstance did not, however, in the 1720's foretell any legal difficulty. In 1724, Robert Brooke as a Jesuit was allowed by government officials to accept his family property for the order under the name of a specific member in Maryland. As it happened, Dr. Charles Carroll, the Annapolis surgeon, and Charles' father were named trustees of the James Carroll estate. The latter throughout the 1730's was striving to carry out the will and effect the transfer of Anthony's share in the inheritance to Father George Thorold, to which arrangement Anthony was agreeable. The surgeon, Anthony's uncle, anxious to enlarge his own family's share of the estate, bitterly opposed this decision. The only hope of the surgeon was to reverse the court ruling in the Brooke case. The grounds for this would be to press successfully the illegality of a Catholic clergyman's acquiring property through inheritance.

The tenacity of the surgeon in going to this degree of opposition resulted from his own conformity to the Church of England. His militancy appeared in the protracted court case. He revealed that he had already used his trusteeship to apply part of the estate to his own fortune. When Charles' father urged the surgeon to repay what he had taken the surgeon responded that to pay it over to Father Therold would leave him open to a charge of violating the English statute against inheritance by Catholic priests. Daniel Dulany was said to have verbally concurred with the surgeon's opinion, even though he had been commissary in the Brooke case, which ruled to the contrary. Faithful to the traditional pattern of conduct of the Founder, Charles' father pressed the case to the assembly during the period of the 1730's and early 1740's. Only later in Europe would Carroll's son hear of the consequences of his father's involvements which brought further repressive measures by the assembly just as the Founder's contest with Hart had done.[16]

Charles' father would not have become the strong character, as he is revealed in Maryland history, had he stood in the Founder's shadow during his early adult life. As it turned out, unusual demands were made upon his initiative and leadership in protecting and expanding the family fortunes. Returning from college in Europe, he assumed his duties as executor of the Founder's will and took part in its legal probate in 1731. All the time, he had been providing for the landed wealth to which he had fallen heir. Operating under the gentry law of "expand or die," he sought to enlarge his inheritance.

As a spirited entrepreneur, he continued the Founder's activities of floating loans at handsome interest returns.

In 1719, British imperial policy had called for the promotion of iron works in the colonies. Charles' father used the new opportunity for profit and joined with three older gentlemen in commerical activity, which increasingly modified the economic character of the planter-gentry society of Maryland; together, they developed the Baltimore Iron Works. Benjamin Tasker had been in the proprietary council. Daniel Dulany, who had handled the Founder's litigation over loans and was a rising light in the legal profession, was a second. Less promising was Dr. Charles Carroll, a cousin and Annapolis surgeon, who was at the same time entering ever more deeply into the antagonisms of the James Carroll estate controversy.[17]

In January of 1731, Charles' father began holding bi-monthly meetings of the Baltimore Iron Works partnership. Each partner subscribed £700, but no technical administrator was employed, so that the partners each saw to certain specific details of the operation. The record keeping was in the hands of Charles' father, and the success of the endeavor here revealed itself over the greater part of his life. Very soon there were annual profits of £400 on each original share and by the 1760's they had risen in value to £10,000. Charles' father was also a major factor in marketing the iron in Maryland, where about two-thirds of the sales were made. Daniel Dulany used his connections in England to good advantage for markets there. The employment and management of skilled workers were left to Dr. Carroll. Stephen Onion was employed to direct the iron works, which was built at the mouth of the Susquehanna River; in time, a sixty-ton square stern schooner was constructed. Dr. Carroll was accused of improper management, especially in using the schooner for his own business. While Dulany was anxious to keep peace in the company, the James Carroll estate litigation made it difficult. Charles' father seemed to find the same dishonesty here in the iron business that he saw in the Doctor's conduct as trustee of the estate. Dulany, who had purportedly stood with the surgeon in the James Carroll case, was critical of Dr. Carroll in the Iron Works controversy. It is a tribute to the business acumen of all the partners, however, that in spite of all of these controversies, their company was to thrive for many years. Only a hard grain of discipline in Charles' father kept the association from collapsing. The Carroll fortunes indeed depended upon such discipline.[18]

The iron works venture as a diversification of the Carroll financial base was very timely. Planters were having difficulty commanding a good price for their produce. English factors with whom they dealt were not competing effectively with the French farmers general (royal marketing agents). Eighty planters who were in the same plight as Charles' father petitioned the Crown for a remedy which they thought could be found in an affiliation to gain uniform practices in sales and the quality of tobacco. His uncle, Henry Darnall II, exercised some leadership in the movement, when in 1729 he published at Annapolis the pamphlet *A Just and Impartial Account of the Transactions of the Merchants in London for the Advancement of the Price of Tobacco.* It was the good fortune of Charles' father that he began to reap profits from the iron works during this period of depression in the tobacco market.[19]

The iron business as a ramification of the Carroll holdings was indeed significant, considering the family's origin in a Tory tradition of landed wealth. Even before the birth of Charles, the family fortune had been expanding. Records showed transactions with Michael Macnamara of Annapolis. Payments were made to Charles' father by kinsmen in Prince George's County, and Benjamin Tasker, Daniel Dulany, Dr. Carroll, and many others during this period. Under Charles' father, the company records were indeed in the hands of a professional entrepreneur. Tasker, although considerably superior to Charles' father on political grounds, felt economically inferior. "I may not be in advance as much as some Gent [lemen] are," he once wrote defensively to Charles' father, "but I believe I am as [satisfactory] as to any paym[en]ts in cash, having lately paid about £80: in cash." Economic relationships helped the Carroll name socially. Those who met bi-monthly in common profit-making enterprises were suitable companions at Reynolds Tavern in Annapolis; and at more formal social affairs, including those of the provincial governor himself. While the Catholic aristocracy was religiously and socially apart, they had a common social life in many other ways. All of this secured a degree of respect which was a benefit to the whole society of such Catholic aristocrats, since they were not radically removed from the social mainstream. They were still very much the great lords of manors which George Calvert envisaged in 1632.[20]

Controversies over land titles were part of the way of life in the planter society. Charles' father had them with his own kinsmen, like Dr. Carroll or Ignatius Digges, and with other business associates like Daniel Dulany in 1739. Quit rents on the five-thousand acre estate of Charles' father in Prince George's County, according to Dulany, had not been paid. Charles' father threatened an appeal to the Crown, but the matter was ultimately satisfactorily settled. Such partially political disagreements were more abrasive than what was experienced in the purely commercial realm. On the whole, however, it appears that the Carroll style was favorable to maintaining congenial rapport with the whole gentry society. Even Carroll's moneylending induced a certain respect among the large number of gentlemen of lesser economic rank who were dependent upon Charles' father in their times of economic distress. Daniel Dulany was at times himself in this position and as a lawyer had handled court cases for Charles' father against defaulting debtors.[21]

Charles' father bore many domestic responsibilities while in his twenties and early thirties. In addition to escorting his sisters Mary and Eleanor from Europe, he was concerned about his brother Daniel, whose affairs he managed even after the latter's return from Europe. In a Virginia land project, he enlisted the help of Daniel and generally aided him in establishing economic security for his newly established family. Daniel had married Ann Rozier of Notley Hall Manor, the daughter of Notley Rozier. Three children, Charles, Elizabeth, and Mary, were born in the early years of this marriage. Elizabeth was to become the wife of Daniel Carroll, signer of the Constitution of the United States, whose brother John Carroll was to become the first Catholic bishop of the United States. The eldest child, born in 1729, was the origin of the Charles Carroll of Duddington branch of the family. Charles' father indeed took pride and satisfaction in his younger brother Daniel's growing good fortune. In 1734, however, a tragic reversal took place with Daniel's premature death, and Charles' father took care of the family which he left. Nor was that the full measure of sorrow that year. Eleanor, the sister of Charles' father, also died, a young woman of twenty-three years; the death was a blow to the Founder's widow as well as her son.[22]

Charles' father, amid all these concerns, finally established his own family. True to the Catholic gentry code of marrying its own kind, with leniency toward prohibitions of consanguinity, he courted and married Elizabeth Brooke. She was of an old Catholic family which prided itself on having given to Maryland one of its first native priests, and of having suffered confiscation of property for their faith. Her father, Clement Brooke, had married the lovely Jane Sewall, whose mother's matrimonial career provides one of the more romantic chapters in Maryland history. The mother, Jane Lowe Sewall, survived her husband and in her widowhood attracted Charles Calvert, Third Lord Baltimore, who in time married her. Charles' father was thus in his generation contributing to the ever expanding but interrelated family lines of the Catholic gentry. As with Lady Jane's son, Benedict Leonard, Fourth Lord Baltimore, crises in the various families sometimes turned on the religious issue of conformity to the Church of England. Dr. Charles Carroll, the surgeon, was at this time another instance, witnessed by Charles' father. Somewhat later, Henry Darnall, III, a Carroll kinsman, also conformed. From marriage to Rachel Brooke, his wife's cousin, would come Henry Darnall, IV, father of the famous revolutionary gentleman son of Charles Carroll of Carrollton's future bride.[23]

Charles' father with his expanding domestic and commercial family fortunes undertook the building of his own mansion at Annapolis. In 1735 he built an imposing three-storey brick structure a block from the residence which the Founder had bequeathed to him. The town setting imposed a simple design on the mansion's exterior, where chimneys at the extremities of the edifice suggested much of the interior. Fireplaces were located in the major rooms at either end and on every floor. The high ceilings invited provincial endeavors at imitating the European style of design and furnishing which Louis XIV had made immortal. An English traveler said that the edifice would not disgrace Westminster, that indeed it was superb. Magnificent terraced gardens commanded a view of Annapolis harbor and bordered Spa Creek, which emptied into the harbor. A 1743 map called the stream "Carroll's Creek", a testimony to the prestige of the ambitious young resident nearby.[24]

On September 19, 1737, Charles Carroll of Carrollton, later destined to far greater renown than his father, was born in this impressive mansion into a family that had been enriched with so much history. His father in the fullness of his manhood at thirty-five bore this family heritage in his dynamic personality, eager to impart it to his heir.

The mansion was the scene of fashionable affairs that attracted many guests from the various elements of the gentry society. The frequent visits and stays of near relatives made the child especially aware that he was part of a clan. Another feature of the atmosphere of group identification centered in the Mass that was celebrated on Sundays in the Carroll private chapel. As a child, Charles could see the uniqueness of this in reference to the majority of the townsmen who attended Anglican worship at St. Anne's Church, where each Sunday the governor and assemblymen took their appointed places. When Charles was six, his grandmother Mary Darnall Carroll died, after twenty-three years of widowhood in the household of Charles' father. She was venerated for her courage and wisdom, and as matriarch and oracle of the family's proud heritage.[25]

In his childhood, Charles tried to understand the separations of Catholics from the rest of society, particularly in his own educational program. It had to be explained why he did not go to St. Anne's grammar school, a few blocks up the hill; and why he must begin his learning at home. An unsuccessful attempt had been made by a Catholic schoolmaster to educate Annapolis boys. James Elson, about this time, had been called before government officials to explain the classes which he had been conducting. His gatherings had the appearance of a papist school, which was forbidden by law. Elson explained that he had both Catholic and Protestant students and that he was willing to instruct each student in his own particular religious faith. He was denied freedom to proceed with his plan, and young Charles, therefore, had to be placed elsewhere. Father Thomas Poulton, S.J., had anticipated such difficulties and made plans for a school for Catholic boys at Bohemia Manor, on the eastern shore of the upper part of Chesapeake Bay. Bohemia Manor, as the extra-legal school was called, was holding classes at this time. In 1747 Charles went to Bohemia Manor to study for about seven months, and went again the following year for a similar period. He understood that this would prepare him for a much longer period at his father's alma mater, St. Omers in France.[26]

As a boy of ten, he found a large circle of friends and actual schoolmates for the first time. Bohemia during this period attracted as many as forty students. Here he met Jacky Carroll, his cousin from Upper Marlboro, and Robert Brent, Jacky's cousin. There were four boys from the Neale family in the school. Charles probably confined himself to writing, at which he had only a rude beginning, and to arithmetic. He may have ventured into Latin grammar with his cousin Jacky, who was two years older than himself. Some students even began the study of Greek at Bohemia. In 1748, on the eve of their departure for St. Omers, these boys had already formed their identity as a Maryland group. This was particularly true of Charles, Jacky Carroll, and their cousin Robert Brent. By competition among themselves, they had been conditioned for future rivalry with their English Catholic schoolmates at St. Omers. By the time that Charles returned to Annapolis for the last time from Bohemia, he was accustomed to separation from his family, and the salt of Chesapeake sailing. He was accustomed, too, to the notion of going to St. Omers, since it was so much a matter of course for the children in families he knew best. All of them had fathers who were alumni like his father. Such education was a requirement of the social class in which he was becoming more consciously involved. It also was necessary since he was destined to be like his rebel father, who had pursued such a course of studies.[27]

The Catholic society in Maryland which young Charles would soon leave for studies abroad, and to which he would one day return had a formative influence on his own life as well as that of his family. The many episodes and significant remarks of his rebel father revealed its characteristic forces. The Catholic community could best be called a "counter-revolutionary" society. Charles' father often spoke of the "late Revolution," referring to the Glorious Revolution of 1688, which put an end to the Founder's claim to the office of attorney general of the province. That event reversed the rule of religious freedom which had prevailed since the colony's founding. The undying hopes and efforts of the Catholic community sought to bring back those halcyon days, subverting the order of things established by the revolution of 1688. In this sense, Catholics were a counter-revolutionary group guided by a set of liberal ideas regarding religious freedom. To this militancy was added a vexed spirit which chafed under their exclusion from public office, public worship, and from acceptance as a loyal civic element in the broader provincial society.[28]

A sharp intellectual vision guided Catholic social behavior. They believed that the Toleration Acts of 1639 and 1649 applied in sound legal fashion the initial provisions for religious freedom found in the Maryland Charter of 1632. The measure of 1639 clearly called for separation of church and state. The act of ten years later took special account of the freedom of Christians in the face of a threat from Puritan migrants to Maryland in the 1640's. In the seventeenth century, furthermore, the Catholic gentry was proportionately greater than the same class of the Protestant population. This admirable legal structure of religious freedom in the Toleration Acts had been very much of their making since Catholic gentlemen constituted a majority of the assembly that passed the legislation. A beneficent Catholic lord proprietor by his generous land grants accounted for the large numbers of the Catholic gentry. This in time became a source of complaint by some Protestants who were not satisfied with the proprietary efforts at correcting this condition. On the other hand, a major segment of dissenting Protestants (Presbyterians and Quakers especially) was outside the favor of the Church of England as established in the mother country and in many of the colonies and cherished the Maryland condition of separation of church and state. The Maryland Charter and Toleration Acts in reality constituted a shield against harsh statute laws passed in England, those of Elizabethan times being most odious to Catholics. However, the "late Revolution" of 1688 had removed that shield of freedom.

A justification and an implementation of the new order were constructed. John Locke said that by their very faith, Catholics stood suspect of treason, whatever an individual's own record might be. In establishing the Church of England, however, leniency was shown toward dissenter Protestants. Anglican gentlemen of the Church of England were not entirely satisfied with the new order. This proved significant to the subsequent behavior of Catholics toward this segment of the Protestant community and the political state which they dominated. They simply challenged the validity of Locke's notion as applicable to Maryland Catholics. Many of the Anglican gentry also favored the return of government under the old proprietary family. They also desired the old legal structure which provided autonomy for political life in Maryland as it had once stood apart from imperial control from London and laws made there. When a Protestant proprietary rule began in 1715, these gentlemen and officials of the new government pressed for acceptance of the pre-1688 understanding regarding the statute laws made in England. Many Anglicans and dissenters thus shared this legal view with Catholics. When the lower house of the assembly sought to enforce English penal laws against Catholics, the Anglican gentry and proprietary party opposed this legislative action. Such laws, they believed, did not apply to Maryland Catholics. Even though separation of church and state no longer existed, early Maryland toleration acts still applied. There was further foundation in theology for the alliance that prevailed since Anglican teaching was more respectful of Catholic doctrine than Puritan traditions were. An intellectual dimension was thus given to the collaboration with the Catholic counter-revolutionary society.

The wealth of Catholic gentlemen greatly aided this collaboration. The advantage of educational opportunities abroad in Jesuit colleges came to many Catholic families in Maryland. Their personal faith was thus elaborated with considerable sophistication, which won the respect of many Protestant aristocrats. Therefore the social structure within which Charles' father moved fostered a patrician style of self-confidence and hope for the future. There would be dark moments when the Anglican gentry failed in its collaboration. Yet, by and large, the favorable condition continued up to the time of Charles' return from Europe. A new phase of intellectual and sociological modification would then rapidly develop, which would give him an even more respectable position in life than his father had experienced. The same intellectual vision of the Catholic society, however, would remain. It would inspire him with a desire to see a complete return of the freedom for which early Maryland law had provided. He would thus have a counter-revolutionary cast of mind, bent upon undoing the mischief caused by the revolution of 1688. Desirous of expanding the horizon of freedom into the civic as well as the religious realm, he would be preparing for a role in the American Revolution.

Chapter 2

SCHOLAR IN EXILE

As July of 1748 was passing, Charles, a boy of eleven years, prepared to board a vessel in Annapolis harbor. This time it would not be a voyage confined to familiar Chesapeake Bay, but out of its mouth and into the open Atlantic, destined for the coast of France. He had discussed the anticipated voyage with Bobby Brent and Jacky Carroll at Bohemia Manor School in the spring. The three boys were finally joined on deck by Stanislaus Hoxton, whose brother Walter was already at St. Omers, looking forward to the arrival of the new group of Maryland scholars. The fact that their parents, except for a father or two, would not see the children again for as long as ten years brought a depressing mood to the departure. The seafarers were prepared for a one-month's voyage. Perhaps they might encounter hostile French or Spanish men-of-war. Rough days of passage on a pitching sea were inevitable. The captain persisted on his course all the same and landed the scholars in their famous place of exile in France.[1]

In their own boyish minds, the Maryland Catholics grasped the legend of the Jesuit English College of St. Omers. It had its most dramatic form in the story of Titus Oates. Oates, in the last days of James II, fabricated a story that Catholics were preparing another Gunpowder Plot, determined to do violence to the Protestants of England. He was to have a part in it, but, according to his account in the trial, he turned from association in the plot and informed public officials in time to scotch it. Some boys from St. Omers, however, gave evidence in court which discredited the Oates version of the purported plot. At the critical moment of its execution, at which time Oates said he was on the scene in London, the students of St. Omers testified that Oates, overgrown boy that he appeared, was within the very walls of St. Omers College. The archway of the older College had borne the legend: "Jesu, Jesu, converte Angliam, fiat, fiat," the Latin legend inspired by Catholic exiles from England, "Jesus, Jesus, convert England, may it be done, may it be done." The Maryland counter-revolutionary Catholic society, however, pleaded for recognition of a time-honored foundation for the freedom of all citizens, rather than for conversion of English Protestants. Even their fellow scholars from England had modified the legend's hope. Unfortunately, they had no legal foundation to sustain their hope, nor, as time was to prove, the means of political change which had developed in the New World to attain it.[2]

"The school, St. Omer" it has been said, "is the historic symbol of the Catholic Englishman of penal times, who went abroad in youth, at lively risk to all his family by proclamation and distraint, to return anon as priest or layman and fill the ranks depleted in his absence." A dominant purpose was to keep the faith alive through an intellectual process. Indeed, Catholic intellectuals in the period of James II's indulgence were preparing to enter existing English universities as professors transplanted from St. Omers. Others brought for a short time the liberal arts tradition of the school into England. It was hoped that the school itself with masters and scholars alike would return in honor to their native land, but the hope was dashed, and the scholars in exile went on in the old heroic mold.[3]

It was a confused atmosphere, where English Catholics in growing numbers were supinely accepting the revolution of 1688 as an irreversible defeat. There was little hope of recovering civil liberties, of becoming a part of the non-Catholic society around them in the world of education, politics, or social life generally. Their main intent was to keep the faith and their wealth, which supported it, and to strengthen family bonds. Among this English Catholic gentry, therefore, Charles found a lethargic spirit that might well kill the force of Maryland's counter-revolutionary society in which he had grown up. Would he develop the acumen required of his Maryland society as critics of existing institutions and persistent protagonists for the original freedoms of Maryland law? Charles was to seek a development in his education which passed beyond that required of an English Catholic gentleman, of one merely fortified for a passive acceptance of civil privations, and of one in need of culture to offset the dangers of total social isolation.

The rector of St. Omers College, Father Nathaniel Elliot, came to that office the year that Charles himself arrived. He succeeded Father Charles Wells, who had served for three years. Both men stood in the shadow of Father Richard Hyde, an eighteenth-century second founder of the college, who in 1725 was the moving force in the rebuilding of the college after the disastrous fire of that year. Father Hyde had died four years before the arrival of Charles, but not until he had left the magnificent structures that resembled in general plan what Montbard's engraving of 1689 depicts, and which surpassed the older buildings in quality and size.[4]

Charles soon found his way to one of the topmost halls of a four-storey rectangular building, where beds were arranged in a dormitory in separate alcoves. From its windows, he could see a large inner courtyard, which was surrounded by the four segments of the building complex. In these structures were the living and study facilities of about 120 students, and 20 or more Jesuit faculty members. A church, student chapel, and large and little theatres clustered along one side of this main quadrangular building and its courtyard. To the rear of both units were a walled garden and park area, beyond which were various shops to service the community. The entire college grounds were placed in the heart of a European metropolis, with college entrances and walls contiguous with the thoroughfare. Charles saw the bastion-like appearance of the town of St. Omers, where a rebellion had driven the Spanish patrons of the college from control in the early seventeenth century, only to be taken by France in the wars of Louis XIV. The French Jesuit college in the same city and with the same name reminded the English scholars that they were exiles from their own land. Louis XV was irregular in the financial aid which had been promised on an annual basis by his father, a great admirer of St. Omers. The walls of the city were washed by the Aa River, which often found the English boys at its banks, fishing in a manner unsuited to their family background. They appeared an alien curiosity to the Walloon folk of the environs.[5]

In the lower years of the college were fellow students ready to give assurance to the recently arrived Marylanders. Charles also made the acquaintance of the sons of English gentlemen, some of them destined for high distinction. Joseph Reeve was one day to become the influential ecclesiastical historian in England; a son of the Webs, a family of nobility, was there. Especially, there were fellow Marylanders among the younger group of about forty boys, such as Watty (Walter) Hoxton, whose brother had made passage with Charles. Watty became his fast friend at St. Omers and remained so through correspondence for several years in the time before Charles concluded his more extended studies. Joseph Hathersty was another Maryland scholar. More would come and future marriages in America would multiply the numbers of St. Omers' alumni.[6]

After a few days, the hardy troup was marching through the detailed regimen of the study day. They arose at 5 A.M. for Mass, followed by study in a common hall, and then breakfast. Jacky Carroll and Watty Hoxton took their place in a class group which was more advanced than the one for the study of grammar in which Charles found himself. Charles' goal at this time was to progress toward the stage of syntax, where the rules of the Latin and Greek language were applied to composing and translating the simpler structures of the classical languages. As soon as possible the speaking of Latin in class, and in some other appointed situations was demanded of him. The response to these requirements was not always what was desired, whether at the English or French Colleges of St. Omers. At the latter French institution a rebellion occurred in 1754, the year that Charles was concluding his studies at the English college. The rhetoric students opposed the rule of speaking Latin, and those in the grade above them revolted against the requirements of Greek. Some of the ringleaders were expelled, but only after a disconcerting inquest. Charles' lifelong delight in the classical prose and poetry did not derive from the experiences of this rudimentary period, but from the long awaited introduction to Cicero a couple of years later. Like the rebel students, he felt the restiveness of discontent.[7]

There were many facets to the training of an English Catholic gentleman, even during these first three years at St. Omers. One of the more pedestrian pursuits, the cult of penmanship, was rather grievous for young Charles. Toward the end of his first year he shrank from the demonstrations he was told to give to his father in the form of letters home, a regular requirement of the college. In a letter at this time he pleaded that an injured arm prevented his compliance with the rule. In explaining that he was succeeding with his studies, he crossed out "my" for "your" in his phrase "to your greatest satisfaction." In March of 1750, however, he demonstrated a great improvement in the penmanship of his letter.[8]

The Jesuits were celebrated for the theatre, and what it achieved in their colleges. Charles found a place on the stage for presentation of a play in Latin which a faculty member had written. This was more than an attempt at extending the classical instruction of the classroom. Boys overcame bashfulness in such appearances in the early periods of their training; they later mastered oral expression, a part of everyday life in the social role of gentlemen. In Charles' first years at the St. Omers theatre, instruction in the dance was part of his regimen, and he made mention of this activity in letters to his father. "Nothing contributes more," his father believed, "to give a gentleman a graceful and easy carriage." The ballet especially was greatly developed in the Jesuit colleges. Dramatic works of a more serious character and in the vernacular, depending on the period of study, took on greater variety, including the farcès. Some alumni had contributed to the contemporary stage, as did John Caryll, a dramatic writer and diplomat of the court of James II. An appreciation of this art form was one of Charles' achievements at this time, in addition to his delight in classical writings.[9]

Literature in the vernacular and histories of the modern nations were subjects which found places in the eighteenth-century modifications of the Jesuit plan of study *(ratio studiorum)*. In his early years at the college, Charles had a taste for these innovations. He confessed that he neglected writing to his father because he was using much of his leisure time reading narrations and what he called "fiction". In his first three or four years, he heard lectures in English history, which he faithfully transcribed in booklets. They were dominantly factual narratives on the eras of English medieval kings, which would be suited to Charles at this stage of his training. This substantially enlarged the usual program in history which traditionally encompassed ancient history in order to provide appreciation of the classical authors. So it was that Charles wove for himself the narrative of the revolutionary reforms of the Gracchi, the formation of Parliament under Edward, and a host of other episodes, which in later years would provide historical references for his philosophizing and revolutionary oratory.[10]

The St. Omers faculty included at this time a very gifted director of the spiritual life, Father Levinus Browne, who had held positions of highest authority in the English Jesuit organization, and who at one time had been master of novices. A Renaissance man, he readily clothed the Christian message in the dress of the gentleman's secular and cultural life. Six years before Charles' arrival he had published *Bossuet's Variations,* a translation of the great craftsman of sacred oratory, who was a literary as well as a religious ornament of the court of Louis XIV. Father Browne was a friend of Alexander Pope and had acquired from Pope the manuscript of his poem on St. Francis Xavier. Although he was an elderly man in these years, the priest was well known for his ability to present the *Spiritual Exercises of St. Ignatius* to laymen. Charles annually made these spiritual retreats of a few days' duration.[11]

While the students all had regular catechism classes, the retreat concentrated on a prayerful, personal grasp of Christian teaching regarding the life of perfection. The *Directorium* and the *Three Conversions of England* of Father Robert Persons, S.J., were influential on both the catechism and most prevailing approaches to the *Spiritual Exercises* among English-speaking Catholics. Persons imparted to his readers the image of spiritual combat in defense of the faith since he wrote in the atmosphere of persecution in the Elizabethan era. Of far more general influence in the spiritual formation of the Catholic gentleman were the French authors Francis de Sales and Jean Croiset, who were read by all spiritual mentors, and in time by many of their protégés. Both had gifted insights into the Christian transformation of gentility toward which young students were striving. The Sodality of the Blessed Virgin Mary further served to link the personal piety of the student to his cultural development. A religious rule of life, adapted from that of the Society of Jesus, was followed by the members in their efforts to acquire and practice the Christian virtues. The Sodality organization called for academies in which the members, in seminar fashion, cultivated an appreciation of literature or other subjects. Here some topic of the general academic curriculum would be pursued in greater detail.[12]

The recognized strength of the Jesuit colleges throughout Europe was the personal influence of a cultured adult upon the developing adolescent and young adult. This plan was implemented by having the same Jesuit teacher conduct the same group of fifteen or twenty boys through the periods of grammar, syntax, rhetoric, and poetry. It was for him to know every gap in the knowledge required at each stage and to see to a complete achievement by his student. This was accomplished in the group situation of the classroom, more than by private instruction which might bring a destructive harshness to the learning process. Competition was emphasized both individually and on a team basis. While this would seem to be an extrinsic motive to learning, it was eminently suited to the temper of juveniles and guaranteed mastery of the tools necessary to the probing of knowledge as an end in itself during the young adult years ahead.[13]

A happy adaptation of this system was made in the case of Charles. Shortly after his arrival at St. Omers, he had for his tutor and master his cousin, Anthony Carroll, who was descended from a branch of the family that had remained in Ireland. He was a central figure in the controversial will of James Carroll, which had settled a portion of the estate upon him and which he received for the Jesuit Order.

At this time he was a young man of twenty-nine, only five years in the order and not yet a priest. The traits of the intellectual later seen in Charles were found in Anthony. He too was enamoured of French literature and culture, and the year that Charles signed the Declaration of Independence, Anthony published *Practical Divinity,* a belletristic translation of the sacred oratory of Bourdaloue. Charles' artistic fluency in French for which he later became famous had its origin in this devoted tutor and instructor, who enriched the classical teaching of his order with excellence in the modern vernacular. On the occasion of Anthony's violent death at the hands of a thief on Fleet Street, London, in 1794, *The Gentleman's Magazine* commented on the esteem in which he was held, particularly as "a man of irreproachable character." This, too, was essential since the personal influence of the tutor and instructor extended beyond the classroom into the rest of the student's life, in recreation, travel, advice, and conversation.[14]

Charles responded to the rigors of both education and adolescence as he approached his sixteenth year. He told his father how much his life was dominated by college rules, but that he was studying hard. Anthony made a slightly different estimate and saw enough juvenile giddiness in him to take note of it in a letter to Charles' father. The son assured his father, however, that he was growing in piety and was active in the college Sodality. In a class of twenty-three, Charles ranked third, which might have given him some sense of complacency; apparently it did not, since he took special note in writing to his father that Jacky Carroll was first in another class. Anthony attempted to take some of the edge off the father's undue ambitions for his son by reminding him that his son was younger than most of the boys in his class. On the other hand, the tutor saw the need to keep the pressure of extra study on his gifted student apart from any rivalry with others, and Charles' father was ready to collaborate. He would send over maps which Charles should study. In an era of wars waged close to Charles' province he should find them fascinating. Anthony thought that they would especially help keep the swift-moving mind of Charles occupied with profitable matters. By October of 1751, it does not seem that the contest of Charles with his two masters was yet settled. "I cannot omit," his father pleaded, "recommending to you dilligent application to your Studies, Piety, and the observation of the Rules of the J. [Jesuit] C. [College] and, making good use of your time and [that] you may lay in such a Stock of Virtue and Knowledge as will give you more Credit and Comfort than the greatest Wealth."[15]

At this point in his course at St. Omers, Charles could sympathize with the young rebels of a decade before who had refused to speak Latin, especially with those heroes among them who fell in action in the noble cause of rebellion. At a time when four or five St. Omers' students yearly went seven miles down the road to the Jesuit novitiate at Watten, Charles wondered, as he did about a decade later, if the regimen with which he struggled was not a pre-novitiate prescription. It was assuring, however, that there was the monthly day of recreation at Blandyke, an acreage about three miles away, where the bare armed and barefooted Englishmen, who earned the townsfolk complaints by frequently fishing along the town walls, could more feely pursue their diversions. Football could be played to the point of exhaustion at Blandyke, something the short periods in the school yard did not allow. The summers too brought extended days of vacations there. There were the visits to Paris in a group with Anthony Carroll, with residence in the overly familiar halls of the Jesuit college there, or to other large cities which they visited from year to year[16] to soften the rigidity of school life.

At this time, everyone was talking about the good old days when the students and the masters lived like true English gentlemen. In earlier days, they rode their horses for sport, hunted, and wore wigs, an impish delight to the students since it annoyed the Walloon townsmen of St. Omers as they saw them parading about the streets, flashing watches and chains across bright colored vests. Then, Father Joseph Constable received a letter from Rome in 1737, in which Father General said in effect, "when in Rome, do as the Romans do". This meant giving up ice-skating on the Aa River, a silly English pastime that provoked Walloon criticism. Now the rule on horses was that they were for going to places at a distance. The Englishman's insight into common law and the Jesuit's acquaintance with moral theology no doubt mitigated any harsh impact of the reform measures, for there were ways of avoiding literal interpretation. Yet in Charles' day things were not at all what they once had been for Englishmen, and he merely resigned himself to a delay in the acquisition of any great skill in riding, hunting, and fishing until later times in England or Maryland.[17]

Each year Charles' associations with the sons of the English Catholic gentry became closer. They were, however, more to be observed than joined by the Marylanders, who clung closely together and gave Charles a sense of security in his first years in Europe. The year 1753 was distinctive in this respect as well as in the maturing nature of his studies. Father Warring, a friend of Charles' father, had come from Maryland a few years earlier and could give reports on the Carroll family and affairs in the colony. Charles found himself still a part of the provincial society he would one day join.[18] About this time, Father William Wappler came to the faculty and told Charles about his missionary career in Pennsylvania, and travels to Germany after leaving America in 1748. The Jesuit's interest in history had led him to investigate the authenticity of a relic of St. Thomas possessed by St. Omers College. In time, he inquired about the matter from the famous Bollandists, an institute of scholars who for more than one hundred years had been studying the lives of the saints with the latest critical procedures and documents. Ralph Falkner, a young Jesuit not yet ordained to the priesthood, was also a native of Maryland; he served as tutor and instructor until he went to Rome in 1755 to prepare for ordination. Then, there was the venerable old Father William Newton (1683-1756), who was well known to Charles' father, probably one of his teachers, and who would die shortly after Charles' departure from the college. There were others less well-known, like Father Carvall, who by their correspondence with Charles' family bound them by additional ties to the college community. All this explains why Charles' father referred to them as "the family".[19]

The most eventful day for the Maryland group in 1753 was the departure of Jacky Carroll and Joseph Hathersty for the novitiate at Watten, when Charles was sixteen years old. It is probable that Anthony Carroll left St. Omers a couple of years before, in order to prepare for ordination to the priesthood at Liège.[20] Charles still required the guiding hand of a tutor, especially with arithmetic. His father suggested that he seek the assistance of the Jesuit scholastic Ralph Falkner, a Marylander. He would later need similar tutoring in law in London. Much more littérateur, he found some of these other studies an outright chore, for his mind was not naturally interested in them. Charles was also dissatisfied with the opportunity to master dancing. His father did not understand the difficulty, even though he encouraged Charles to get a better dancing master. Undoubtedly

Charles was looking for more than "a graceful and easy carriage." He was aware that contemporary dance forms would be demanded of him at future social gatherings. The present offerings gave him no preparation for this situation, and he later regretted that it had not.[21]

Charles' father continued to play an active role as quasi-tutor, however far removed geographically from his son. He learned from Father Wappler that his son was still at the same rank that he held in his first-year class. He urged Charles to rise from third place to first, *"aut Caesar aut Nullus"*, either be a Caesar or nothing at all. This was a bit of Gaelic as well as classical rhetoric. It was not easy to put this injunction in proportion, least of all for an adolescent. In other ways, however, Charles' father showed insight into the intellectual state of his son, who was groping at the edge of young adulthood. "When an impression is made by reason," the son was told, "it will last as long as you retain your understanding." The last year at St. Omers was a rewarding experience for a boy who had endured the mnemonics of vocables and grammar in three languages. "Your judgment," his father now pointed out in reference to the current emphasis on classical eloquence in literature, "will enable you to enter into the reason of the rules and lessons you are learning." The style and literary devices of Cicero in the setting of the Roman Republic offered meaning beneath structure for the articulate gentleman who would one day take his place in public life and controversy. Both father and son had a genuine appreciation of Cicero as the classic type of orator, and Charles was truly grateful for a biography of Cicero which he received from his father at this time. The pride and satisfaction in a collection of books of merit now began naturally to develop in the young student's culture values through these rich days spent with some of the great prose of Western civilization.[22]

Yet all the parental and tutorial pressures to become a gentleman of parts were reasonable, even if the urging to rise to the rank of a Caesar did need some explanation. "Ambition to excel in virtue and learning," his father hastened to assure him, "is laudable." The priggish, the pompous, or the snobbish type of gentry need not come of this. But this was not easy to understand either, since Charles found such defects among his follows and masters, according to the ordinary laws of human frailty. His father had his own way of deterring him from such eccentric turns in gentlemanly conduct. "Fops are the object of contempt and ridicule everywhere," he wrote to Charles, "but it is from the fine gentleman you are to take example." Charles for his part responded with determination, professing that he would devote himself to "virtuous education alone." He was motivated by his father's contempt for the counterfeit as well as his esteem for the harvest in the good life that awaited the true Christian gentleman.[23]

In the late spring of 1754 Charles prepared to move further into the world of mature men, and by fall found himself in a new college for study in the year of poetry. He was not at all reluctant to leave the restrictions of St. Omers; but left behind among the masters and students, were many friends whom he cherished in the memories he took with him. Both he and his father felt assured in the prospect of spending the next year in the company of Anthony Carroll, now a priest, and once again his faithful tutor and instructor. The College of Rheims in northern France was not far away. There, studies in poetry were a part of the orderly curriculum he was pursuing with adequate preparation at each stage. He would study Greek and Latin authors with the added excitement of mastering them in association with new professors, French Jesuits, of whose accomplishments he had already heard at St. Omers. Marked with so many dramatic and crucial chapters in Western civilization, Rheims provided a stimulating environment. The commanding landmark of the cathedral epitomized the drama of the city as well as the nation born here with the crowning of the Dauphin by St. Joan of Arc. A maid Charles' own age was the moving force of the revolution which had driven the British out of France and had created a political form of nation that had for so long only smouldered in the hearts of Frenchmen.[24]

The College at Rheims had declined somewhat in size and quality as a result of a controversy which led to the formation of the *Collège des Bons Enfants*. When Charles arrived at Rheims its president was Father Jean-François Vayriot, and there were only 175 students enrolled, only fifty of whom were laymen. Classes began on October 18. The course of humanities or poetry continued until September 14 of the following year. The revised curriculum by now included a fuller treatment of history, geography, and heraldry. Remnants of the old glory of the college dedicated to Henry the Great in the seventeenth century still remained. A magnificent library of 18,000 books also remained as well as the famous theatres, the productions of which had long been of the finest among the Jesuit colleges.[25]

Charles and his small band of English scholars were introduced into the usual dormitory that was a unit of the whole larger cosmopolitan complex. As he entered into the study of poetic forms, he felt ill at ease, and had little interest, and, according to his own estimate, less success than he had experienced with prose studies at St. Omers. The atmosphere of greater freedom compensated for all of this; for he was no longer among a group which had a number destined for the seminary. Now, he was not concerned with choosing new dancing masters but with deciding if he would like to take up fencing, as his father had suggested. A wig at St. Omers may have been a fad to satisfy juvenile giddiness. His appearance now meant much more to him, and he had to decide if the natural appearance of his hair better suited the young adult than the full wig or the periwig. These were the stirrings of eighteenth-century male vanity. In their pride, both parents became anxious to learn more about their son's appearance. He finally had to heed his mother's entreaties that he have a fifteen-inch drawing sketched of himself. It was, after all, the proper thing for all young gentlemen to do at this stage of their development. The plans at this time called for only a couple of years more in Europe, and he had better attend to the matter.[26]

With his changing age and locale, Charles stood in need of advice during these difficult years. His father commended Anthony Carroll to him anew as his tutor and master. "Never be on the reserve with him," he tells his son, "or backward in asking his advice in everything, though to you seemingly insignificant." He would have personal problems in the new experiences of himself. "Look always upon him as your Friend," he says, "and not as your Tutor." While there would be no social affairs in mixed company, that day was only a few years away. His natural interest in women was now taking place in a setting where Charles was much freer and independent of both the college and his tutor. Heretofore, the father had left all direction in the hands of the "family" at St. Omers. Now at Rheims College and thereafter, he felt the obligation to give much more instruction and guidance to his son, although one could hardly say that he had ever been disinclined to do this from the moment his son left Annapolis.[27]

The program of studies was having its proper effect upon Charles, and in the fall of 1755 he was academically and temperamentally ready to proceed to Paris for his philosophical studies. His modest view of his achievements in poetry did not reveal the benefits he received, which would further elaborate the littérateur's temper, now so much a part of his personality. A sense for words, for the feeling they communicated, and their reflected enlightenment, which one of his intelligence gained from the poet's view of life's profoundest realities and experiences, all left his mind altered and prepared for what was ahead. The delicate thread of a propensity for reflection and analysis appeared between the lines of his letters which make up the narrative of his early years. This intellectual trait would now have fuller scope.

The fullness of cultural life was found in Paris in the eighteenth century, but there was also an aura of civic majesty, which provoked reflection as well as mood. The College of Louis the Great was in the midst of it all, and the Sun King had made it his favorite benefaction. The Jesuit theological and cultural tradition was hostile to the Jansenist message of this era which originated in its most eloquent seventeenth-century spokesman, Blaise Pascal. His *Provincial Letters* returned the volleys from Jesuit Colleges; Louis XIV shrewdly saw the Jesuits as a citadel against this theological enemy of the state, which prompted his patronage of the college named after him. The Jansenists, long after Louis' death, sought to change the prevailing Jesuit influence on party and policy in the royal chambers. In philosophy, the college stood against the stream of Cartesianism, now considerably turned aside from the main current of French thought when Charles arrived at Paris. Finally, Protestantism had long been under counterattack by Jesuit polemicists, and its French manifestation in the Huguenots literally drew the fire of Louis XIV's armies at LaRochelle. The edict of toleration favorable to them was revoked in his reign. Yet ironically, the French and other Bourbon court conspiracies would in time work against the Jesuits and their college as they formerly had against the Jansenists, who in the future would aid the court in process. The very enlightened despotism which had founded the school would destroy the Jesuit Order. This irony revealed the complicated intellectual condition of the Order and the college.[28]

It is not strange that during the period of alliance the Jesuits never yielded their ideology of limited civil authority. Francisco Suarez' liberal theories of the seventeenth cenutry never lost currency. Even the radical Juan Mariana was restudied in his justification for rebellion and regicide. The new natural law trend, well under way in the eighteenth century with Locke and Montesquieu, also constituted a rich enlargement of the more traditional Aristotelian and Thomistic studies and would be pursued by Charles at the college. There were many other subtle adjustments in the traditional Jesuit intellectual orientation. Just as the study of French gained emphasis in Charles' earlier years, so now the nationalism of eighteenth-century France called for patriotic themes in the Jesuit theatres at the college. The Jesuits formerly had asserted the primacy of *res publica Christiana,* the Christian political unity of Europe under papal auspices, but now after the breakdown of medieval forms they were preoccupied with the nation over which presided his Christian majesty. The over-tones of this realignment expressed much in the realm of Church-state separation and the national character of the Church in each European state. Some of the resulting enlightenment revealed the tradition of tolerance as a need for the state under the changed conditions. The French court was not left untouched by the trend, much less the college.[29]

The fluid state of things came home forcefully to Charles. There was structure enough in the college scheme of philosophy. He had to learn the outlines of logic in the classic style which became the pattern of colonial and revolutionary rhetoric. Concurrently this first year, he strove to master the systematic metaphysics of Aristotle and Aquinas. Mathematics in the dress of Sir Isaac Newton was also studied and given further development with programs in physics his second year. Charles would not find the same sureness here that he would in his other second-year subjects, such as morals and the main philosophical extensions of basic metaphysics. If his readings are any indication, this final year in which a comprehensive public defense of philosophy took place was also rich in seventeenth- and eighteenth-century thought, especially as it stemmed from John Locke. The whole dimension included not only relationship to the developing humanism of the era but also exploration of new Christian implications in the prevailing intellectual horizons of study and contemporary cultural developments. Here indeed is found in formation the distinctive lineaments of Carroll the public figure of the Revolution. Bourges, his next location for Roman and French civil law, and London there-after for English law, did not lead his mind from the contour im-pressed on it at Paris at this time.[30]

The social life of Charles was now cast in a very new setting which made him part of the intellectual life of the city. He resided at *L'Hôtel de Saint-Louis Rue,* in the district of *Saint-Antoine,* where other English students stayed in greater privacy than they had previously enjoyed. Father Edward Galloway served as master and tutor at the residence, a role in which he had some distinction. Having been at one time the tutor of Sir Robert James, Eighth Lord Petre, he was greatly familiar with conditions in England, where Charles might possibly pursue further studies. Lord Petre's son, Sir Robert Edward (1742-1801), was about this time entering St. Omers College. He would one day be a member of the historic Catholic committee which influenced passage of the Catholic Relief Act in 1778. Yet he kept his ties with Marylanders. By this time his friend Watty Hoxton had returned to America, where now as a correspondent Charles learned of his resumption of provincial life. It was from his mother, rather than Watty, that Charles heard of his friend's forthcoming wedding, "to an agreeable young woman of a good fortune and a Roman Catholick." Charles now found himself very much in the social life of the scholars in exile, but the confining chains of wedlock were far from his intentions. Instead, he was in the carefree way of collegians such as his friend Willoughby.[31]

Occasionally, there were visiting friends of his father, whom he entertained, some from far-flung places. Whether by design on his father's part, or not, they were frequently clergymen, a useful balance of adult fare to offset Willoughby. Charles must have found Father Rozolina from Italy interesting company. He should have been grateful for the glowing praise the Italian had for the recently arrived scholar at Paris as a highly refined and bright young gentleman. An atmosphere of excitement was found in his meeting with a clergyman from America recommended to him by his father. He had been in the Pennsylvania area in the first years of the French and Indian War and came into Charles' company fresh from an escape after the English debacle at Monongahela.

His father's letters commenting on the changing fortunes of the colonies further prepared Charles for a fuller understanding of these developments as they affected Maryland. He was by now aware of the unfavorable implications the war had brought to Catholics in the colony. Pierre de la Rue, another friend of his father, was in Paris at this time. As Vicar of Louisiana he was known as Abbé de l'Isle Dieu. He had recently seen his father help French Acadians expelled from Nova Scotia find a haven, as well as financial assistance, among Catholic families in Maryland. From him, Charles could learn the

French side of the controversy as well as the opportunities which Louisiana offered to Catholics who had been discriminated against in the English colonies and were in danger of further penalties as the war with France spread. Anthony Carroll retained his friendship with Charles even though he resided at Rheims at this time. He was also in correspondence with Charles' father and occasionally gave assistance to Charles. In time, he would take steps through the abbé with Charles to apply to the French government for a plantation in Louisiana, in the event that conditions in Maryland took a disastrous turn for Catholic estates like his father's.[32]

Chapter 3

THREAT OF AN ALIEN LIFE

After his sixteenth year, Charles became increasingly informed of events in the New World, particularly as the Great War for the Empire between France and England, also called the Seven Years War, moved to a crisis in 1755. His father's letters initiated him into the subtle pressures which the war, called in America the French and Indian War, brought to the Catholic counter-revolutionary society in Maryland. When Charles took up residence in Paris, his father soon involved him in the Catholic gentry cause. While he studied theories of the state, the nature of civil authority, and human rights in the academic halls, Charles also took part in the social struggle of his province. The conditions hostile to Catholics in Maryland led them to maneuver with the intention of securing permanent exile. Father and son together energetically and responsibly exercised leadership in this endeavor.

While Charles was still at St. Omers, his father had revealed his premonitions of an impending crisis. The assembly in 1753 stirred with militancy against the Catholic colonists. His father assured him for the moment with the hope that authorities and influences in London would curb the assembly's belligerence. Charles and his father must learn to stand as seasoned captain and tyro mate on the quarterdeck, ready for what might be ahead. "A continual calm in life," his father philosophized to the youth of seventeen, "is no more to be expected than on the ocean." In 1755, the storm broke. French forces in western Pennsylvania moved on the English settlements, together with Indian terror units. The atmosphere of hysteria which anti-Catholic forces in Maryland had been educated to use took hold of the colony and its assembly. Bills to put a double-tax on Catholic property to support the war were introduced over the opposition of the governor, councilmen of the upper house, and the proprietor. To remove this opposition, pressure could now be effectively applied by popular appeal to the notion that French and Maryland Catholics were of one piece. The latter were susceptible to sedition and should not be indulged by the proprietary party.[1]

Charles was able to get a complete picture of the military fortunes of General Edward Braddock from his father's clergyman friend who visited Charles in 1755 and had been on the scene a few months before. Young George Washington, together with Governor Robert Dinwiddie of Virginia, strove to stop the advance of Coulon de Villier. They constructed Fort Necessity at Great Meadows, after winning a skirmish with French forces from Fort Duquesne on the Monongahela River. By July, however, Washington had to give up the outpost. He devoted a year to organizing a larger force, which ultimately took shape under General Braddock in April, 1756. With 450 colonials Washington advanced with Braddock's force of 1,000 to within eight miles of Fort Duquesne. There an uncanny force of 900 Frenchmen and Indians in motley array confused and turned back the English, leaving Braddock mortally wounded on the field of the Battle of the Wilderness. Charles' friend retreated with the ranks of Washington to Fort Cumberland, Maryland, and proceeded to the Chesapeake Bay area, where he met with the elder Carroll and subsequently left for Europe. Had he gone to Annapolis with good news from the Monongahela the hysteria would have receded and weakened the hand of the double-tax protagonists.[2]

Shortly after this English fortunes took a better turn at the mouth of the St. Lawrence River and the Bay of Fundy, but this only further aggravated the condition of the Catholic community in Maryland. Colonel Charles Lawrence then succeeded in occupying French Nova Scotia for England. Seven thousand Acadians there who refused to take the oath of loyalty to the King were expelled. Having trouble with oaths himself and being of the same faith, Charles' father strove to win a chance for survival for those who were dispersed in Maryland. Such interests only confirmed his Maryland enemies in their mania for suspecting conspiracy and sedition.[3]

The Acadian episode and the defeat of Braddock convinced Charles' father that he must prepare for the worst. He did not cease to ply support for his defense with the proprietor, governor, and upper house, but he knew very well that only men of heroic stature and high principle could save him and his estate from the killing tax. The proprietary party proved men of another stamp, when the double-measure became law with their connivance. The price of curbing the hostile lower house was too high. Charles' father would continue his appeal to them, however, since a favorable turn and the ultimate success of England in the war would mitigate the anti-Catholic feeling. It would thus be easier for the proprietary party to do its duty and fulfill the fundamental law of the colony. He led the Catholic community in this effort. He could not, however, entirely count on such a probability. Indeed, there was even fear that additional penal laws would be imposed. So he had to face the awesome decision of exile in order to secure the future of his son in a way of life which he himself had fortunately inherited from the Founder. By his own correspondence and Charles' personal contacts with the French government he sought an estate in Louisiana, or a plantation on a French Caribbean sugar island. It would in addition be advisable to initiate the transfer of heavily-taxed landed wealth to another form.[4]

By the beginning of 1756, after seeing the implications of Braddock's defeat, Charles at his father's encouragement began to negotiate with the French government. As a young man of nineteen he met with Anthony Carroll to make their plans. Anthony himself had a close connection with one of the situations which had brought on the hostile Maryland legislation. He was heir in the James Carroll estate and Charles' father held his powers of attorney. This controversy had spurred Dr. Carroll into leading the anti-Catholic attack in the Maryland Assembly. The Church played a major political role in Louisiana as it did in France generally; as a mission land, this was even more the case. Charles and Anthony, therefore, first approached the vicar of Louisiana, Abbé de l'Isle Dieu, who was an elder churchman of about sixty-eight and a good friend of the Carroll family and who administered his office in Paris. The abbé was no longer uncomfortable in the presence of a Jesuit like Anthony. More than ten years had elapsed since the Bishop de Pontbriand of Paris settled the Jesuit-Capuchin controversy over jurisdiction in Louisiana by removing vicars of both orders there and giving full authority to Abbé de l'Isle Dieu. Charles' father was pleased by the initial efforts of his son and Anthony in which the abbé assisted.[5]

In the early fall of 1756, Charles heard again from his father. Charles had feared that his father's estates in the western part of the colony were in danger from the French advance in Pennsylvania; but the loss of his capital fortune as a result of the double-tax on Catholic land was a more serious danger. The sale of his Maryland property might also leave Charles' father a poorer gentleman. Land prices at this time would bring a loss of £10,000 in terms of the original valuation. Emigration from Maryland seemed the only alternative against greater loss over a period of time. Hope of relief coming from a swift English victory in the war faded. The Indians had taken only twenty-five Marylanders captive in the Braddock debacle, but this undoubtedly would further the hysteria against Catholics. The fall of Oswego in New York also contributed to this feeling. This English outpost "obstructed their [the Indians'] irruptions into the Southern Colonies," his father explained, while relating the other reversals of England. The treacherous massacre of English soldiers by the Indians in New York had created horror in the minds of Marylanders; but Charles' father was skeptical of the role assigned the French as instigators of that barbarity. The whole episode intensified the anxiety of his father's community, for it further fanned the suspicions that Maryland Catholics were on the point of collaborating with the Indians and the French.[6]

Charles' father was not without sympathy for the French Canadians, both in their territorial claims, and especially in the cause of the Acadians. He had an exaggerated view of the number of Acadians expelled, placing it as high as 15,000, more than twice the actual number. The same was true of the number said to be dispersed in Maryland. He was exasperated that he could not acquire fourteen Acadians for his own manor because the government intended to exclude Catholic estates in its allocations. Even though they had now taken an oath of loyalty to England that was not offensive to their religious beliefs, they were not treated as citizens or protected from great want which claimed the lives of some. They would have been better treated as prisoners. He realized that Charles would not read this view of the situation in the general press. Charles' father found the Acadians an admirable people in their religious life. Their agricultural and industrial skills were remarkable and their industry inspiring.[7]

Charles' father was favorable to the legitimacy of English territorial claims in the war, but felt that the situation of Nova Scotia, the home of the Acadians, did not make it a legal possession of England. Using the French exploration of waterways as a basis of reasoning to legitimate possession, he therefore considered the mouth of the St. Lawrence River region French territory Yet, a series of Anglo-French treaties greatly modified this application in favor of England. He left no doubt in Charles' mind that the French were unlawful aggressors in Pennsylvania. The Appalachian watershed, long possessed and settled by Englishmen on both sides, gave them undeniable title to it. This, however, did not displace the French claim to the Mississippi Valley through discovery and settlement. The claims of Virginia and other colonies that their boundaries extended from sea to sea, therefore, were not sound. As for his devotion to the English cause in the war, there was little doubt of its intensity; his love of Maryland and his country was strong beneath his narrative of the war. All of this in juxtaposition to a project of lifelong exile and a new world for Charles in Louisiana provided deep pathos to the lives of father and son, now on the verge of desperation. Even in distant Paris, Charles had tasted bitterness and despair.[8]

The French government had not responded to the Carroll project by the end of 1756. Nor were friends in England having much influence with the proprietary court or the privy council of the king. Strenuous efforts, therefore, would be required if Charles and his father were to succeed on both fronts against their enemies in Maryland. France was the primary objective, but England still claimed attention. More than before they now had to continue in England efforts at redress and disallowance of the new legislation, as a safeguard in the event of failure in France. Still there was a prospect of a declining fortune under heavy tax while petitioning in England dragged on. Persistence, however, had been a constant requirement in the counter-revolutionary society's discipline during the Founder's generation. Charles' father had been faithful to it in his own era, and he was instilling it in his son now as a scholar in exile in Paris. With Charles, he would pursue the Louisiana project there.

Beyond the world of politics another matter was calling Charles' father to Paris. He remembered his own hope that his father, the Founder, would come to the ceremonial climax of his career in the intellectual world more than thirty-five years before. In 1757 Charles was to have his own moment of philosophical defense in the public hall of the College of Louis the Great. Anthony Carroll encouraged young Charles' father to come, even though the Marylander hesitated at the expense of the ceremony and his voyage to Europe. He finally decided to go by force of the added motive of wishing to treat with French and English parties who might yet save his fortune by their governmental influence. Postponement of the voyage, however, was necessary until the end of the summer or early fall of 1757.

Charles' father arranged to have Richard Croxall administer his affairs in Maryland. Croxall was at this time ably managing the Baltimore Iron Works, the records of which Charles' father kept among his other duties as shareholder. The confidence was well placed on family grounds as well as others; for Croxall was the son of Joanna

Carroll, a sister of James Carroll who had written the famous contested will.

On June 2 Charles' father departed from Annapolis on a long voyage of seven weeks, which he logged day by day. He wished to preserve for his family a picture of the sea at the time of the Great War for Empire, technical details reflecting the gentleman's acquaintance with the laws of navigation, the exhilarating and prideful joy at first sighting Ireland, and the arrival in England on June 18. Charles retained the log after receiving it upon his father's arrival in Paris; and its contents undoubtedly provided the first pleasant conversations between father and son.[9]

Both anxiously bore the burden of the grim business at hand and turned to it as soon as family news had been told. Charles questioned his father about many details of Maryland politics which letters and other reports from Maryland had prompted. As father and son stood in Paris in the summer of 1757, they symbolized the Catholic counter-revolutionary society in full retreat. Their own kinsman, Charles Carroll the surgeon, had led the attack that turned them back from their progress toward freedom before 1754. Charles now learned how Dr. Carroll had stiffened his opposition to his father in an effort to recover a portion of the James Carroll estate. The surgeon drew upon the critical weapon of the statute laws, so effective a maneuver in the lower house, which he led. One of these laws *(praemunire)*, he contended, made it illegal for him to honor James Carroll's will where its trustee, a Roman clergyman, was named a beneficiary. When a special commission with Daniel Dulany as a member was indecisive in the case, he threw it into the lower house, only to be pursued there by Charles' intrepid father. Governor Horatio Sharpe wanted to avert such a setting for the controversy; his view of statute laws favored Charles' father but offended a large number of the assembly. Daniel Dulany had earlier been unwillingly implicated in this phase of the controversy and contended that Dr. Carroll had misstated his side to make him appear on the side of the surgeon.[10]

At this juncture, the estate question and the double-tax legislation came together as a force against Charles' father and his fellow Catholic gentlemen. He was accused of plying public officials, Dulany among them, and lower house candidates with entertainments in order to win and maintain their legislative support. Dr. Carroll did not need to explain that some of these men had long held judicial and political views to which Charles' father adhered, that they were of a common court or proprietary party. The clergy of the Established Church, a target on occasion of Governor Sharpe's criticism, came to the assistance of Dr. Carroll. Although the surgeon died in 1755, the anti-Catholic movement which he had led reached its full degree of needed momentum, to which the pulpit imparted a final thrust. The father of Samuel Chase, future compatriot of Charles in the Continental Congress, gave the attack its full rhetorical measure at St. Paul's Church shortly after the defeat of Braddock. He recalled the massacre of Protestants in the Pretender's rebellion in Ireland about ten years previously and warned that a Catholic conspiracy in Maryland was bringing its colonists ever closer to the blow of the French-directed Indians and their tomahawks. The warning was repeated by others, even in the assembly. Although an investigation by Governor Sharpe removed any reasonable grounds for fear, the pitch of hysteria and hostility did not abate.

In the tradition of the Revolution of 1688, a Protestant Association was formed to take the decisive action against Catholics which the conniving proprietary and court party were avoiding. Under this unrelenting pressure, however, the governor and his council of the upper house capitulated and helped pass the odious double-tax law, even though it was against their principles and the instructions which they had received from the proprietary court and the privy council. In the wake of this debacle, Charles' father arrived in Europe. He and his son now sought a disallowance of the law by appeal to the authorities in London and thus to provide against the possible failure to win a Louisiana or other French plantation in the New World.[11]

The Dulanys, father and son, were deeply involved in this complex contest, now strengthening, now compromising the cause of Charles and his father as well as the principle of freedom upon which it rested. Charles' feeling toward the elder Dulany was not without a mixture of gratitude. Dulany had justified the entertainments of Charles' father which the lower house had censored. When badgered about his having been educated at St. Omers and having once been a practicing Catholic, he acknowledged the facts without indulging any narrow hostility toward a religion which he said he had rejected by following a mature conscience. He further vindicated his allowance of an occasional mass in his mansion for the benefit of his wife, who maintained her practice of Catholicism. Like Governors

Bladen and Sharpe, he respected Maryland Charter rights and the Toleration Act as part of the early laws of the colony. He did not believe that the Catholics of Maryland were prone to sedition, as were Catholics of Elizabethan times; and this reasoning rather than the mere acceptance of the religion, whatever it might be, he believed, had been the basis of any such Elizabethan statutes against Catholics. He dared to argue these questions with Dr. Carroll.

As for his brilliant son, Daniel Dulany the Younger, the double-tax and other anti-Catholic measures fell on his own household as well as his father's. His sister had married a Catholic gentleman named Heath. About this time, upon the death of her husband, she was honoring her promise to him that she would send two of her sons to St. Omers even though it was against English statutory law to do so. All the same, the moment of reversal and retreat left Charles' father bitter about Dulany, even though the younger Dulany had lost his lower house seat in the assembly for voting against the double-tax. It was not strange that Charles inherited this aversion as part of the general grievance against the proprietary party for their conduct in the crucial hour of the double-tax law.[12]

Having heard all of this, Charles understood his dispirited father very well and he knew he himself was in a full retreat as part of the counter-revolutionary society. He helped his father get established at his residence in Paris. The business with the French government his father was about to pursue did not greatly appeal to Charles. He could understand how his father in the wake of the recent reversal of fortunes with the double-tax law sought a swift solution to his family's problems by exile on a Louisiana plantation. Here, a friendly government would be experienced for the first time in his life. Charles, his father, and Anthony Carroll planned their approach to the French government to petition for the plantation. Father and son met and dined with the Vicar of Louisiana, Abbé de l'Isle Dieu, and were assured of his support of their project. The Carrolls had in the past and would in the future prove his faithful benefactor in the cause of the expelled Acadians.[13]

In Paris, Charles' father could better appreciate the previous lack of French interest in his Louisiana project. He knew well enough that John Law's South Sea scheme, an extravagant investment venture in Louisiana, had met with disaster. Now he was fully aware that the French government had been extensively implicated in it, and that it had created a financial crisis. With hardly ten years to recover from the national calamity, the French farmers-general and other departments concerned with colonial projects were understandably ill-disposed in 1757 towards even such modest ventures as the Carrolls were proposing. These at minimum called for a grant of substantial acreage resembling the Maryland manors. If the Carrolls were favored, further requests would be made by them and others who were in the same plight. His Christian majesty was already faced with a disheartening array of Acadians pleading merely for alms. Their lot was far worse and as Frenchmen their claim on the royal favor was far greater. Munificence became the king, but at the height of a losing war, carried on in three hemispheres, he himself stood in need of benefactors.

Charles was far better prepared than his father for the outcome of the subsequent conversations with the French officials. In his distress of mind, his father had constructed what was in reality a utopian dream. The refusal of a grant now came; but because Louisiana was an emotional attachment Charles' father never fully believed that it had vanished from the realm of future realities; not so his son. He had not endured his father's trials in Maryland, and his imagination was not so easily taken. Maryland still stood and with it what his father and grandfather had built, however much it was threatened with diminution by hostile tax laws. The force of the colonial constitution had been weakened by the crisis of 1756; but it was not dead, nor were men like Dulany entirely drained of its spirit. Paris in the era of the Enlightenment left Charles with hopes and aspirations which were not a part of his father's generation. At the height of his public defense of philosophy, he was not without its spirit himself. He was not unlike the young reformers of the Roman Republic who set about rebuilding their society in its true and ancient form. This vision Charles would take to England and then to Maryland, where his father would soon return. Father and son would again urge the old proprietary party to recover the integrity shown on occasions before the capitulation of 1756. Charles now had to remind his father of the words he had received from him in a period of juvenile adversity; that peace and calm are not to be expected by those who pursue an ocean voyage, let alone on the course a minority had to travel. For Charles' part, he was still burdened with pursuing as far as possible the dream of a Louisiana utopia, since his father had not relinquished it.

Charles' father attended his son's formal public defense of philosophy; for Anthony Carroll had sought a postponement since the elder Carroll could not arrive for the usually appointed time in June. It was a delight for him to hear Charles execute the intellectual feat in French and proudly receive his son's thesis sheet to be framed for the walls of Doughoregan Manor. Conversation in this language of the eighteenth-century littérateur was natural to father and son, and carried over into their correspondence.[14]

The previous year, Charles' father had gone to great pains to enlarge his son's library, making possible personal copies of works by Newton and Locke. What should they say of Locke's philosophizing on toleration? This English philosopher believed that it should be extended to all Protestants, but many reservations were made regarding non-Christians and Catholics. The position of the elder Daniel Dulany was more acceptable to Charles than Locke's claim that the Catholics' belief in itself involved them in suspicion of sedition. As a member of a counter-revolutionary society Charles found little inspiration for reform of the English political system as it fell upon his Catholic fellows in England and Maryland.[15] Locke canonized a single revolution of 1688 without providing any rich vein of thought on toleration for future revolutionaries. While governments might be formed by social contract of the people, the majority once established were not clearly bound to respect those minority elements which might bring about future change and revolution. For reasons of state and on plea of public safety, Locke would say, a plausible case could be made against such dissidents as Catholics living under penalty at that very moment. This seemed no more than the Leviathan state of Thomas Hobbes. It was understandable that the young philosopher should turn to French masters whose thoughts probed the frontiers left open by Locke. The lecturers at the College of Louis the Great had introduced him to traditions of thought rich in meaning for his own revolutionary bent, notably in their commentaries on Suarez and Mariana. At least outright tyranny had an immediate, if violent solution, in their philosophical scheme. Locke would spill no blood with the Glorious Revolution of 1688, but there might be other days requiring violence, which Mariana certainly saw.

These matters were not all settled in Charles' mind at this time, but he would soon go to Bourges for the study of Roman and French civil law. Here the brilliant contemporary, Montesquieu, would provide him with insight into the intricacies of political systems, especially England's, and cast them in the light of the law of nature. Charles would pass into a realm of reflection beyond Locke, one rich in Montesquieu's empirical knowledge of society so much needed by the statesman. Already Charles had examined the French constitution as his father had directed, and they discussed its present operation in the throes of the Great War for the Empire. Together they visited the great historic landmarks of France, the *Parlement de Paris,* Versailles, and countless other scenes of stirring events.[16]

The provincial gentleman's interest in science was largely satisfied by the study of botany and experiments in the garden of his manor. While Charles expressed gratitude for a copy of one of Newton's works which he had received from his father the previous year, he wanted to know about the crops of the ever improving Doughoregan Manor and the botanical gardens at Annapolis. Charles admired the energy and courage of his father, who had the past few years set about building Doughoregan Manor in Baltimore County. The art and science of architecture also claimed the gentleman's interest; quarries and design were pleasant topics of conversation for Charles with his father.

French economic thought was now dominated by the Physiocrats. They exalted the agricultural society of the nation and the landed gentry which ideally should provide its leadership. This became the frame of Charles' economic mind, which he would share in future years with such admirers of French thought as Thomas Jefferson. Undoubtedly, Charles heard his father tell of his plans for mills and even manufactures on Doughoregan. All of this was not so much to be for the future of the father but for the son as heir. In these dark days, however, both were drawing strength to see that the dream would not vanish in the turns of political fortune in the Old and New Worlds. Since permanent exile no longer seemed realistic, at least to the son, the counter-revolutionary society must reassert its tradition of persistent legal attack in Maryland and England, in an attempt to recover the rights inherent in the Maryland Charter and fundamental law as a social contract.[17]

Not only in philosophizing, but in the other intellectual pleasures of the cultural and social life of his class, Charles and his father could find satisfaction in spite of their trials. There were the refined conversations pursued at this time with Abbé de l'Isle Dieu. The residence of Charles with his father's friend, Father Galloway, provided the setting for a pleasant supper hour and an evening of conversation. Charles had occasion to give his father a fuller appreciation and insight into his college associates. They met and dined with his student friend Willoughby, whose debonnaire manner stood in contrast to Charles'. He was introduced to Charles' friend M. D'Auge, kinsman of the Countess of Auzoüer. Father and son both found satisfaction and assurance in Father Alexander Crookshanks, with whom they associated at this time. This native of Scotland, once president of Douai College, now assumed special responsibilities for what guidance Charles needed in the present setting of his gentlemanly formation. He was a source of abundant information for Charles' father on a whole range of subjects—academic, book acquisitions, and even personal information about his son. Father Rozolino provided further cosmopolitan flavor to the associations of Charles and his father. Charles had other visits with this gentleman, who continued a friendship with his father by correspondence upon his return to Italy.[18]

The sun had not yet set upon the French theatre, which Molière had made famous a generation before. Pierre Augustin Caron de Beaumarchais, a future patron of the American Revolution and a contemporary of Charles, would soon become a dominant figure of the era. Charles' father seized the opportunity of his visit to attend the productions in Paris at that time. He noted the French eminence in staging and choreography. "Their Stage," he said by way of comparison with the English, "is also much more chaste." He was in general agreement with the lifelong esteem Charles held for the land and the life that had given him a cultural foundation in taste and values. "I have always entertained a high opinion," his father said to him on one occasion, "of the generosity and Politeness of the French." These pleasures of the mind and spirit in Paris soon became a treasured memory of father and son who had experienced them together and confirmed Charles in the high value which he put upon them. "I think of you very much," Charles would later write," and the agreeable time we spent together." This social feature of the aesthetic and intellectual life provided a beneficial counterpoise to his strong penchant for solitude with his books. As his education in

France turned out, he was left with these two poles about which his life and personality would always turn. They also held a wholesome attraction, even as now in times of trouble.[19]

During the last weeks of his father's visit in Paris, they had to decide upon the final details of Charles' education. His mother had earlier intimated in her letter that Charles might be expected to return after his defense of philosophy, just as his father had done. His father's regrets at the lost opportunity to study law in London were still with him, even though he was a highly successful man of affairs. Since the desperate dream of permanent exile in Louisiana had only receded and never disappeared from his mind as he conversed with Charles in Paris, an English legal education would not serve its purpose in the event the Louisiana dream materialized. His hope was that the next year would settle the question definitively. If the French affair continued in the present direction, it would be doomed to failure beyond hope. Charles had undoubtedly seen that this would be the outcome and realized that he would have to take up his place in the Maryland counter-revolutionary society armed with a London education in law.[20]

A very profitable choice, suited to both eventualities, appeared. At Bourges, Charles could spend a year in the study of Roman and French civil law. Montesquieu had made the intellectual world in which Charles moved aware of the deep roots which European societies had in Roman law and the classics. He had further shown how the laws of the modern nations and their reform could be brought about by an analysis of law in those times. This great philosopher of jurisprudence, who had died but two years before the arrival of Charles' father, enjoyed renown in the halls of the College of Louis the Great, where its eminent scientist and philosopher Father Louis-Bertrand Castel had provided critical companionship to Montesquieu in his last years while composing *The Spirit of the Laws*. Charles' studies at Bourges would further encompass the developments of basic law in France as it derived from the period of Roman dominion, thus preparing for the contingency of a future life in a French province. It was therefore agreed to make arrangements for a program at Bourges which would also be a suitable prelude to full study at the inns of law in London. Before his father's departure from Paris, Charles, with Father James Power, who was living at Bourges, made arrangements for his new studies. By the end of September, the

Jesuit informed Charles' father that he had found a private instructor.[21]

In November, Charles prepared for the departure of his father from Paris for England, where the elder Carroll would take into his own hands the cause of freeing Maryland Catholics. His father had not been satisfied with the efforts of his merchant friends with the proprietary party and its court. He would now personally strive to bring about the proprietor's disallowance of the double-tax. To this business of state, Charles gave his full support. He was even willing to play his own role in London

Though excited about his own plans to move to Bourges, he felt great sadness at the moment of his father's departure in the late fall. This was not the child's farewell of many years ago at Annapolis, but that of a young adult, who had deepened the relationship that had been kept alive by correspondence and by nearly four months of companionship. The prospect of a permanent French exile, although affluent compared to what might be ahead in Maryland, seemed fortunately to be passing from his father's intentions. His battles for English legal rights in London and Maryland would go on in the effort to stem the inroads into the Carroll fortune as well as to achieve and secure Charles' future well-being in Maryland society. Father and son parted, firmly agreed on this common cause.[22]

Chapter 4

STUDENT OF REFORM AND GENTILITY

In November of 1757, Charles departed from Paris in a more genteel manner than when he had arrived. A fuller measure of gentility also marked his living circumstances in Bourges, where he now proceeded, especially in its social adjuncts. He would learn to make practical judgments about the gentry code which was taking root in his mind and manner. The foundations of legal reform could also be found in the studies he was about to pursue at Bourges; he had absorbed the reformer's *esprit de corps,* which his father had communicated in his Paris visit. The gentleman's role was at a more advanced stage than that of the legal reformer; he needed only greater scope to apply that code. As a legal reformer, it is true, he was but entering the ivory tower; but there had already been instances of acting in the gentleman's role. Others would come at Bourges and at Paris, to which he would return for some months before his departure for law study in England. The pursuits of both ideals, the legal reformer and the gentleman, complemented each other.[1]

"I never in my life made so dull and melancholy a Journey," Charles complained of his trip to Bourges. Had he foreseen the consequences of riding a public coach he would have hired a private one. That would surely have seemed more suitable in view of the fact that he had a servant with him. But there were limitations even here to the standards of the grand manner. The servant lad was honest and helpful, but awkward and simple; so many directions were necessary. When Bourges came in sight, he experienced further disappointment. Hardly 15,000 souls inhabited the city; to one who had forgotten Annapolis but seen Rheims and Paris, the anticipation of a social life calculated to improve a young gentleman was slight indeed. The carriage stopped in front of the modest private home of M. Carré Medeur, where he would reside, a place which Charles described as discreet and regular. The residence of his private *docteur professeur* of law was but a short distance away.[2]

He arrived on a Saturday and with the help of his servant established himself in his new residence. His tutor, Father Power, had done well enough in what he had arranged thus far. After mass the next day, he learned further what the social setting of Bourges would require of him and what he could gain in return. The important figures of the city came to the church on Sunday. After mass, they and ordinary people of the town by custom individually greeted the chief official of the city, *Monsieur l'Intendant.* It was not long after such acquaintances that Charles made the financial calculations regarding his social demands. A capital budget of £130 *per annum* would perhaps do. There were new requirements of elegance beyond what he had had in Paris. He needed twenty-six shirts. "Some of 'em," he wrote to his father, "must absolutely have work'd ruffles: for nobody here weares plain ones when he goes into company."

Father Power now had a chance to explain the purpose of the academic arrangement which he had made for Charles. He was himself only a part of the small Jesuit College community which was but a unit of the whole University of Bourges. One of its Jesuit scholars, Guillaume-Francois Berthier (1704-1782), won fame in the university and throughout France as editor of the *Journal de Trevoux* and contributor to *l'Histoire gallicaine*. At one time he was master or tutor of King Louis XVI. The lecture halls of the faculty of law were not without distinction. About the time of Charles' enrollment the brilliant young François-Michel Vermeil (1732-1810) was studying at Bourges. He was one day to become famous for his treatises on criminal law; he eventually held the offices of highest adviser to the king's ministry of justice and was counselor of the court of highest appeal. The private lectureship provided Charles would bring far more than regular attendance at the lecture halls; and more would also be demanded of him. A private residence was therefore desirable. Because of his status as a scholar under a *docteur professeur,* his own genteel origins, and family connections also gave him entrée to the social and cultural life of the city. All of this, Father Power was convinced, would give Charles "the acquaintance of the most genteel folk of the town [*la connaissance des plus honnêtes gens de la ville*]," over which the *l'Intendant* presided. Charles' former tutors also assisted him in these first ventures into a place in society. Father Anthony Carroll at Rheims and Father Crookshanks in Paris had collaborated to bring some fine and useful volumes to Charles. Father Power needed a dictionary to help his English along, even if Charles needed none for his French. Father Crookshanks sought out two volumes of the Greek poet Pindar for Charles' father. Charles was encouraged by his father to live with liberality and not to fear incurring expenses for useful academic or social benefits.[3]

After Charles had become well established in his quarters and his servant initiated into providing for his needs, he ventured forth on a series of social occasions. On December 18, he went to the anxiously

awaited dinner with *Monsieur l'Intendant*. The appropriate conduct
was indeed not yet second nature, as he candidly confessed. There
were sixteen guests in attendance. Distracted by shyness and the new-
ness of the experience, he was unable to recall later whether there
were five or six women at the affair. Fond of conversation, he felt
himself out of place when the men became engrossed in a card game
for stakes. "I do not much like that diversion," he later told his father,
"yet I must absolutely know how to play to go into company." On
December 19, he had dinner with Father Power and his guests, which
was more satisfying. "They are all my friends," he believed, "and I
am persuaded very sincere ones." It was still possible for him to visit
the Abbé de l'Isle Dieu for more refined entertainments.[4]

It was not long before Charles was able to gain better acquaintance
with the young ladies whom he had met during his first weeks in
Bourges. In addition to his initial shyness; he had other handicaps
which he admitted. "I was a perfect stranger," he said, "and not well
acquainted with their dances." He was determined to learn the
popular dances, so different from those he was taught at St. Omers
and Paris. Charles was swift in removing this barrier as well as that
of his standing as a stranger in the city. "I had the pleasure of accom-
panying and danseing with one of the most beautifull young ladies
I ever saw," he reported in February of 1758. "Don't be afraid now
that I am fallen in love with her," he assured his parents. "There is
no danger; she is going in a few day's time to Paris to be married
there to a handsom [sic] gentleman of a pretty fortune: her's is but
very inconsiderable." His father should have been satisfied that Charles
had an eye to the financial ingredient in any marriage of a gentleman.[5]

His new associations brought him to others outside of Bourges, one
of these being the charming household of an English manufacturer
at Chante. Charles accepted an invitation to tour Monsieur Alcock's
button factory and marvelled at its industrial techniques. Greater
fascination was found in his daughter, who reciprocated the interest
of Charles. His meetings and infatuation with Mademoiselle Alcock
made him bold in telling his parents how independent of parental
authority love for her might make him. If he wished, such beauty and
wit could lead him to put aside objections which his parents might
make to a proposal of marriage. Fortunately for them, he had no such
wish. After a few months the philosopher in him neutralized the
volatile ingredient of the romantic, an affliction of reformers. He

knew that he was not in love, yet for the first time he felt that he now knew what love might be. By August he discovered what was yet needed in a woman to win his heart. "The qualities of Mademoiselle Alcock are very mediocre," he explained, "or rather I should say she has nothing better than her vivacity and her beauty." Charles' ideal woman should be styled to the pattern of his gentry code, which said she must be "sensible," and able to profit by the conversation of a gentleman. This was the meaning such formulae of gentry literature implied for him. Quite simply, Mademoiselle Alcock could not sincerely enter into the excitement of those intellectual, literary, and artistic interests that were by now so much a part of himself. Could he ever find a woman to share such a heart?[6]

In the course of the summer of 1757, when Mademoiselle Alcock claimed Charles' attention, he introduced her to his friend Willoughby. It was not like Willoughby to look beyond the romantic realm, as Charles had done. He was entirely taken by the wit and beauty of the young lady. The romance was in full bloom at the end of the summer, helped by several social affairs under Charles' sponsorship. One of these found the two young gentlemen at the Alcock villa for a party. Willoughby was carried away by the conviviality of the evening, and by the free flow of strong punch. When the ladies retired, he continued in his cups. After Willoughby had gone to bed, he soon awoke and felt the need of relieving himself. By mistake, he entered a maid's room and used the bed which she occupied in accomplishing his purpose. Her shrieks awakened enough guests to mortify Mademoiselle Alcock. Charles played consoler of his friend the next day, confident that he would survive his hapless joust with cupid. As his French narrative of the episode reveals by its comic vein, the wound would mend, since Willoughby's affection for this proper young lady probably was not much deeper than Charles' own. Charles was confirmed in his own good habits; for they were calculated to avoid the loss which Willoughby incurred as a rejected lover due to this comic event and the carelessness that caused it.[7]

Charles became restless with life at Bourges by the end of the summer. Not only did the legal studies tire him but the round of parties as well. The thought of travel relieved him of tedium, and so he began to make plans for a trip to Lyons. It would be proper to take this with Father Power, in order to secure instruction and suitable accommodations as well as companionship. Willoughby would also go along and assure that the travel would be a vacation for students and young gentlemen in need of variety in the pleasures in which they were being educated.[8]

From London, Charles' father viewed his son's initiation into Bourges society. He was, of course, intent upon reforming Maryland law and removing the double-tax. William Bladen, who had been appointed governor in 1742, now resided in London. He and his father had been neighborhood friends of the Carrolls at Annapolis. Charles' father was hospitably received by the Bladens, who sympathized with his cause. The former governor, who was married to Lady Baltimore's sister, promised a favorable influence. George Plater, another Marylander residing in London, was also visited. Charles' father had many contacts with London English merchants, such as William Perkins, and they were also enlisted in his cause. These were special moments for the father to instill further in Charles the ideals of gentlemanly conduct, which heretofore were largely confined to the books Charles had read. The father seemed to view Bourges as a laboratory, where he sought to induce the proper form of activity and measure its effects on the young gentleman. He had lingered a considerable time in London, unable to find passage to America and did not leave until April 1, 1758. On leaving, he gave his son an account of his own cultural experiences in England. He had already seen three performances at London theatres. The stages were more confined than those of Paris, he felt, but the dramatic power of David Garrick, now in his fortieth year, completely captivated him and made him forget the pageantry of the more spacious stage productions in Paris. His father noted for his son's moral instruction, however, that some of the plays which the English chose to produce were scandalous and left a bad effect on society, particularly on women. *The Provoked Wife,* which he saw performed, would have offended a virtuous woman's modesty, at least in such a public setting, but not the least blush came to the women whom he observed in the audience. Charles could see that this commentary put Mademoiselle Alcock's conduct with Willoughby in a better light since more was demanded of a woman's modesty than a man's on whom rested the obligation of propriety in her company.[9]

Charles had already accepted his father's understanding about the formation of friendships even before he received such advice in a letter of January. He should not make too many acquaintances. "A return of civilities is to be paid to all," his father explained, "an intimacy is not to be contracted with any, until you are well acquainted with their characters and manners and until you are convinced they are in the esteem of good men." So he had proceeded in the formation of his friendship with the Alcocks. In time, however, he would have to expect certain unhappy incidents to occur. With Willoughby in mind, Charles could have commented on this refinement of an ideal. Thoughtfulness and munificence foster friendships once carefully made; polite letters of thanks, the gift of a volume on Horace to *Monsieur l'Intendant,* and other civilities, were all gestures which Charles made at this time under his father's encouragement.[10]

Reports of his progress as a gentleman pleased his father, who heard of his "Pious[,]Prudent and regular behaviour[;]. . . sweet temper and disposition[;] proficiency and figure in Studies. . . ." The father felt assured that his son had discovered the wisdom which was productive of such excellent conduct. "The beginning of wisdom is the fear of the Lord [*Initium Sapientiae timor Domini*]," he observed. "Always remember this." He encouraged him to spend some time in the company of women, without engaging in any intimacy; for this "will contribute to soften and polish ye manners." The sociability which all of this required was not incompatible with the fear of the Lord. "A cheerfull, lively, easy and polite behaviour is [in] no way inconsistent with Religion or your Duty to God," he explained. "Nothing contributes so much to your comfort here as Innocence and a clear Conscience; it heightens all ye pleasures of Life and enables us to bear as we ought ye Crosses and Afflictions incident to it." Trained so thoroughly to the manner of a Christian gentleman as he was, there was no danger of an affectation which tainted the foppish or the cynical gentlemen, who were then having their day in European society, particularly in England.[11]

Only candor on Charles' part made possible this free expression of idealism by the father. He did not resent his advice, so much so that his father felt free to say: "I often wish it was possible for me to inspect and direct your conduct." They both understood, however, that this would have deprived the son of the rich measure of maturity which he gained during these years at Bourges and Paris. The ties of correspondence were ideally suited for bringing about the good effects that were so visible. The gentry were envious of their good name as it lived on in their sons, but Charles' father was far more intense than most in his devotion to the training of a worthy heir to the Carroll name, traditions, and fortune.[12]

Charles had become accustomed to excursions into various parts of France even during his days at St. Omers. Those who had a hand in his academic guidance later recommended travel, and his father was especially encouraging, seeing it as essential to the gentleman's formation. At Bourges, Charles' reading and his growing knowledge of Europe's past and present added depth to the visual perception of what he had previously found only in books. Early in his residence at Bourges, social acquaintances extended invitations to nearby places, like Chante, where he visited the Alcocks in the summer of 1758. In June, he viewed the beautiful valley of the Loire River, which captured his imagination and inspired him to set down in a letter to his mother a very artistic description of its magnificence.

The Province of Sancerre also enchanted him. Here was set a nostalgic episode reminiscent of the Pretender's rebellions. A Scottish lord resided there, a melancholy victim of the abortive rebellion of thirteen years earlier. The agony of exile had driven him to excessive drink, a misfortune known to the townfolk with whom Charles spoke. The gendarmes discouraged Charles from visiting the pitiful man, who once in his power enjoyed an income of £3,000 a year. Having faced the prospect of exile himself, he charitably judged the Scot a "good, honest, man, unhappy 'tis true but worthy of a better fate." That he was a rebel did not condemn him by one given to revolutionary thoughts himself, and Charles was also sympathetic to those who would change the practices of England's dealings with such citizens.[13]

The October journey of Charles, Father Power, and Willoughby to Lyons became very extensive. They set as their destination the ancient city of Toulouse in a southernmost province, whose vitality had existed even in the days of the Roman Republic. The path of their leisurely journey was filled with fascination as they passed to Charité, Nevers on the Loire River, and Moulins on the Allier. They continued southward through Airnion, Nîmes, and Montpellier on the Mediterranean; then westward along the coast of Posenas, Péciers, and Narbonne. They proceeded northwest by way of Carcassonne, Castelnaudari, and finally entered Toulouse. The return northward held special interest for the young scholar of French jurisprudence, for Charles and his companions passed through the Province of Guyenne, over whose *parlement* Montesquieu had presided a few years before. On the left bank of the Garonne River, stood La Bréda and, not far from the city, the ancestral estate of Montesquieu. In the south of France, he found the marvels of Languedoc with its industrious peasant farmers, so much like the Acadians, and their ingeniously constructed canals. By Limoges, he returned northward to Bourges, much refreshed and renewed in his enthusiasm for the law his masters had waiting for him.[14]

At the outset of his stay at Bourges, Charles had found the necessary solitude, which his father had told him study would conquer, depressing. The right amount of social life was added to the formula, along with the exhilaration of travel at reasonably appointed times, so that a pattern of life was set in these days. From such a way of life, would come the gentleman of mature and well informed judgments based upon a peaceful and thoughtful spirit. Charles indeed came to move as a true and self-possessed humanist. His sallies into politics with the inspiration to reform society had their source and fruitfulness in this balance of life. In this carefully constructed social and intellectual setting, it is not strange that Charles had a mature intellectual awakening. He had found a social code of Christian orientation; an intellectual life which encompassed the aspiring young humanist. The character of the man which the American Revolution would one day know was cast. Beneath his social life, were forming the ideas of the reformer. The intense study of these days gave the decisive impetus both to the intellectual and the reformer.[15]

Since the winter of 1757, Charles was meeting frequently with his *docteur professeur* of Roman law. The tutorial and other assistance which Father Power provided facilitated complete application to the study of Roman law, and his servant freed him from further practical details. His rich background in the history and literature of classical times had enlarged his background perspective for this study. At the same time, he was able to keep alive his broader interests in the arts, letters, and history with reading which provided diversion as well as intellectual improvement.

In the summer of 1758, he moved on to the demanding study of French civil law. The ramifications of Roman law reached into French legal traditions as it did into English law. For this difficult pursuit, he fortunately came upon a very excellent master in Professor Champion, a friend of the Duke of Norfolk. The Carrolls were known to the Duke, who had recommended Champion. It was not entirely certain at this time that Charles would proceed as far as a formal study of English common law as it was usually treated. The great master of both Charles and his professor, however, was the eminent French scholar of jurisprudence Jean Doumat (1625-96), who had completed his monumental work *The Civil Laws in Their Natural Order* in 1694. With so challenging a study and such a master *("clair, net et précis")*, Charles wrote to his father in August that he "would like much better to live as a hermit like Diogenes", absorbed in studies. He was ready for the complex study of the scholar who had sought to reform French law as it had grown up in tangled fashion from earlier Roman and provincial law. French law was not unlike the course of recent Maryland law, which had obscured the original trunk of fundamental law and right. Doumat cited the unequal application of the law as it stood. Charles must have found the example he gave of this in the Duchesse du Bouillon a striking motive for a reformer. Jealousy drove her to murder the actress Adrienne Lecouveur, having her barber deliver the lethal potion. The hapless agent was executed; but in the court decision, the Duchesse, though a conspirator, was untouched. In a less dramatic way, the double-tax on Catholics in Maryland had defied fundamental justice found in the seventeenth-century "Conditions of Plantations," which required that all property be uniformly taxed without discrimination.[16]

As Charles moved by instinct into the philosophical reflections about the foundations of civil law, he readily turned to Montesquieu, whom he was reading at this time. Each nation, according to Montesquieu, tends to elaborate a system of authority which stands behind its laws. In his *The Spirit of the Laws*, published in the middle of the eighteenth century, he explores how the law of nature operating in each nation demands specific systems of authority in order to avert the arbitrariness which Doumat depicted in the unreformed French law. The court in itself is not a comprehensive fulfillment of justice for the citizens of a country. Those who make laws and those who execute them for the good of a society exercise authority in a way that affects the conditions of justice in the life of the citizen beyond the action of the courts. Tyranny can become entrenched in either of these three quarters. In the conditions of Western Europe nations, such as France and England, a check and balance of these authorities can prevent tyranny and the arbitrary application of the law by the particular authority behind it.

Charles had made the acquaintance of Montesquieu earlier in the general perspective of his philosophical studies at Paris. In pursuing the author further at Bourges, he now became anxious to secure his own personal copy. Looking forward to the possibility of the study of English law and life in a province of the Empire, he found special interest in the extensive treatment which Montesquieu gave to the English structure of authority. He had personally experienced the inequities of its legal system, and throughout his life, his father had struggled to reform it. Charles had by now become determined to play the reformer himself. Though at present in the role of Diogenes, he foresaw that the role of Gracchus might not be far away. All of this added to the vitality of his intellectual pursuit and the richness of his philosophical awakening.

He was not in the climate that breeds the hack lawyer. Montesquieu and Doumat brought him into the vast panorama of Western civilization as an historical process. The one was rich in delineation of classical times, the other of the growth of a nation. Charles had by now become familiar with the far-reaching portrayal of New France in the pages of Pierre de Charlevoix, who had himself seen the vistas of the Mississippi Valley and the Louisiana Province.[17]

At Bourges, too, Charles came under the commanding view of civilization as an organic process of growth. In the optimism of the Enlightenment, he vested civilization with the law of progress, which as an idea animated the social reformers of the day. He was clearly beginning to take his place among them in the vision of the future with which he now began to wrestle. As in the case of Montesquieu's writings, he was determined to buy his own copies of the works of Voltaire.

Voltaire was in the midst of the headlong career of heterodoxy, and Charles followed his intellectual adventures of the day with zest. Was Voltaire not educated in a manner like his own under the Jesuits at Paris? Charles was excited at this time by news that the brilliant intellectual, wielding a cudgel against orthodoxy, was preparing *L'Insprit,* which was said to be written *"avec peau coup".* Charles told his parents that Voltaire was under judgment of excommunication, and that *L'Insprit* was about to draw hostile fire from the Church's citadels in France. It was trouble enough to espouse principles contrary to religion, as the prelates judged his work. When the royal court found itself also under attack from Voltaire, a typical Gallican collaboration of Church and state to repress it boded ill for the career of the iconoclast. In 1756, Voltaire wrote his *Essay on the Customs and Spirit of the Nations*, which was diet for any reformer. The striving of the human race in its long career is outlined and interjected with biting attacks on episodes of tyranny. It was destined one day to be nourishment for the apostles of the French Revolution. In 1758, when Charles was following the rumors about *L'Insprit*, Voltaire's most popular work, *Candide*, was published. Using Leibniz' philosophical remark that this is the best of all possible worlds, Voltaire portrayed Candide in his career as evidence to the contrary. In his best satirical flairs, evils of the day were seared by his social commentary.[18]

Voltaire was what the young reformer required, since Charles saw much that was wrong with his own world. Was not his own father an iconoclast in that world? His was not the world which was the target of Voltaire, nor was Voltaire's Church and its religious doctrine entirely what Charles had known. The course of English Catholicism, particularly in Maryland since the seventeenth century, had been in a channel of freedom. It was neither the Ultramontane nor the Gallican Church of France. Doubt arose in Charles, as his complicated mind confronted Voltaire's passages so hostile to the revealed religion of Christianity. But such a mind had a critical context in which the negative chaff of the iconoclast was sifted. Voltaire's own dogmatism did not escape Charles' discerning mind. In the intellectual crucible, the case for tolerance in Voltaire undoubtedly meant the most to Charles. He saw that English Catholicism had stood for it, while the rationalist tradition to which Voltaire adhered had in England experienced blind spots. Application of that theoretical toleration had not benefited his own Catholic society in Maryland. Standing within that Catholic counter-revolutionary society among English people, Charles had reform grounds which were similar to what Voltaire theoretically articulated in France; he hoped to see their realization in greater freedom.

Charles revealed the tough fiber of his mind as he thought through the Enlightenment writers and their humanistic ideal. He made it clear to his father why he could be both a complete gentleman and a good Christian, with a freshness and creativity that his own intellectual experience of the Enlightenment produced in him. "If I practice what you teach," he wrote from Paris in 1759, "I shou'd not only be a compleat gentleman, but a good Christian, which is much ye most important of ye two." Such a Christian was judged by a good conscience, intelligently formed and reflected in a virtuous life. Charles understood the virtues of the mind as well as those overtly revealed in moral conduct. These are "ye greatest blessings we can enjoy on earth." He confessed that he did not aim at canonization to sainthood as popularly understood. "I detest served up devotion, distorted face, & grimace," he wrote of a common misconception of the full Christian life. On the other hand, he attacked the very authors whom he had read and who to his mind were not convincing in their satirical assaults on the essence of his religion and the life it was intended to produce. "I equally abhor those," he said, "who laugh at all devotion, look upon our religion as a fiction, & see its holy misteries as the greatest absurdities."[19]

Charles himself showed no small measure of achievement as a Christian gentleman and modestly acknowledged it. "I observe my religious duties," he said humbly; "I trust in ye mercy of God not my own merits, which are none, & hope he will pardon my daily offenses." He was honest about the stage of his spiritual progress and saw it in both theological and philosophical dimensions. "I retain as yet that salutary fear of his Justice," he candidly revealed, "which by ye wisest of men is stiled *initium sapientiae* [the beginning of wisdom]." Yet, his relationship to God was not without the warmth of charity, which stood in the context of reverence and humility: "I love him [,] tho' far less than his infinite goodness deserves & I would wish to do."[20]

Judging from the general reading of Charles at this time, Voltaire's prose satisfied his taste as littérateur as much as philosopher. His letters show a penchant for the satire and the rhetoric of his era which exalted trenchant criticism. He employed both in his career from this time forward. Some of his time was devoted to the delights of French dramatic literature.[21] He said that he was more refreshed by the company of the French playwright Racine than the social set of Bourges. The setting of *Britannicus* in ancient Roman times was congenial, and the theme indicting imperial tyranny struck a note of accord with his reformer temperament as he read the play of the seventeenth-century master. He was anxious to buy his own copies of Jean-Baptiste Regnard's comedies, and the tragedies of Prosper de Coepillion. Charles was at the height of a great intellectual awakening as he began to conclude this period of study in Roman and French civil law and in these other ever widening intellectual interests.[22]

There was still a menial chore to which Charles must learn to attend: keeping a ledger. He had, at this time, fretted about his budget and how he could reconcile twenty-six shirts of linen, some with ruffles, with the money alloted by his father. The accounts-master of the Baltimore Iron Works could instruct him in this matter, and his father as usual was not reticent about doing so. Charles should pursue this business of bookkeeping with as much regularity as his lofty legal studies and reading of literature. It would not harm the latter pursuits. "Keeping regular accounts need not restrain you from things necessary and decent," read his father's instruction. "It will rather enable you to procure them [necessities] with greater satisfaction." If careful records are kept of expenditures, his mind will be in better order for a peaceful pursuit of higher things. "As by a review of your accounts," he explained, "you will see whether your money has been well or needlessly expended." He should especially make use of his affluence, which will free his mind from concern with trifles. His father's agent in London would increase the amount of his budget if he should decide that this was necessary after careful computations. So it was that the final detail of a gentleman's way of life was being mastered as part of the whole man which his father hoped would be formed by this time.[23]

The thoughts of Charles, in exile though he was, were never allowed to stray from his beloved Maryland, still in need of legal reform. Of this, he learned from his kinsman, good friend, and former tutor, Father Anthony Carroll, who was still involved in the litigation of his uncle James Carroll's estate, which dragged on under the discriminatory treatment of the colonial government. Charles' father continued to assist the cause at this time acting with powers of attorney for Anthony. Anthony referred to Charles as the reason for such loyalty. "You are the first gentleman I have ever known," he remarked pleasantly to Charles' father, "to be thoroughly content with his son's governor." The devoted master now had a more troublesome charge in the young son of Ireland, the man who oversaw a Carroll manor in Maryland, and who now made him appreciate even more his former charge. Charles sympathized with the boy, putting the blame on the seminary-like atmosphere of St. Omers, which in time would drive the confused lad back to Maryland. The generous Anthony also became involved in the welfare of the son of the deceased Doctor Charles Carroll, the very source of all the mischief in the James Carroll estate.[24]

Further enactments of the Acadian tragedy now fell as a troublesome burden upon both Charles and his father. Charles had continued his cordial visits and letters to the Abbé de l'Isle Dieu and was disposed to good offices in his favor. The Abbe's letters to his father portrayed the latest harsh treatment which the British had inflicted on the missionaries in conquered French territory. He revealed that young Charles had been most generous to him, giving financial assistance to help his priests in the crisis. The Abbé, at Charles' father's request, gave Charles accounts of the war which his father had sent to the Abbé along with his responses to earlier letters. The following year, Charles was told by his father that he must prudently restrain his generosity. "You are likely to be cheated," he stated quite baldly. The people of Maryland had tired of supporting the Acadians, and they cost his father more than 2,500 *livres*. Charles should let the Abbé know of this situation. "I should not mention it," he told his son, "but I am provoked at ye injustice done you." Fortunately, by this time, Charles was on his way to London from Paris and did not have to make the reproach verbally. As it was, he could politely decline further finances by writing a letter. The generosity of the Christian, all the same, was unmistakable in these dealings with the Abbé. Works of mercy stood high in the scheme of Anglo-Catholic spirituality, and Charles had been well formed in its ideals.[25]

Charles now found that his father again carried the same troubled mind which he had when they parted company a year before. Evidently, the negotiations with the authorities in England earlier in the year were not promising. The Louisiana project still haunted the horizon, inviting new efforts at a settlement but his father saw there was no hope there. His father's Italian friend Rozolino had chided him for the lack of spirit which the English commanders showed in the war with France. They had a greater destiny. Now the poor progress of the war only dampened hope of relief from hostile Maryland laws. Charles learned from his father's letter of that month that the picture to the north brightened somewhat in July of 1758. England had taken Louisburg. Charles should get out his maps in Charlevoix and see how strategic that post was. Impressive naval statistics were cited. Ticonderoga appeared to be a focus of attack for the English, but reports were too uncertain to learn if there was further hope there.[26]

By November, Charles had acquired an optimism which his father lacked. In his growing maturity and respect for his work at Bourges, he boldly stated his own view of his father's future in Maryland. He should stay there and put away the unrealistic dreams of moving away; rather harsh words to one who had weathered the most difficult battles of the counter-revolutionary society. The young reformer, however, was reading the signs of British fortunes more accurately than his father was. He took into account the European forces at work in the Great War for the Empire in his evaluation of the war in the New World. British victory was more than probable in these terms, and with that victory the excuse for discriminatory legislation in Maryland would be removed. Then too, was there not hope to be found in himself as a promising recruit to the Maryland campaign for legal reform? His father began to awaken to the potentials of Charles whom he had nourished and encouraged to the stature as the young man now had. He could look back a year later in August of 1759 and see that his son's optimism was fulfilled. Under the emerging leadership of William Pitt in England, General Geoffrey Amherst was assigned the American command; Ticonderoga had fallen to the British, and General James Wolfe drew up his forces before Quebec.[27]

Charles was not anxious to delay in Bourges, where provincial society had become boring. He planned to conclude his studies in French Civil Law at Paris. He was not entirely satisfied with his study under Professor Champion, even though he was pleased with the *docteur professeur* who had guided him through Roman law during the first stage of his program at Bourges. In January, 1759, he confessed that the professor was really unequal to his task. When Champion died about this time, Charles did not seek a successor at Bourges, but felt it more promising to go to Paris and profit from the lectures of the law faculty of the university. With renewed enthusiasm, he arrived there on January 8, 1759. Within the environs of the College of Louis the Great, he recaptured the excitement of three years before. Father Galloway welcomed him to the hostel in Saint Antoine. His tutor of philosophy days, Father Crookshanks, greeted him and once again assisted him in concluding his studies in Paris. He welcomed the company of the young men near whom he would reside for eight months, some of them already his acquaintances from earlier days. Charles saw that his expenses would be greater in Paris, especially those for books, so he dismissed his servant.[28]

A cloud of sorrow and anxiety, however, had come over the community of Jesuits, for they had learned of the assault of the Portuguese Minister, Marquis de Pombal, upon the Jesuit Order in that country. The same Bourbon ruling house which dominated Portugal held in its power the destiny of France, and the fortunes of the Order there as well. There were signs that hostility had grown up in these high places that had for so long patronized the College of Louis the Great. Charles' father wanted to know the true nature of the plot against them. "I know ye Envy their superior Merit draws on them," he wrote a few months after Charles' arrival. There had been rumors that the radical philosophy of revolution found in Jesuit writers, especially Mariana, gave plausible grounds for accusations that the Jesuits were plotting violence against the throne. "They are not only too virtuous," his father believed, in opposition to this rumor, "but too wise to engage in Assassinations, however illy treated."[29]

Charles and his friend Father Crookshanks had very much to occupy them at this time. He was to observe the French legal system at work and his father urged him to analyze the *Parlement de Paris.* He wished to be enlightened by his son as to whether it was entirely a judicial body and hence unlike the Parliament of England. How were other courts related to it? How much power did the king have over the *parlements?* "In the course of your Studies," his father advised, "I doubt not but you will think it necessary to obtain a pretty good insight into ye Constitution of France." In his answer, Charles summed up the jaundiced view which he held of the French civil Constitution. Theoretically, he said, the *parlements* were accountable to the king; but he could find no authorities who could explain in what way this was so. "Ask a minister," Charles said satirically; "his answer is ready at hand, . . . Sᵣ. ye King's power is boundless. . . ." He answered this way, "because by this means he [the minister of the king] hopes himself to be [boundless in power]." If a parliamentary act violated a man's rights, he could go to the great council; but there was no evidence that the council was a higher authority, and hence there was no assurance of redress. Checks and balances, in Montesquieu's terms, were certainly lacking.[30]

Reflecting on these matters a few months later, Charles found

France and other Catholic countries thus bereft of "that greatest blessing [,] civil liberty." Nor was England any better. He could not conceive "how any Roman Catholick especially an Irish Roman Catholic can consent to live in England or any . . . British Dominions, if he is able to do otherwise." Privation of either civil or religious liberty is a curse. "Now where is the man of spirit," he asks, "that can behold the rod lifted up, tremble, and kiss the hand of him that holds it?" One would judge, however, that England had more advantage in terms of civil liberty than France; and this seemed more important to him. To continue living in Maryland, therefore, is the best arrangement, especially when family ties are considered. "Not withstanding my natural aversion to all such oppressions," he explains, "and to an humble, silent, groveling submission, I cou'd even rather bear all this, than be deprived of the pleasure and comfort of living happily together [with my family]."[31]

The pursuits of the gentleman in formation were a welcome relief and variation for the mind of the reformer which wrestled with these dilemmas of political life. Charles' father gave his usual encouragement to travel about France, and Charles heeded his suggestion. He was told to see Versailles and the king's court once again and not to neglect the spectacular park garden at Chantilly. The young littérateur took increasing delight in his language ability. "Your French letter," his father noted, "is prettily wrote; I don't doubt but you will be a perfect Master of that Language." But there were newer pursuits. St. Omers did not provide all that was needed to develop the horseman because of the restrictions imposed before his arrival. Now, he enrolled in a riding academy. At Bourges, he had found that despite his dancing lessons in his years at St. Omers he had not yet mastered some of the usual dances found at social affairs; he must remedy that defect. He was also reminded that even a seventeenth-century gentleman could sketch pictures. Charles felt that a gesture toward this acquisition was required of him, although he had little confidence of achieving more than the minimum requirement.

His strong bent for books again manifested itself but in more sweeping fashion. Seeing the day of departure from Paris, the book-publishing center of the world, not far off, he energetically sought out new volumes at the stalls of Paris often accompanied by his friend Crookshanks. A provision for future days in Maryland as well as in England was systematically collected. "Only books most noted," his father advised, were to be purchased; Livy, Cicero, Horace, Virgil, and Caesar were the authors of first rank in the listing. His father's agent in England would send sterling generously for such expenses, Charles was assured by his father. A magnificent library was in the making, built upon the one his father and grandfather had accumulated and with the money that his father now provided. That his father's tastes and values were at one with Charles' proved fortunate as future years would show. The ivory tower of the reformer and revolutionary would be well provisioned.³²

In 1759, the final turn of good fortune came in England's war in America, and with it a final change in the thinking of Charles' father about the future. "Upon ye whole," his father triumphantly announced in February, a month after the arrival of Charles in Paris, "our Campaign in America has been a glorious one." Fort Duquesne has been taken, and "ye Western Frontier of Virginia, Maryland and Pennsylvania is secured against ye Cruelties of ye Savages." By June, Amherst in upper New York, and Wolfe at Quebec were on the verge of victory. There was similar success at Guadeloupe in the Caribbean. France held little hope of retaining her possessions, even in Louisiana and in the Caribbean.³³

And what of his father's dream of exile in Louisiana? By April, Charles was told to think of it no more. He surely needed no encouragement, for it had for some time ceased to be vested in any reality for him. The war had now dispelled his father's last cloud of fatuousness. "The success," he confessed of the Louisiana project, even with a different turn of events, "would depend much on my life." The years were slipping away [*"Fugaces labuntur anni"*], he philosophized to the young classicist. Charles' father no longer had the physical vigor to face long travel, transplantation, and the hostility of a strange climate and land. There was yet a deeper force, stronger in him than ever, rooted in his keen mind and strength of character rather than in his body. From the time he parted company with Charles in Paris, the elder Carroll was creatively elaborating an alternative plan, which was most honorable to his son. If a hostile government would double-tax his land, he would move his fortune away from the land, increase his sterling holdings by sale above the price that had prevailed at the time of original acquisition. He enthusiastically told Charles of a recent transaction which brought £2,000 sterling, a handsome amount with which to bring to him as debtors hard pressed gentlemen in need of credit. The Iron Works was progressing prosperously as usual. Yet, Charles need not fear that the physiocrat's ideal of the country gentleman was slipping out of his future inheritance. The estate at Annapolis and one nearby would remain; so would two country estates of 13,000 acres each. Among these, Charles could create a life like his father's with the summers at Doughoregan and the rest of the year in the mansion at Annapolis. If he would carry on labors at reform, he would do it in this gentlemanly fashion. There was a heretofore unexpressed warmth for all Marylanders in his father's letter, which he hoped would further lure his son to the province, even after his taste of the fine company of Bourges, Paris, and what was ahead in London had passed. Return would be certain, he tells Charles, "If you should ever know our people."[34]

Chapter 5

A PROVINCIAL'S LEGAL STUDIES

To pack a young gentleman's possessions after ten years of residence in France was burden enough. When he was an energetic humanist who loved the classics, made a special study of philosophy, specialized in Roman and French civil law, and delighted in *belles lettres,* the task was far greater. Small wonder that Charles was distressed at the expensive transportation of his belongings from Paris to London. The matter settled, he put his mind to the elevating contemplation of the French countryside, as his carriage took him northward on September 11, 1759. He would not pass through St. Omers, but he had heard from his cousin Jacky Carroll who was now a professor of philosophy at the college in Ghent. Charles was delighted to meet with him there and renew his old friendship, learn of old college acquaintances, and hear about distant Maryland and their mutual kinsmen. The young priest reminded Charles that he must soon begin his own state of life. The last turn in his road to it was London; but the distance of four years to the final goal by way of legal studies did not look short from the vantage point of Ghent.[1]

As usual his father had eased the transition to life in London, where he arrived, September 24. His agent Perkins, other friends, and his tutor Father Jennison had arranged his quarters at the Temple, near the inns of law. A servant would make life more comfortable for him than had been the case in Bourges. His stay in England would bring a demanding social life, which would now be added to the burden of his law books and services to the counter-revolutionary society. As in Bourges, he would receive private instruction a few times a week and devote the remainder of his time to reading the masters of English law. By the end of the year, Charles was established in London and well into his studies, contrary to the schedule recommended by his father, who had urged more travel in France. Thus Charles independently made his own decision to leave for London. He revealed a firm desire to accomplish his last stage of training and entered enthusiastically upon the first phase of his study of English law.[2]

Characteristic of his broad approach to studies he settled upon a specialist named Twinkio as a guide to English common law, which was the very foundation of the whole legal system. "Neither its difficulty or dryness frightens me," Charles wrote his father, who must have recalled Charles' bouts with the legal history of Doumat. If French law was a morass with no legal passageway from one province to another, English common law had its own forbidding features with which Charles was already acquainted. Its general force was to secure specified rights like trial by jury to every Englishman in whatever county or province he might find himself. It was not fixed once and for all in a Magna Charta in 1215, nor in a Bill of Rights in 1688; but, common law was all of these written testaments to freedom and many others to be found in the oral tradition of Parliament, the language of the courts, and in the customs of the people as sensitive barometers of the rights of Englishmen. The details of freedom as they were delicately elaborated in the daily practices of justice alone made England great as a lawgiver. There was room for legal growth and adaptation to new situations in the evolving society of England, which now was possessed by thousands of Englishmen in provinces beyond the sea in America. This was a vast horizon from what King John and the barons at Runnymede knew when they signed the Magna Charta. To reconstruct common law system without losing the threads of enduring fundamental rights was the law scholar's chore for the present. In time he would come to see its meaning in his own environment as a legal counselor and a leader of English society. Charles responded with a touch of poetry: "I am convinced of its utility and therefore am resolved at all hazards to plunge into this Chaos."[3]

After a year of such study, Charles thought he should modify his program. With his growing number of friends, the social life which this demanded, and numerous business activities now undertaken he saw that too much time was being spent apart from his main pursuit. Though he might have book in hand as he studied in his residence, he found it difficult to convince his frequent callers that he was fully employed. He therefore considered placing himself more formally under the program of lectures at the Temple, where he would be protected from these intrusions. At the same time he would not depart from his plan of extensive independent work under a tutor. Several months later, however, he saw the need to attend additional lectures elsewhere, which would bring his knowledge of law closer to its practical applications. Gray's Inn was unsatisfactory because it required considerably more lectures than he wanted. Instead, he found that Westminster had a better proportion which would allow him to follow the plan which Lord Coke, the eminent seventeenth-century English jurist, had recommended. Such an arrangement would provide considerable time for private reading, a practice to which Charles was attached, while studying common law instruction by Twinkio a few times each week. As his legal studies moved toward the practical details of law in his second year, he saw the advantage of joining a practicing law office in the manner of colonial legal training. In all of this planning, he had consulted with Daniel Dulany, who together with his father was probably more responsible for his final plan than Charles.[4]

Neither Dulany nor his father fully realized the obstacles before Charles in attempting to follow these plans. The Disabling Act of 1696, like a similar Maryland provision, disqualified a Catholic from legal practice and to some extent from full access to training for the profession in England. Influence in high places might make an exception in a particular case. Apparently Charles' father had assumed the possibility of this regarding access to specific lectures in common law at Oxford and Cambridge. After more than a year in London, Charles had not benefited from such lectures; the reasons are not clear. Even before going to England, he had been prepared for the restrictions on his study and use of law. He was not discouraged at the developments that now came. On another score, Charles found an advantage in living somewhat apart from the inns and the commons in which they were placed. The class of legal scholars who strolled about the commons arguing the cases of the morning repelled him by their moral laxity. He did not wish to take up life in their inns, which he regarded a danger to his own moral life. Even had the law clearly allowed him, he probably would not have resided at the inns. This still left the possibility of staying at accommodations nearby, called *ordinaries*. Here, throughout his stay in London, Charles maintained his far more comfortable quarters, benefiting from the law offering of the Temple, or elsewhere, as he chose. With such a residence, Twinkio and other instructors in the law could easily visit him.[5]

By choice, then, rather than by legal exclusion, Charles sought only limited access to the usual regimen that formed the English lawyer. At the inns, young scholars prepared their lectures on English statutes and read them to the morning assembly of their fellows. In the afternoon, they put cases to one another as they walked about the commons, dined at the inn's tables, or conversed in rooms they shared. No doubt, there was some of this in Charles' studies, particularly in his second year when he frequented the Temple. He thus acquired the well-known benefit from law and case analysis as a method. It prepared the young revolutionary to argue the logic or lack of logic of laws in terms of cases, just as he had come by his rhetorical and liberal college education to speak with persuasion on the injustice of a law. Charles all the same recognized the limitations in the situation which unfriendly laws imposed on him. As his education progressed, he sought one final remedy. When students moved to the more advanced stages of legal study, they often found a place in some law office. Here, they might see actual cases and participate in the preparation of counsel for the barrister in court. Charles failed, however, to secure such an arrangement, which would have led him to prolong his stay in London. As a result, a process of self-education developed once he had established the foundations of legal knowledge through his private instructors. Understandably, by this time he found it advisable to continue this regimen of private and independent study at home in Maryland. At the same time, Charles felt that he could compensate for lack of access to practicing law offices. At Westminster, where Parliament convened, was the great hall where litigation was transacted by lawyers and judges. He moved freely in this gathering, observing law in the practical process of resolution.[6]

Prominent men stated what training best suited the lawyer among the inns of law and the books of their favorite authors. Charles had his own view of what he should be. Obstacles placed in his path by the London institutions only forced him to clarify the scope he intended to give his knowledge of the law. As a littérateur he was critical of Coke's jargon-laden prose, and his father criticized Charles for not carefully following Coke's procedures for mastering the law. Charles feared the traditional formation of the English lawyer, lest he one day resemble those whom Cicero described. He did not want to be "an insignificant petty fogger, grubbling all my life in the mean but gainful application to all the arts of chicane." Charles felt he already had an antidote to the ailment. "Without a perfect knowledge of history and mankind," he explained, "which latter is acquired from the study of history and personal experience, there is no possibility of excelling in the law." After all, a good master of common law knew that the history of mankind was in its roots, and its contemporary application could be discerned only by those who had tapped these roots.[7]

So, Charles' first two years of law reached out in many directions in pursuit of this grand vision. The core of English law revealed the trials and triumphs of her people, their bouts with despots at home and abroad. Hume's multi-volume presentation of this saga was becoming popular at this time, and Charles turned to reading the account. His enthusiasm was not disappointed. He was fascinated with the story of the Tudors and the Stuarts and urged his father to read Hume's volumes. They both agreed that a complete set should find a place on the Doughoregan shelves, and Charles arranged the purchase. He vitally experienced the current events of justice in England and cast them into his own historico-philosophical context. The Earl of Ferrers, he observed, had been brought to feel the full weight of the law against his crime; this was not always the case with nobility according to Doumat. "Great men may see by this," Charles moralized, "that the laws are not made only for the poor sort, that they extend to all and cannot be transgressed with immunity. The ancients, at least the wisest ancients," he noted in reference to universal history, saw "that the property, Liberty and safety of individuals could not be too secure from power and its natural ally, injustice." Charles sent his father a current London magazine to maintain their instructive exchange of comments on the times.[8]

The broader intellectual interests of Charles continued amid the stimulation of legal studies. He and his father had delighted in the theatre, and they found that it expressed the society from which it came. The colony of actors was close to the inns of court, and the Carrolls took a special interest in a popular actor and playwright of the day who also succeeded in becoming a lawyer. Arthur Murphy (1727-1805) had other things in common with the Carrolls as a student of St. Omers for six months, and as a native of Ireland. His pamphleteering at the height of the Wilkes controversy had placed him at the center of events which Charles closely followed during his last year in London. Charles had read, and possibly had seen produced, Murphy's *The Way to Keep Him,* a comedy of manners of the kind his father had seen in London.[9]

Before he went to London, his father had sent him his impressions of a modified production of John Vanbrugh's *The Provok'd Wife.* It was Colley Cibber's version under the new title *The Provok'd Husband* (1729), which had scandalized the elder Carroll. Murphy did not receive the condemnation which the Society for the Reformation of Manners had passed on Vanbrugh; but his work *The Way to*

Keep Him followed the trend of jocose moralizing which charactered mid-eighteenth century dramatic productions in England. Murphy humorously complained of the little effort which wives made at securing their husbands against the arts of seduction cultivated among English gentry society. Charles' harsh criticism of the English gentry during these years gave him a natural interest in Murphy's plays and confirmed him in his social reform mentality. He found little value or entertainment in Murphy's political lampoon of 1761, *A Letter from a Right Honourable Person,* which he read a year after the play. Murphy's biography of his mistress was not mentioned in Charles' letters, nor his success in gaining enrollment at Lincoln's Inn through the influence of Lord Mansfield. Charles might well have commented sardonically on these facts as instances of Murphy's conformity to the age and to the Church of England. Yet, it is doubtful to what extent Murphy was raised as a Catholic. As a playwright, he was in the eyes of Charles part of the world of English culture, which the Marylander could appreciate because of his excellent liberal education. The English theatre, after all, was greatly influenced by France and authors like Molière and Regnard, whom Charles had read.[10]

Charles' reading continued on a wide range beyond the theatre and law. He acquired for Doughoregan library the eighteen-volume work of the eminent professor of the College of Louis the Great. Jean Croiset's *l'Année chrétienne* was a remarkable offering of religious reading, which drew on the Scriptures, liturgy, and his own sophisticated insights into the Christian gentleman's secular world and the related spiritual values of the Catholic gentry code. Within a year of his arrival in London, Charles pursued the same systematic process of acquiring new books which he had employed in Paris. He had in hand his father's list of Doughoregan books so that he might avoid duplication. With the growing taste of a collector as well as the intellectual curiosity of a highly cultivated reader, Charles sought out better editions of books that he already had, or that might be in poor condition. Known as a man of books, gifts to him often took this form as when Lord Arundell of Wardour gave him a handsome *Royal Almanac.* Amidst all of this Charles still planned for travel. Toward the end of his second year in London, he was looking forward to a trip to the northern counties of England, and especially to Yorkshire, which had been the scene of sixteenth-century Catholic uprisings against Queen Elizabeth.[11]

He gave more than a token gesture to pedestrian learning. He employed a master for mathematics at this time, in order to learn decimals and thereby acquire mastery of the Venetian method of bookkeeping, which would be a daily employment for the rest of his life. His father saw to his initiation into the dry realities of legally maintaining his great landed estates. Every successful gentleman must be a pettifogger of sorts, spending his time in court over litigation regarding boundaries, land titles, and a host of other minutiae. Like a good pedagogue, his father sent cases for consideration by the lofty-minded scholar in London.[12]

The lofty-minded approach, however, was to leave its mark on the times and the society through which Charles moved. He was now finding his destiny in the counter-revolutionary society of Maryland. When Charles moved to London from Paris, the quarrel of his fellow Catholics with British law was no longer remote. With the encouragement of his father, he plunged into the relevant controversial literature of the day. His father listed the better known apologetic literature, much of it already at Doughoregan, such as Challoner's *Why Catholics Cannot Conform to the Church of England;* all of this Charles should study. Much of this was cast against the English Catholic's century-old lot in England rather than in the provinces. Yet, Charles reflected on these matters in the context of Maryland penal laws which were the result of the "late revolution," as his father referred to the 1688 overthrow of the Maryland Constitution by William and Mary. The young legal reformer was already casting his own counter-revolutionary mentality, and he carried his creative thought beyond the terms of the old anti-Elizabethan constructions of Catholics in England. His father motivated him to the endeavor. "Your estate for this part of the World," he wrote at this time, "will be a Considerable one, and of course liable to many Disputes, especially as a Rom. Cath. stands but a poor chance for a Justice with our Juries in particular." Charles needed little encouragement. More than a year before, when he had been scarcely six months in London, he realized how much he had to learn. "I am perfectly ignorant of the Maryland government", he wrote in April of 1760, "its laws, and power of the Proprietary." He asked his father for complete texts of the Maryland laws. Within a year, he had an abridgement of the Acts of the Assembly of Maryland, wherein he could read the Charter, the early toleration acts, and the Conditions of Plantation. Two months later, he ordered a new edition of the statutes at large.[13]

This was the framework of study and books against which Charles developed his reform ideas and activities. At this time, he began to resolve the dilemma he found on the road to freedom for his family and to legal reform in the colony. On December 19, 1759, a few months after his arrival in London, he described the frame of mind with which he entered upon a study of Maryland law. In France, he had seen the law of a Catholic country at work, and found it religiously beneficial to the Church and its adherents. Yet, it did not satisfy him, for France did not have "that greatest blessing[,] civil liberty." On the other hand, he could not conceive "how any Roman Catholick especially an Irish Roman Catholick can consent to live in England or any [of] the British dominions, if he is able to do otherwise." Charles and his father had unsuccessfully tried to do otherwise by planning to live in a French province, gaining religious liberty but being without civil liberty. In both countries, his aspirations were confined. "No where is [there] the man of spirit," he had earlier lamented in the tragic dilemma, "that can behold the rod lifted up, tremble, and kiss the hand of him that holds it?" For the moment, he saw that he must stand with his own, wherever they were; and they were then in Maryland. "Notwithstanding my natural aversion to all such oppressions, and to an humble, silent, groveling submission," he wrote to his father, "I could even rather bear all this, than be deprived of the pleasure and comfort of living happily together." He was much like his Catholic fellows in England, who in the eighteenth century were a people withdrawn from society and the contests which they would otherwise have been compelled to join in a militant fight for fredom. Within a year, however, Charles had weathered this intellectual crisis and saw the promise of enlarging the civil liberty indigenous to English institutions by resorting to reform activities. He would labor to mitigate religious oppression. Perhaps in his lifetime it would be removed entirely, and freedom in Maryland would be restored to what it had been before "the late revolution" of 1688.[14]

Charles consequently initiated social relations with the proprietary party in London, where during the first two years of his residence provincial officials made prolonged visits. The family of the former Governor Bladen was still in high standing with the lord proprietor. Within a few months of his arrival, he had already paid a visit to the governor's son. "He was civil to me when in London," Charles' father reminded him, and it was expected that Bladen would pay the first visit. "If he makes the first advances," he was told, "be polite and civil." This family had shown respect for the Carrolls and had been of assistance when the elder Bladen was in power in Maryland. Charles, within a few months of his arrival in London, repaid Bladen's visit. Others, however, provided the first entrée to the lord proprietor himself. Rozier, Charles' kinsman from Maryland, was in London in the summer of 1760 with his friend Plater. Charles' father had encouraged his son as well as the visiting Marylanders to meet Bladen. It was not long after this that Charles attended an important dinner at the home of Perkins, his father's agent in London. Lord Baltimore was present on that occasion, and Charles accomplished a very cordial meeting. The young scholar was invited to visit the lord proprietor. Both Plater and Rozier accompanied him to the proprietor's home in the late summer of 1760. After visiting for a time, they all went to a dinner given by the brother of Governor Horatio Sharpe of Maryland. Charles was most pleased with Sharpe and wrote of him to his father in complimentary terms. Soon, Lord Baltimore invited Charles to be his guest during the Epsom racing season. Charles, while accepting, prudently manifested some reserve in socializing with the high dignitary. He did not venture to stay for any more than one day with the proprietor at Epsom. Undoubtedly, the matters of greatest moment between the two were no more than touched upon on these occasions. Propriety suggested this, but so did the state of Charles' incomplete knowledge of Maryland law and the reforms that he might effectively recommend. A few more months of study, and his case for Maryland freedom would be ready.[15]

For the present he knew what he was about in .this alliance with the proprietary party and was determined to use his social acceptability as a means of legal reform. His father had only recently lapsed into his familiar jeremiad on the theme of Maryland injustices to him; the vague lure of exile in a French province as an escape from them again drew him. Charles, on the other hand, was looking to the future in the hope of reform. He was already aware of the political strategy out of which would come a recovery of former Maryland liberties. When he wrote to his father about this matter on September 16, 1760, he did so in the spirit of an adult aristocrat. As part of an aristocracy, he hoped to turn back hostile forces in Maryland; the proprietary party was his ally for this very reason. In the past, he noted, the governor and the upper house as the focus of gentry power and interest had on many occasions stood firmly against the meaner and middling sort of folk in the lower house who were intent upon further infringing the freedom of Maryland Catholics. Unworthily some gentlemen of the better sort of society had curried favor with this lower element and the constituents who gave them their power. Yet, Charles had confidence that the solid gentry as the fiber of society would bring ultimate victory. "Clamours of the mob," he moralized, "we may laugh at and despise its insolence: its giddy fury will turn to his own shame. I despise the insolent mob, and keep it at a distance. '*Odi profanum vulgus, et arceo*'," he wrote in Horace's words. The malicious double-tax had originated here with the meaner sort of society. They surely were "an ignorant, base, contemptible rabble," he wrote satirically. "Yet, time may perhaps polish and soften their manners," he said hopefully. "Wealth acquired by their own industry may satiate their avarice, and correct [or] at least moderate that eager longing after other men's property." He knew all the same that compromise with the lower house and its element was the only realistic view to take of future politics. Since his lot for the present was cast with the upper house and the proprietary party, he would have to thoroughly establish his alliance with them and bring their power to bear on a favorable compromise regarding issues of greatest importance to himself.[16]

Upon his arrival in London, Charles learned that his father's visit there a few years before had borne fruit among the proprietary party, and with Lord Baltimore himself. In all of his scheming to leave Maryland, his father had been moved by the fear that laws more discriminating than the double-tax measure were likely to come upon the landed wealth of the Maryland Catholic gentry. Charles now learned from a gentleman named Hunter that this would not be so. The lord proprietor himself had told Hunter that he had given orders to the assembly to bring no further harm to Catholics. Baltimore further assured Hunter that he found Catholics without fault as citizens in his province. This had encouraged Charles' father to put aside his plans of removal. These developments paved the way for his own efforts to improve the lot of Catholics, removing the double-tax itself if possible. Toward the end of 1760, Charles prepared himself to take further steps with the proprietary party in London. At his father's encouragement, he arranged a meeting with the lord proprietor. He was well equipped for preparing his case. He had the Maryland laws at hand, and from them the chief issue clearly emerged as he read the charter, early toleration ordinances, and the Conditions of Plantations. By this last constitutional provision, the first settlers secured for themselves and their posterity a uniform tax. Charles could show that the Catholic Carroll family for three generations had proffered unwavering loyalty to the Lords Baltimore; and that Catholics, as the elder Daniel Dulany himself had stated, in no way resembled the people who were the target of Queen Elizabeth's penal laws. The double-tax was therefore an undeserved penalty, a violation of the foundations of Maryland law, and a breach of honor among gentlemen of the English aristocracy who were expected to be the pillars of justice and order in Maryland society.[17]

Shortly after January, 1761, Charles met with Lord Baltimore. The discerning young man sought out evidence of good faith in the proprietor and eventually was not disappointed. In the course of their conversation at this time, it became evident that Lord Baltimore had not maintained detailed knowledge of provincial affairs. In the case of the double-tax and other recent legislation, he had relied almost entirely upon the word of the governor and other advisers for information. He was led to believe, he told Charles, that Catholics had not openly opposed the double-tax. He did not see that it was a sop to the militant anti-Catholic element, used by the proprietary party to avoid trouble for other policies of greater importance to them in the lower house. The proprietor had not adverted to Charles' contention that the law violated the Conditions of Plantations and early Maryland law. The law, Charles charged, was "subversive of the Maryland constitution." On his own initiative, Baltimore assured the young Marylander that his fellow Catholics had always been most loyal to him and his government. He expressed gratitude for this, particularly for the Carroll family and its long service to his lordship. Charles felt that he had brought new knowledge to the proprietor from which he had been previously kept. The good effects on him seemed to have justified the great pains which Charles took with this mission. Baltimore said that no such laws in the future would meet his approbation. If the governor and upper house would not act with honor, he seemed to be saying, he himself would. At least further repressive measures stood less chance of tolerance by Baltimore, even if he made no immediate move to disallow the double-tax. His father had always feared such additional measures. Charles could now reassure him.[18]

This aspect of the meeting assured Charles to a great extent that his hope for improvement of civil liberty in Maryland was well founded. He was astute enough to see, however, that the restrictions on religious freedom in the future would not be energetically opposed by Lord Baltimore. Charles had noted, for example, an abiding and veiled suspicion of Catholics in him. Baltimore had said that he would not allow any such laws as the double-tax in the future, but he hastened to add: provided Catholics gave no occasion for them. They stood unfavorably judged as a group, in other words, rather than as individual English citizens. This was alien to the ideals of English liberty to which Charles adhered. He could not with propriety and prudence urge immediate action by the proprietor against the current laws discriminating against Catholics. He did, however, leave this burden of obligation with Lord Baltimore as a result of the whole tenor of their discussion. The anticipated end of the French and Indian War would make the removal of the double-tax by the governor and upper house easier, especially now that the proprietor had so committed himself.[19]

In the course of the discussions with Baltimore, Charles had brought up another important matter which further brought out the tensions in the alliance which the Catholics had with the proprietary party. He sought to advance the appointment of his kinsman Henry Darnall III, to the office of Secretary for the Colony. Darnall had conformed to the Church of England and had already served as attorney general of the province. There was particular distress in this for the Carrolls, Darnall being a cousin of Charles' father. In addition, Darnall's son, known as Henry Jr., or the Fourth, had married Rachel Brooke, who was the niece of Charles' father. The gambling of Henry Jr. brought grief and separation to the marriage. Rachel and her daughter, Molly (Mary), came to reside at Doughoregan. In all of this is seen the loyalty of the Catholic Carrolls to their community even in these difficult situations.[20]

To his surprise, Charles found that Darnall's conformity to the Church of England carried no weight with the lord proprietor, but instead created the major obstacle to his appointment. Baltimore professed contempt for one who took such a step from self-interest, which he felt was the case with Darnall. Baltimore, Charles wrote in February, 1761, "had heard strange reports of that gentleman: then, he added with great warmth and seeming emotion [,] 'I can't conceive how a man who has taken ye oath can be so deep a disembler as to appear a Protestant, but at heart remain a Papist.' " A month later the proprietor confirmed his opposition to Darnall because of his own "disaffection" and the "Papistical inclinations" of Darnall. Charles in time revealed his own "disaffection" for his conforming kinsman, which was similar to his father's violent aversion for the conforming Dr. Charles Carroll over the James Carroll will. In July, Charles revealed that Lord Baltimore had warned him of Darnall, to whom Charles had made a loan which went unpaid during this period. Baltimore was not surprised. Charles now turned from advocate to plaintiff in the Darnall case. He wrote to his father urging that action be taken against the Darnall estate to recover the debt. Poor Charles, who had succeeded so well in pursuing legal reform in his meetings with the lord proprietor, was now distressed by the outcome of his gentlemanly offices in favor of an undeserving kinsman. Yet he maintained respect in the eyes of Lord Baltimore, who saw that he pursued his religion apart from self-interest. Baltimore saw that he must deal honorably with Charles if he had any conscience at all.[21]

After some initial reluctance, Charles continued to include the Bladen family in his social life, since the family still might have influence in Maryland politics. Although he had reservations about young Bladen's friends who played cards for such high stakes he had none for the family as a whole, particularly after his acquaintance with Bladen's sisters. His visits grew frequent after two years in London. More clearly than Bladen, however, Daniel Dulany the Younger seemed already destined for high office in Maryland, and his friendship was sought out by Charles and his father. Dulany's stature as a lawyer more than his personal qualities attracted them. Both found him vain and lacking in candor; but as an aspiring politician these defects were understandable, particularly since it was clear by December of 1761 that he had long had his eye on the governorship of the province. It was not possible to forget that he was one of the few in the proprietary party who did not capitulate on the double-tax issue and had lost his seat in the lower house as a result of his vote against it. Then too, Charles' father was still a partner of Dulany in the Baltimore Iron Works, whose market in England depended upon the influence of the Dulanys. The relationship was so satisfactory, considering everything, that Charles was encouraged by his father to get advice from Dulany regarding his program of legal studies.[22]

Young Dulany's father had been a law partner of the disreputable Michael Macnamara. Macnamara had married the sister of Charles' father under the scandalous circumstances of a pre-marital pregnancy. The Carrolls retained relationships with Macnamara and his son, who like his father had conformed to the Church of England. The younger Macnamara, Surveyor General of Maryland, was at this time in London. He was negotiating the sale of that office to Lawson, a friend of Charles, and was seeking to acquire a better office for himself with assistance from Charles. In dire financial distress, Macnamara went to the young scholar, who fearing his kinsman would be put in the debtors jail, made a loan to him. Charles conveniently left to his father the task of exacting repayment, since Macnamara was to return to Maryland at the beginning of 1762. "He has little thought and no prudence," Charles commented. Yet, such men, he knew, were part of the proprietary party and could at some time play a part in supporting the legal reform for which the Carrolls were striving.[23]

Charles at this time involved himself without any political interest in the welfare of provincials more deserving than Darnall and Macnamara. Ireland, the overseer of a Carroll estate, had failed to win benefits from an inheritance in England upon which he had relied. The burden of this loss was falling upon his son at St. Omers, who had not benefited as Charles had from a program without any practical learning. He was now in need, and Charles was trying to reopen the claim to the inheritance. He also attempted to assist another Marylander in a similar condition, a son of the MacCullam family of Elkridge. The unfortunate lad was trying to make ends meet in England as a domestic servant. Charles was trying to recover an inheritance for him or at least to obtain a more suitable employment for him.[24]

These business concerns, however, were all of less importance to Charles than his own family estate. The enhancement of family interests was gradually becoming part of his obligation as his father advanced in age. Involvement in the double-tax controversy made Charles feel the urgency of his responsibilities, so that he willingly took up many financial transactions for his father. Acumen on the part of father and son might avert an attrition of the landed wealth, particularly as it now became necessary to gradually transfer the base of capital from land to other assets which in turn were suitable for investment and loans. During his first year in London Charles reported a number of debt collections and other negotiations. About a year later, he told of his efforts at securing objects of new investments. His father frankly confessed that he was counting on him to multiply his business relationships in London. Charles competed for social engagements with such merchants as Maire and Hutton and did not overlook association with the Virginia councilman Ludwell, with whom he eventually established a friendship. He investigated the assets of the debtor Gallot to see if they might meet the demands of the Carroll creditor Edwards.[25]

Charles was not aware of the full extent to which his father was diversifying the foundations of his future inheritance. He did know of the usual transactions to increase wealth by slave ownership, sale of grain, annual loans to Marylanders, and the complex expansion of the Baltimore Iron Works. The persistent controversy over land titles, many of which Charles would inherit in an unsettled state, came more and more to his attention. From his conversations with Michael Macnamara at this time, he became alarmed at the extensive rate at which his father was said to be converting his landed estate to other forms of wealth. Macnamara had told Charles that his father had sold the extensive acreage near the Monocacy River in Frederick County for £12,500. Charles had understood that this land was to be part of his inheritance, and he did not want any disposition of it until he had returned to Maryland. At it turned out, Macnamara, against whom Charles had been warned by his father, had been speaking irresponsibly from rumor; Charles' father assured his son that such a transaction had not taken place. It was clear that Charles did not see the wisdom of a wholesale transfer of landed wealth. He evidently hoped that in the near future the attrition of double-tax would be brought to an end because of the proprietary party's interest in his cause of repeal. More favorable conditions for this now appeared with each English military victory over France. His father was, as a matter of fact, at this very time acting to secure the major portion of his landed inheritance to Charles. Under a codicil of June 15, 1761, he had made a draft of his will. It even extended to the condition of Charles' dying before his father. His father named his niece, Eleanor Carroll, daughter of Daniel Carroll, of the first Maryland generation of that branch of the family, and Eleanor's brother Daniel to his conditional inheritance.[26]

Charles was not confined by the narrower view of the war which his father inevitably had as a resident of Annapolis. He was at the seat of empire in London and that vision always affected his opinions about the future of the province. He responded to the excitement of the war years, seeing how they would affect all Europe as well as the colony; and he viewed the execution of imperial policy with a discerning eye. He had arrived in London at the very time that General Wolfe stood before Quebec. He fully realized that if France had something better than flat-bottomed boats, she might land a force of 50,000 men, subdue all of England, and sue for peace. Charles shrewdly wrote in 1760 that such a settlement would not establish a new dependent dynasty in England, not even one of the old Stuart line. French diplomacy correctly strove for mobility, and such a prolonged occupation of England would only leave France a prey to her continental enemies. These were reflections in a moment of elation over Sir Edward Hawke's victory over the French at sea. Charles saw better than his father that the French ministry was unequal to the demands of the war. It was the victim of *fatalité*, that blindness and stupor from which Pitt had delivered the English ministry and set England on the path to victory.

By the beginning of 1761, Charles was so confident of England's progress toward ultimate victory that he put stock in the rumor that her offensive in North America had penetrated into the Mississippi Valley. The European theatre also inspired optimism. The Prussian forces were so impressive that France could not hope to win out against the Landgrave of Hess Cassell, where an engagement was imminent. She would thus be forced to a peace settlement. By the end of the year, he praised the English ministry for committing English forces on the continent at Colberg, even though this required a tax on windows and dogs to support the expense.[27]

Despite all of his enthusiasm and optimism over England's prosecution of the war, Charles had a critical eye of the counter-revolutionary for the internal affairs of the British Empire. An unhealthy instability still threatened the government regardless of its current success. What an incongruity, he noted, that it conducted a peace congress as battles raged on. He regretted that violence and power were the arbiters of international disputes over rights and titles. He spoke in the vein of Hugo Grotius' vision of international order. Charles was versed in Montesquieu and Pufendorf who had used Grotius' writings in their own commentaries on European institutions. In the summer of 1761, England was looking forward to the coronation of George III, and front seats for the event were worth twelve guineas. "Do you advise me to give away so much money to gratify my curiosity," Charles asked his father, with a note of sarcasm for the House of Hanover from which George was descended. The Hanovers ultimately owed their dynastic power to the Revolution of 1688, which had disinherited the Carrolls from their English liberties. Understandably, he was not without sympathy for noblemen who were turned out of state positions by the Revolution, or for others who were regarded as rebels in the British Isles and on the Continent because they retained their loyalty to the deposed House of Stuart. He never lost curiosity about the lot of the last of the Stuart line, then in exile in Pouillon, France. Scottish rebels also drew his observation and comment. The scars of the late rebellion were seen at Portsmouth, where 500 Highlanders were awaiting deportation to the Indies. Instead of their conduct resembling the reasonableness of Bates, Charles wrote, mindful of more prudent Scottish rebels, their careers were "all blunders & nonsense."

Charles planned to visit the northern counties of England, the scene of Catholic uprising in the sixteenth century. From here, had come many Maryland Catholic settlers in the seventeenth century. As for the Acadians, his father was at this very time signing the certificates of death of the unfortunate folk in Maryland, victims of their exile's hardships. And what of poor rebel Ireland? "The present situation of that Island," Charles wrote pathetically to his father, "will only renew the memory of past wrongs. . . . [H]ow unavailing to remember what we can not revenge! [H]ow melancholy to see old, ancient, noble, and once flourishing families now reduced to beggary." Indeed, he could number his own kinsmen among the victims.[28]

Yet, Charles still stood by his judgment on Catholic countries, which was reinforced at this time. In France, there was none of that civil "liberty & freedom that satisfies & becomes an Englishman." She had now disregarded justice and launched an attack on the Jesuit Order. France was set on the same tyrannical course established by the Portuguese minister Pombal and was on the point of overthrowing religion by the complete expulsion of these worthy men. "They have hindered them to print or publish any thing in their own Justification," Charles reported of the French *parlements*, "while at the same time libels dayly appear loading them with all the infamy malice can invent & in some measure authorized by our Judge & party, for their place of sale and distribution is the *sale de Palais.*"

Charles had thus clearly placed himself in the vast international arena of social forces and was developing the instinct of a comprehensive reform thinker. He avidly studied current affairs, at the same time persuing his academic books in this context. After two years in London he was also initiated into the practical politics which any would-be social reformer must master if he would leave a stamp on his era. Proprietary politicians provided him with a suitable first encounter, and he gained sureness from the progress which he was making with them.[29]

Chapter 6

AMONG ENGLISH GENTLEMEN

Charles was very much at home in the company of English gentlemen as he came to maturity. He knew that upon his return to America his life as a gentleman would not be radically different. The affluence of his father was reflected in all of his letters to his son, and his description of the provincial social life of the aristocracy assured him of its desirability. Charles was, for example, encouraged to provide himself with a wine suited to an aristocrat, no less a part of that social life in America than in England; his father on occasion sent him choice pipes of wine. The wit and worldly wisdom spoken in the light manner of the London tavern was also heard in provincial Annapolis. About this time, his father wrote this bright piece of banter to his friend Clement Hill: "Well you are to have a pipe of wine; some men perhaps would chuse to drink water all their lives rather than accept a pipe of wine. Are they not fools? A Pipe of Wine is a Pipe of Wine, but honour is an empty-sounding thing like an empty Pipe."

Englishmen were proud of their gardens, but Charles was anxious to show them how they could be improved by the varied growth of the New World. He wrote to Maryland for indigenous seeds, and for orchard products which he had tasted years ago as a boy.

Charles also learned the trials of extending hospitality as well as its joys. Two gentlemen from Maryland were expected in England, who would probably complain of his father's treatment of them when they stayed at the Carroll mansion. Charles was advised to defend his father among their own friends in England and explain that the two gentlemen in question had prolonged their welcome at the Carroll household five months. That was too much for any man's sense of privacy, as the most rollicking English gentleman would agree.[1]

And so, it was in 1760 that Charles as a London resident with roots in the province was a man of two worlds and could see their unity in the gentry class. He continued the practices he had learned in France, taking a vacation at Portsmouth in April, for which he acquired a riding horse. He entered more fully into the social life of London and the counties, but by correspondence he gained a vicarious experience of gentility at Annapolis and Doughoregan.

Without obscuring the essential unity of the gentry class and English culture on both sides of the Atlantic, Charles' day in London threw light on the many nuances in that society which became increasingly important to his own life. He also did not lose his identity with the Catholic counter-revolutionary society among the Maryland gentry into which he was born. Catholic aristocrats in England obviously had much in common with that Maryland society, especially through their education in France. It was not necessarily a narrow social loyalty in the case of Charles. He enjoyed the company of the Protestant Bladen family. His Protestant cousin, Michael Macnamara, reported that Charles was generally accepted by all, that he had "great applause from all his Acquaintances." The many transactions of his father with Perkins gave Charles entrée to the merchants. He became a close friend of Christopher Bird, who won Charles' esteem, as he said, "both by his Character, & polite, friendly behavior to me." Bird was a country gentleman, cut very much to his own style of gentility. Charles was at home in Bird's manor, playing chess with his father or conversing with his aunt. The frequent visits to Bird and and Perkins revealed, however, that Charles was not narrowly attached to the former, a country gentleman who was his ideal. He could judge the man apart from his group, and he therefore grew to a cosmopolitan outlook in the making of social ties. A lasting friendship was formed with another young man named Bradshaw. He also made the acquaintance of the Baker family, who derived their wealth from extensive Caribbean plantation holdings. Here, too, was an acquaintance passed from father to son, and Charles benefited once again from his father's stay in England in 1757. The Corby family became his friends.

Charles had met socially with the nobleman Lord Baltimore, but these occasions were strongly tainted by politicking with the proprietary party and by state-business purposes. This was not the case with Catholic noblemen. Charles' tutor and master Father Jennison was a chaplain at Wardour Castle, where Lord Charles Arundell resided, aware of its ancient Catholic traditions. The Third Baron of Arundell (Lord Henry) was imprisoned at the time of the Titus Oates Plot, but after six years was released by James II and made keeper of the Privy Seal. Lord Powis, whom Charles' grandfather, the Founder, had served as a lawyer, had been imprisoned with him. In the spring of 1760 Father Jennison paid Charles a visit and their conversations were a delight for two men of books, possessed with the same sense of history. In the early fall, Charles went on an excursion with Jennison which took them to Bath, where the Bakers resided,

Crystal, and Oxford. The highlight was Charles' stay at imposing Wardour Castle, standing as a proud battlement, a symbol of his own staunch determination to hold to his beliefs and turn back the hostile laws which attacked them. The meeting with Lord Arundell meant as much to him as it did to Charles. The young Marylander was deeply honored in the spring of 1761 when he received a handsomely bound atlas from his lordship. Charles also desired at this time to seek out his kinsmen and their friends among Ireland's aristocracy.[3]

Charles showed initiative in seeking the company of such high personages. He was already acquainted with the Web family through one of their sons who had attended St. Omers with him. In December of 1761, he was planning to visit his friend's brother, Sir Thomas Web, and his chaplain, Father Molyneaux. The Russell family was another source of interest for Charles, particularly the daughters. He soon feared that his visits were too frequent; they had too much appearance of courtship in the eyes of one of the daughters. Charles, according to his plans at this time, saw that he was near the end of his education and that his carefree friendships with women were about to conclude. The permanence of matrimony threatened. He confessed to another uneasiness about his social conduct. He saw an undesirable timidity in himself, which others may properly have regarded as laudable modesty. To move in such high society without some moments of anxiety at his age would have indeed been unusual. He especially felt uneasy with the London gentry and the nobility. There was another station among gentlemen which was more congenial to him. The country gentry had a less spectacular existence, simpler way of life, and more elevated conversation. In his grand life, he found relief in thinking about his cousin back in Maryland, Nancy Cooke, who had had a bout with the smallpox. "I hope her beauty is not impaired," he wrote to his father, "by a distemper so fatal to the charms [of her] fair Sex." He never failed to see that his life would one day be among this provincial gentry society. His sophisticated life in England did not, even at this time, take away his taste for the company of England's country gentry, which was closer in spirit to Maryland's provincial society.[4]

Charles made friends among his fellow law students and established members of the profession, whose friendships he retained years later by correspondence. They were often from important families. Daniel Barrington was the brother of the illustrious Daines Barrington who had a distinguished career on the bench of Wales. At the time that Charles was pursuing his studies, Daines was concluding his volume *Observations on the Statutes (1766)*, which some jurists have called the link between Montesquieu and later developments in English law. An admirer of the Frenchman and an adherent to Charles' ideal of a full historical approach to English law, he advocated reform in statutory structure by explicit repeal of outmoded laws.

William Graves, a young scholar at the Inns of Court and Chancery, was a great admirer of Charles, who he said had the "evenest & best temper I ever met with." The two were congenial companions on a journey to the continent. They made pleasantries of their differences of faith, and of such provocative topics as the Titus Oates Plot. From the Graves family, would come English admirals of the Revolution. One of Charles' best friends was his fellow native of Annapolis Edmund Jennings, who like Graves pursued a longer period of study than did Charles. Correspondence with both men upon his return to America would often have Charles debating the colonial case against the mother country much the way young law scholars argued in the commons.[5]

He was well prepared for his social successes in England by his life on the continent. His cousin Jacky reported the "great improvement he has made in France, & his elegant way of living at London." Charles wrote of his pleasant associations with new acquaintances while he was visiting Portsmouth in the spring of 1760. He found "friends & good natured and cheerful, so you may easily imagine that the time we stay here, will be spent agreeably." This expresses some satisfaction with himself; but he still speaks of the work of further improving his personality, in a way that would in the future enhance both material fortune and personal satisfaction. To his accusations of shyness, he now adds that he is "stiff and reserved." This introversion was only partially explained by his growing responsibilities and experience of maturity. The English environment was different from that of France, and his sensitive disposition responded to it. Deeper thoughts deriving from these experiences showed that he was further developing an intelligible social code of conduct. His gentility was based on what he had read and been taught, it is true, but the active mind of the young reformer made a creative work of what he constructed by his actions. He proposed to deal with the simple matter of his shyness on a complicated basis. Openness and affability awakened good will in others, he reflected, and he must therefore bring himself to such reasonable conduct. He believed that these efforts were the work of a "great [,] very great mind," which seemed a surprising statement to most gentlemen, but not to Charles.[6]

All of this was but the surface reflecting deeper and systematic reasoning about his own social conduct. After a year and a half in London, he was able to sketch his ideal on a very broad canvas. He could not fall into the inferior moral pattern of a London gentleman's life, but must construct his own clear and unique ideal. His Catholicity was one of the determinants. "The Laws of my country," he explained, "exclude me from acting in any public capacity. I must endeavor then to be esteemed in private life." The affability which he cultivated to bring about this esteem was only a secondary part of the effort at compensation in the gentry structure. With concreteness he based his way of life upon a conscious choice of the country gentleman as opposed to the London version. Like Wardour Castle the country manor was a retreat but it was also a bastion. Reflecting both the idyllic coloring of classical antiquity's exaltation of the yeoman farmer in the days of the Republic and the scientific French physiocrat's moral philosophy, he painted a rather grandiose image of the country gentleman to which he aspired. "Innocuas Amo Delicias Docamque Quietem [I love simple pleasures and I will profess seclusion]," he wrote. "Moral amusements such as farming & other country occupations united to Philosophy (its best allies) form that plan of life *wh.* [which] to me appears of all others ye most eligible."

Such a personality perpetually in a town thriving with civic activities and politics would be a man at odds with the moving current of an unreflecting stream of society. His irascible father had long slashed his oars against such turbulence at Annapolis. Had this sight brought the son to a wiser choice? Neither surrender to hostile forces, nor continually wrestle with the torrent; find rather a country manor as a Wardour Castle from which forays could be made at strategic moments into the social stream. He could then be aloof in his dignity, his lofty intellectual pursuits, and his other elevated pleasures. What was happening to the reformer who had emerged from Paris, seat of the Enlightenment's intellectual revolution and social reform? He had now adapted shrewdly to the environment of a Catholic in the British Empire, to the anticipated provincial society of Maryland which lay before him.[7]

It was not like Charles to be without suffering the experience of reducing generalities to conclusive judgments on particular instances. The grandiose sketch on his canvas depicting society took on flaring color. The tobacco merchants were a tawdry lot in contrast to his idealization of the gentleman. His generous sampling of London society in other quarters was no better. "The only thing I dislike in my present situation is want of company," he complained. "Instructive company," as he designated his ideal type, was rare. Lesser company, "cannot but be attended with great expense, great distractions and loss of time." He censured "the prodigous vacumm that reigns thro' the conversation" of such company. This "is insupportable to men of a certain stamp." Such men among whom he would stand desire "an undisturbed, serene, composed mind," which cannot be attained without leisure and solitude for uplifting the mind and spirit. At Bourges Charles had aspired to the lot of Diogenes, and in London amid his social activity, he never lost the value he had set on quiet and reflection. Like Montesquieu, he found a book in hand the best weapon against the enemies of the "undisturbed, serene, composed mind." Perhaps he could not for the present entirely avoid the long card games at high stakes with Bladen and his friends. He knew why he could not conform to their prevailing pattern of life. Fortunately, his day of independence on a Maryland manor was not far off.[8]

The passion for dissipation and useless activity prompted a turn from human frailty to reflection in some men; in others, ceaseless and unreasoned indulgence. Each response brings its own distinctive sting to the spirit of a man. So it was with Charles, and his letters tell that he struggled shrewdly. Delinquencies did not find telling in his letters, but his philosophizing cast them in a different light. Charles told his father of his other attractions, and the way in which he pursued them. In the case of women, he did so in delightful fashion. His philosophizing about this passion was in his usual style. "Young persons' passions are strong in themselves," Charles solemnly declared after a few months in London, "& need no outward encouragement; but when roused by occasions, strengthened by example, fired with wine and Jovial company, become almost irresistable." This was from the book. "Who can promise to others [,] even to himself," he added more revealingly, "to remain always virtuous." This was how the young man who had experienced the warmth of a woman's company at Bourges candidly expressed it. Beneath the veil of humor now stood a deeper wonderment. "I have frequently remarked that the most beautiful are always the most powerful, at least to me. I wou'd defy an uggly woman endowed with all the sagacity of a Sphinx ever to entrap me. I have often wondered," he wrote proceeding from his commonplace, "why Providence has bestowed such art, such sagacity on that sex, and at the same time so much beauty." There is no doubt that he finds himself in the midst of an earnest endeavor to keep his way with women and passion as it should be. It may well have been a great struggle.[9]

His father's words on these matters are again at hand and they congenially fit into this context of Charles' idealization. Charles had already read them before his own observations were made. "Now you can only rely on God's grace," he was told shortly after his arrival in London, "your own prudence and ye good principles instilled into you by a virtuous Education." Charles should be on his guard against even the crass transgressions of the moral life. "Avoid them," his father said of women of the town, "as you would a Rattle snake." The elder Carroll had seen them rob English gentlemen of their virtue, health and fortune. He must take care that his gentlemen friends, as well as the women in whose company he placed himself, are deserving of one with such principles as his. Toward the end of his first two years in England, his father gave a broader perspective to such remarks, casting man's whole drama of dealing with his passions into a lofty theme. "Ye only serious business of life is to make thᵗ. [that] eternity a happy one & ye certainest pledge of a happy Eternity is a lively habitual faith." His father wrote, "Pray earnestly for this precious faith & cherish it; having it you cannot act so inconsistently & irrationally as to offend yr god." Charles was inspired from his college days to make a Christian philosopher of himself and he now sought to fulfill that role in the setting of passion and principle. It is understandable that father and son were both concerned at this time with getting a recent book by a favorite author who explored the current meaning of the Christian gentleman, Jean Croiset's *Exercices de piété*. Charles had seen his other works when he was in France.[10]

He had other deep experiences of the heart which tested the Christian philosopher as adapted from Croiset. Sorrow and anguish have no less the force of passion behind them than the attractions for social pleasures and women. After his arrival in London, he visited two Maryland women and their husbands. The Roziers and Platers provided him news and details of domestic affairs closer to the heart than what he had heard from Captain Henry Carroll, whose vessel made so many voyages to England. Charles must have gained more knowledge from his visit with these Maryland women about the tragic affair between Henry Darnall and his separated wife, Rachel Brooke Darnall. After the visit with the Maryland ladies, he wrote to his father condemning the harsh treatment of Rachel by her husband. Charles revealed his great sensitiveness to this domestic sorrow more fully a year later when Rachel's serious illness put her in danger of death. He shared the common anxiety of his father's household during the crisis which fortunately did not claim her life.[11]

Charles had a remarkable affection for his mother, even though he had not seen her since he was a boy. His father chose to write only briefly of her in his letters, lest he awaken too great a lonesomeness. However, Charles learned much about her from Maryland travellers to England and France. The recent visits with Mrs. Rozier intensified his attachment. In these young adult years, he enlarged and deepened his boyhood recollection of her, so that it became what his father put down as salient traits of her personality: a "Charming woman in every sense, remarkable for her good sense, eveness and sweetness of her temper, patience and resignation." His father spoke of her graceful physical features and clear complexion. She reciprocated Charles' warm expressions of concern and attachment and begged him to have a sketch of himself made both in Paris and in London. She regretted his failure to give a fuller account of his personal life.

Charles found an answer to these importunities when he encouraged Mrs. Rozier to give his mother all the information which she sought. He was clearly won to her affection by all of this interest. "Parents, like lovers," he wrote in a light paraphrase of Horace, "are apt to be so much blinded as not to discover the faults of their children, may often imagin[e] those very faults to be good qualities." He therefore had an excuse for not revealing his personal failings. He could count on any which were noted by Mrs. Rozier to be turned to his credit as virtues. When Charles forcefully described his stay abroad as a banishment, the warmth of parental love strongly displayed itself.

He did not learn at this time that his father and mother had agreed not to speak of him when they were together, in order to make their separation more bearable. His father noted that Charles' mother would break off her conversation about him with Rachel Darnall when her husband entered the room.[12]

During his first two years in London, Charles developed a growing sense of anxiety about his mother. By his philosophizing, he revealed the turmoil of his heart. "Our solicitude is always proportionable to our affliction," he wrote; "absence even heightens our anxiety and makes us generally apprehend those evils, which we stand the most in dread of." In the fall of 1760, Charles had heard some rumors that his mother had been ill and even in great danger. He acknowledged that concealment of her condition by his father might have been with good intention. "Pray don't deceive me in the future," Charles begged. "In all your letters you mention her being in good health and that she sends me her blessing: why can't she tell me so in her own handwriting?" It had been rumored that his mother had experienced a swelling condition, but which had declined without further impairing her health. Several months later, in March of 1761, Charles revealed the deepening state of anxiety when he philosophized on death. While his mother grieved over the loss of her own mother, Charles could not but be fearful that she too might be near the end of her days, robbed of the longevity of Charles' grandmother. He revealed the effect of all this on his own feelings. "I hope my Mama enjoys her health and has recovered her spirits," he wrote to his father. "I long to see you both, to see Maryland. I have more reason than one for returning home. . . ."[13]

Charles' mounting anxiety had firm foundation in fact, and the sentiments of the heart proved prophetic. On December 20, 1760, Elizabeth Brooke Carroll was confined to her bed with a distressing illness. She never left her room during the following two months. Fevers afflicted her from time to time, and she was greatly weakened by vomiting; periods of constipation brought about further deterioration. As Charles' father sat beside her sick bed, he had to listen with agonizing sorrow as his wife's speech trailed off into delirium, which her acute suffering and weakness brought on. He saw the painful application of eighteenth-century medical science by the best physicians available in the colony. There was small consolation in the process of bleeding and administration of the physic, which were applied to the delicate, suffering creature. In the last week of February, 1761, Charles' mother was entirely confined to her bed. Lingering on for nearly two weeks, she was finally administered the last rites of the faith to which she had devoted her life. Death came shortly after this, on March 12.[14]

It was ten days before Charles' father could muster the courage to send his exiled son notice of his mother's death. When he did write on March 22, he put aside all caution and reserve, of which his son had earlier complained, and gave all the distressing details of her last days. Charles had need of this kind of revelation from his father even under the oppression of his grief. Elizabeth Brooke Carroll's great courage and resignation to God's will had communicated strength to her husband, and he told his son of it in order to give him courage. It was unimportant that he received his father's sorrowful letter in July, four months after her death, for it would only have replaced his anxious fear of imminent death with a longer period of deep sorrow at the accomplished fact. Yet, the feelings of his heart and soul could not have been stronger. Anxiety had mounted and with it the intense desire of seeing his mother. In his response to his father's letter, he confessed without restraint the "earnest [,] vehement desire of seeing her."

This unfulfilled desire fused with the widening distress of soul that now opened up before him. "You are my only support," was his pathetic response to his father, "my almost only friend in Maryland." Now, a new anxiety took root. What if his father should die? For his own future, he knew, this would be an even greater tragedy, since the household which he hoped to form would be even more difficult to compose. He had been relying upon his father's assistance in this. The burden of his gentlemanly formation in Europe and the further task of finding a lady for the manor which he would soon take up, were weight enough. Death insinuated itself prematurely into earlier thoughts on his marriage; he feared that his frail health made him an easy prey to the thief in the night, which might rob him of time to provide an heir to the Carroll name and fortune.[15]

The Renaissance man had exalted nobility in the way of dying and even made heroics of it, which affected the manner of bearing with death by those closest to the hero. The more gentle manner of the eighteenth-century Christian man of parts, in which Charles formed himself, was not alien to this tradition, nor to the classical touch of the Stoic as he encountered this supreme passion of sorrow and fierce love of life. Charles would philosophize in a familiar vein of his personality and make his own adaptation of the traditions in which he was bred. His father had been brought up in a similar Christian summation of this culture and was now at hand with his own articulation of it. "Philosophy alone cannot administer any solid comfort," he wrote in his sad letter. "Her religion is the only solid comforter of ye afflicted, [;] by it we know tht. [that] ye God who has created us has a right to dispose of us. . . ." These were in a way reflections of religious retreats at St. Omers, which both father and son had made in the past. "Life is but as a Twinkling of ye Eye to Eternity," he reminded Charles. "Ye only serious business of life is to make that Eternity a happy one." He prayed that his son would have "a lively habitual faith. Having it you cannot act so inconsistently & irrationally as to offend any yr God."

Toward the end of that sad year, Charles assured his father that his own thoughts had moved along a similar line in response to their experience of death and sorrow. He had passed beyond Stoicism and the Renaissance style in this formative encounter. Christian humility was joined to gentleness, both of which were so familiar to him as a reader of De Sales and Croiset. "I must expect from time," he candidly reported of his state of soul, "that remedy wh [which] greater firmness than I am possessed of, might, and Christian resignation ought to administer." It was in this way that the mind and manner of Charles were emerging from his struggle with the profoundest of the passions. The experience left its mark on his character in a way that later expressed itself in encounters of lesser magnitude.[16]

By the end of 1761, Charles had emerged with a new maturity of heart and soul. He now estimated that he must make decisions regarding his return to Maryland sooner than he had formerly realized. The specific purpose of his stay in London, the study of law, he now felt was near accomplishment; to stay on beyond the spring of 1762 would be a scholarly luxury in which he could not prudently indulge. He must compose his manor while his father was still in good health; besides, family affection in the wake of the recent sad event also drew him to Maryland. The young gentleman had by now satisfied his curiosity and taste for the intellectual and social pleasures of life in England. These were now cast in a new atmosphere that was sombre by contrast with the air he had when first experiencing them.

Chapter 7

COURTING AN ENGLISH LADY

In planning his return and settlement upon a permanent residence in Maryland, Charles thought it possible to take a bride with him in order to make his manor complete. He did not turn to the Russells and Bladens, in the carefree company of whose daughters he had once delighted. He thought he knew what the lady of his Maryland manor should be, one suited to his own complicated and self-conscious taste. Formal as his approach was, it was not entirely alien to the times nor impractical for him. He had been acquainted with the Bakers, a family of substantial means, loyal to the Catholic faith, and with a young marriageable daughter then studying at the Ursuline Convent in Paris. What he had heard of this young lady of seventeen through Father Crookshanks, his tutor of Paris days, who encouraged him to request a visit with Thomas Baker, was highly favorable. Through the Jesuit's good offices a meeting was arranged with Baker's daughter, Louisa. The journey to Paris in the fall of 1761 was good for the spirit of Charles, who had been burdened by anxiety and sorrow over his mother's fatal illness. He had the congenial companionship of his law student friend William Graves. There were friends along the way, and he found others in Paris. By the middle of October, Charles had paid Louisa Baker visits and found her company pleasant, even though she was nearly ten years younger than he. Charles was satisfied with the impression that he had made and was assured by the fact that his attentions were upon one who was "unpracticed in the wiles of artifices of worldly women." "Her genuine candour & simplicity," Charles told his father, "will unfold her true character, all her virtues, & her imperfections." He had never before reported first impressions of women in such terms. His relationship now was altogether different and clearly directed at marriage. His intentions were clear when he said: 'It will require time to sound the lady's inclinations, to know her well, & to settle matters with the father."

Already, he anticipated obstacles to her consent, even though he had not yet finally judged her suitable from his own standpoint. He expected greater disinclination for living in Maryland from her than from her father. Her sheltered life had kept her from strong ties with her countrymen, which otherwise would have made it unlikely for her to go to America. The wealth of the two families and other financial considerations were normal ingredients of any such marriage. Here Charles' nobility protested the primacy of loftier considerations. In doing so he revealed less the philosophical strain in him than a heart that was being drawn to young Louisa. He must not be selfish in his financial requirements of the match out of thoughtfulness for Louisa. "If upon further acquaintance with the young lady," Charles said, "I should change my mind and think the match [to be] not suitable [,] her fortune however great shall not tempt me to sacrifice my or her happiness to ambition or avarice." He was not yet in love. It was, however, a promising courtship for he knew that he might soon be.[2]

He put off his earlier plan to depart for his beloved Maryland in the spring of 1762. He would further submit to the increasingly arid pursuit of English legal subtleties in his law books. At least the hope of love, if not love itself, was necessary to win this decision from him. There were the usual trials and numerous legal complications to which Charles had to attend while pursuing his courtship. "In case of my death," Charles wrote to his father regarding the harshest realities of the marriage, "my widow may marry again & by so considerable a jointure carry off the great part of the estate onto another family. . . ." Aware of her years and what he called his own delicate health, a long widowhood in the event of his death would be unfair to the Carroll family. According to the usual technical arrangement for such marriages, known as jointure, Charles with his father's approval was willing to grant an annual income from his own estate should Louisa become his widow. The amount of the jointure was determined by a consideration of the estates of both parties to the marriage. The Baker estate was tentatively evaluated at £30,000. Charles would have to assure Louisa in her widowhood of six per cent of this, or £1800 a year. It was necessary for Charles to show that his own estate upon his death could bring Louisa this annual income for life.[3]

This was very serious business of a new sort for young Charles. Before returning from France, he used a last opportunity to take up the social pleasures which he had known as a student at Bourges and the College of Louis the Great. The candor and simplicity of the French prelate Abbé de l'Isle Dieu had always attracted him to his dinners, and Charles had a chance at this time for another of these. The occasion led him to make some very uncomplimentary characterizations of the French, to which the Abbé was an exception. "He is the only frenchman I ever knew susceptible of friendship,"

Charles satirically wrote to his father. Paris also gave him an opportunity to buy clothes whose quality was lacking in English textiles.
He bought velvet material for a suit which would be useful in the
courtship upon which he was embarked. The journey to Paris did
not sufficiently satisfy his taste. Before returning to England, he
arranged an excursion of a few days into the neighboring countryside.
At the end of November he finally departed for England. He was sure,
however, that he would return again within a year, for Louisa would
stay in school for some time. In the meantime, he could reflect on her
character as well as his own and see what further knowledge he
might gain by such a future visit. In view of the financial settlement
required by a marriage of this sort, he needed to be in England as
much as in Paris. Having decided to enter courageously upon a
difficult courtship, he would now deal with Louisa's father at Bath.[4]

Charles returned from France refreshed from travel, and its wholesome distraction of the mind. "The knowledge of men and matters
of different countries," he once said, in paraphrasing Horace, "polishes
and improves the understanding." In this case it improved the
understanding of women, and one in particular. Charles now returned
to his customary ways of gentility, which would go on for another
two years. He read his *Gentleman's Register* and arranged to have a
suit cut from the elegant velvet cloth which he had bought in Paris.
His horsemanship had finally become respectable, but he still needed
a "good, sober, understanding groom." A gardener or some other
servant would hardly do now, "as either the ignorance or the sloth
of such a fellow might be fatal to the Mares." His parents had always
suggested sitting for portraits. A new awareness of his importance
as an heir to the family name, honor, and fortune led him to seek
an artist to do a three-quarter length portrait of himself. A man
named Connolly agreed to do such a work for twenty-five guineas. Such
a fee was considered respectable and he would have paid more if
it were not. Charles did not omit the opportunity to vacation with
his fellow Marylander Edmund Jennings at Dunbridge Wells in
November, 1762.[5]

Shortly after sitting for Connolly in March of 1763, his vanity and
health were sorely tried by an attack of smallpox. Charles had
feared for poor Nancy Cooke's complexion after such an ordeal,
and his own illness was no less harrowing. The treatment of his doctor
called for shaving his head, which according to eighteenth-century

diagnosis was necessary to complete a treatment that called for many physics. A wig was now necessary and Charles was not pleased with his appearance in one, even though he had been in juvenile days at St. Omers. It may have become some gentlemen who had not his handsome crop of natural hair, but not Charles. Because Charles had great confidence in his practitioner, a Dr. Reeves who was president of a college of physicians, he endured all. Etherington, Charles' trusted apothecary, had guided him to Reeves. Charles showed that he feared his ailment as more than a wound to his vanity. He was deeply grateful to Reeves, he said, "to whose Care [,] Judgment & assiduity, I owe under the Divine providence my recovery. . . ." The experience confirmed his belief that he had delicate health. This conviction was urging him to marriage, so that he might have the most of what he feared would be a short life.[6]

When Charles was given a bill of health by Reeves in May of 1763, he turned to Horace's treatment of travel. The country gentleman possessed the most salubrious as well as the most virtuous domain, so he wrote to his friend Christopher Bird, who enjoyed a manor life in a county of England, to see if he might provide the hospitality of his cherished possession for his afflicted friend in London, now pitifully deprived of his strength as well as his hair. Never under even normal conditions resembling a Samson, Charles won the sympathy of his good friend Bird. He also had a confidante in Bird's aunt, Esther Bird Browne, and was most acceptable to Bird's father. Charles also knew that hospitality came easily to the country gentleman, who required the visits of friends like Charles to fend off the monotony which always threatened the country manor however affluent it might be.[7]

Charles completely recovered his health, and, strangely enough, acquired a liking for the wig which was originally inflicted upon him. He put the best interpretation on the compliments which he received from his friends, that he looked as well in it as in his natural hair. Charles was not entirely pleased with Connolly's portrait. With what he now considered his improved appearance, he sought greater excellence in another artist and with a fee that was more than respectable. This led him to one of the rising masters of English portraiture, Sir Joshua Reynolds, who agreed to do a three-quarter length portrait. It was no small compliment that the finished young intellectual and gentleman won the master's consent, assured that the subject would not leave him uninspired and liable to producing a work unworthy of his demanding standards.[8]

Charles continued his well established career in the social life of a gentleman. He was still found in the company of women of the important families whom he had customarily visited before his recent trip to Paris. Though primarily concerned with Louisa Baker, he did not lose his appreciation for the Bladen daughters. He even felt them entitled to an invitation to matrimony, "if Beauty and sense improved by the best education, command esteem & inspire love." Of course, the invitation could not now come from himself. At the same time, he fully understood his father's words which had meaning in their case since they were Protestants. There could be no enduring happiness in a Catholic's marriage with one of another faith, he had remarked in 1762. Even should the one party take up the religion of the other, there would still be disadvantages since the religious background of the parents left its mark on the children. It was even better if a convent education were added to a Catholic family background, since the early impressions of such a bride promised to safeguard the union by religious training and a "virtuous education." A modest approach to courtship was important, his father continued in his disquisition on courtship, both in concealing the intentions of marriage and in the frequency of visits, lest passion obscure the understanding. The virtues of the bride, furthermore, would supply any lack in her material fortune. Great value should be attached to the traits "good natured and sensible."[9]

By the end of 1762, however, Charles was impressed with the importance, if not the necessity, of a fortune in the bride whom he would take. Father and son alike had difficulty stating their formula of the proportionate importance of wealth. "It ought not to be preferred or even put in competition with other good Qualities," his father remarked. The matter of wealth, however, affected both families and not merely a member of each. It did not seem right to Charles' father that there be any risk of one-third of his fortune's falling to his son's bride in the event of his prior death as could happen under some legal arrangement. An expensive jointure could do this and even pass the fortune on to a second husband. Father and son were proud of the aristocratic origins of their family and were determined to perpetuate its financial foundation. "We derive our descent from Princes," Charles' father wrote, "& until ye Revolution [of 1688], notwithstanding our suffering under Elizabeth & Cromwell, we were in affluent circumstances & respected & we inter-maryed with ye best Families in the Kingdom of Ireland." If the Baker family seemed similarly great in this aristocratic tradition, all the more reason for seeking a marriage. Perhaps such greatness might be demanded.[10]

It was with a sense of duty, then, as much as attraction to a lovely lady which led Charles on his course toward a Baker marriage with a reasonable regard for family wealth. His words reflected the complications of mind and heart inevitable in such a courtship. He joked about the ideal woman. In distress at his labors, and in doubt of his affection for Louisa, he hoped that he would never be in love. He soberly protested family loyalty which would never let him marry without his father's consent. "The reasons for being the same Religion," he says, recalling his father's advice, "are so strong that no consideration whatever shall prevail upon me to marry a protestant." At the same time he is not sure that there is yet any Catholic lady who will please him.[11]

By February, 1763, Charles candidly criticized the personal life of the Baker family in writing to his father. No doubt he was thinking of the society from which Louisa came when he described their view of family fortunes. "Their love of pleasure," he judged, "is stronger than their love of riches." His father had carefully cultivated the proper pleasures, it was true, but he had attended to enhancing with hard work and attention the riches of the Carroll inheritance. Thomas Baker was not a London merchant, nor of that particular town's gentry; but the gentry of Bath was different only by degree. Charles was now finding less congenial even the country gentry of English stamp, with a few exceptions such as Christopher Bird; they were not suited to his ideals of life in a province like Maryland. It was now not a question of merely getting on amongst them as a provincial who was more urbane than what the English expected of him. He had to prevail upon such a family to permit their daughter to return with a provincial gentleman, "to a barbarous and uncivilised world," as Charles stated it, reflecting their terms and feelings.[12]

In the latter part of the summer of 1763, Charles set off once again to visit Louisa in the Parisian convent which sheltered her from the society of which he was now so critical. He carried his mental notes on jointure with him and what affection he had for Louisa. He may have received a letter from his father before departing. Its contents if received earlier would have impelled him to make the journey, even if his heart did not draw him to Paris. His father defended the virtues of women, which Charles treated so jocosely in his own letter, and said they were more substantial by comparison than those of men. If that was not enough to see what he was in danger of losing by lack of earnestness in his courtship, let Charles consider the belated marriage which ultimately leads to "fond doting Husbands . . . past their grand climacteristic. . . ." They lose a greater physical fulfillment by a late marriage and the benefit of a numerous offspring. If Charles was not expecting to fall in love, at least let him hope for the blessed occurrence![13]

Charles left London July 17 and arrived at Calais two days later. His leisurely pace to Paris permitted him to examine military installations at Dunkirk and stop for a few days at Bruges, Ghent, and Rotterdam. At Antwerp, he passed a few days with his cousin Jacky Carroll, exchanging news of their kinsmen in Maryland and their own experiences in Europe. His fondness for St. Omers and his many friends there led him to stay a few days. He found his old preceptors a sorry lot, evicted from their old familiar buildings, and living in exile in a dilapidated building at nearby Watten. They had little hope of returning to their former residence unless the King of France passed away; he had capitulated to the *parlements* and Bourbon courtiers, who clamored for their expulsion in hope of ultimate extinction of the order. Charles passed from this depressing scene to Rotterdam and then to The Hague, where, on August 8, he sent his father an account of his travels. He was already planning his return trip, which held special interest by an excursion to Nijmegen, Cleves, and Düsseldorf; there was no prospect of visiting Berlin as he had wished. He would sail for England from Calais after a visit to Lille and St. Omers.[14]

By early fall Charles returned from Paris with greater admiration and affection for Louisa than before. She merited that comprehensive description of the bride he desired, "sensible and sweet," which had its own eighteenth-century connotation and the personal meaning Charles further gave to it. He expressed the hope of being in love. The meeting, however, gave one unfavorable turn to the relationship. "The situation of our affairs," Charles wrote with sadness, "absolutely require[s] my residence in Maryland: and I cannot sacrifice the future aggrandisement of our family to a woman. . . ." He leaves no doubt that he believes America holds great promise for his own fortunes and he will not sacrifice them. Louisa had disappointed him in not understanding that. Was her own attachment to kin and country any different? Charles had not considered this as he did his own case since as eldest son he bore his family fortunes by the law of primogeniture. It was the rôle of woman to have a detachment from family, since she did not bear such a burden. Still, he did not feel that Louisa would long fail to appreciate his point of view, especially if her attachment to him grew and her parents could be brought to accept the separation. From Baker's standpoint, why could not Charles as he himself be an absentee planter, benefiting himself and Louisa by a life in England? Other Marylanders had done so. Should Charles accept such a proposal by Baker, compensation would reasonably be required by Charles in dowry and jointure as the case might be.[15]

He now put his mind and heart to these distressing personal and financial problems. He had little choice in facing up to this business because toward the end of December, 1763, he received a letter from Louisa's father requesting a visit from Charles. With depressed spirits he arrived at Bath, where the Bakers lived. Louisa's father gave great attention to Charles, who now found himself somewhat ill, experiencing "weak nerves," as he diagnosed his ailment. He felt that the journey and brief stay at Bath would be good for him. He submitted to treatment by Baker's physician there. His father later ascribed his illness to a condition common to the lovelorn. The doctor's prescription of donkey milk hardly agreed with that diagnosis, but it seemed to strengthen him for the business with Baker, dispelling his "weak nerves." Charles also became better acquainted with Louisa's sisters and brothers and learned that they had become important factors in his courtship.[16]

Several circumstances, he now saw, were decisive to any final agreement about the marriage. Baker explained that his own fortune was to be divided evenly among all of his children. Unfortunately, he had recently sustained some financial losses, which would further reduce the dowry of Louisa. Charles had hoped that the parents would try to persuade Louisa to go to Maryland. He was not entirely disappointed on this score. Charles took this as a show of genuine affection for him by the family and felt it should be graciously acknowledged in the jointure. "The going to America," he wrote to his calculating father, "will no doubt be made a reason for demanding a large settlement on my Wife in case of my death. . . . Father, mother, & all her relations out of love for her husband deserves a handsome jointure." This was said after returning from Bath as he collected his impressions in January of 1764.[17]

One serious factor was always present in Charles' courtship and that was the age of Louisa. He had met her in Paris when she was fifteen. He had even assumed the possibility of concluding the marriage agreement a year later. A bride of sixteen was not unusual for the eighteenth century and Louisa, like Charles himself, was by her education in Paris initiated into a life separated from parents. He was, however, unrealistic in estimating this obstacle of Louisa's tender years. Her father confronted him with this consideration and used it to suggest postponement of the marriage. At Bath, Charles learned how much Louisa's mother desired postponement. Baker wrote to Charles' father shortly after this expressing the hope that a delay would be acceptable to him. He took the occasion to emphasize the importance of postponement by expressing his satisfaction with the other significant circumstances of the marriage, especially the size of the Carroll fortune. Baker made it appear that the Carroll marriage was praiseworthy except for the youthfulness of his daughter. By allowing time to take care of this perhaps the question of Louisa's removal to America might also be resolved.[18]

Charles' father expressed sentiments similar to Baker's, which went beyond what Charles himself felt. He gives complete freedom to Charles to take Louisa as his wife. He is willing to see Charles become a gentleman of the British Isles; not an absentee lord of Maryland manors, but one presiding over a whole revamped fortune that would be placed in England. He had already begun to sell a considerable amount of his property as a result of the double-tax policies. A full elaboration of this scheme, which had never appealed to Charles, continued to intrigue him, and he now found a new opportunity to see it through with advantage to his son. The scheme assumed at this time a very deep attachment to Louisa in Charles, which did not actually exist. His father undoubtedly was aware of this. In the same letter which makes Charles feel free to live in England, he upheld his son's attachment to Maryland and hopes that it will be fulfilled. He did not fail to express how the present separation from his son and the possibility of its permanence affects him deeply. Charles was drawn all the more strongly by this to his native Maryland and his family there.[19]

He was in the midst of assessing all of these ever-growing circumstances of his courtship in the spring of 1764. He was able to get more exact estimates of the Baker fortune, which would ultimately determine how much income Charles must assure to Louisa in the event of widowhood. Her dowry would be determined by the portion of the total estate of her father, which therefore had to be exactly computed. Baker had prepared Charles for some disappointment in his initial hopes when he first visited Louisa. He had mentioned some recent losses in the preliminary conversations at Bath in December, 1763. Charles had now been provided records which showed Baker to be worth about £50,000. This wealth was largely based upon about 350 slaves and 480 acres on the Island of Saint Croix. Undoubtedly the income from sales in sugar and rum which these plantations yielded was included in the aggregate sum. The jointure ratio of six to seven per cent would be applied to this sum of the Baker fortune to determine the amount of money from Charles' estate to which Louisa would be entitled in a widowhood. Charles, therefore, would have to assure her an income of about £3,500 a year.[20]

The total Carroll estate substantially exceeded that of Baker. The records which Charles' father sent him were indeed impressive. The total wealth amounted to £88,380, or nearly 40 per cent more than Baker's. The Carrolls felt that their fortune could favorably be converted into assets other than land. Diversity of value in land possessions, however, was significant. Country land of 12,000 acres, for example, would bring £20 an acre. Annapolis and related property was worth very nearly £40,000. The 285 slaves were valued at £8,550. Livestock, tools, household items, etc., at Annapolis and Doughoregan were other sources of wealth. It is not surprising that this massive fortune found outlets in loans. In 1762, they attained the amount of £24,230, and the elder Carroll profited by the practice of compound interest as well as the prevailing high interest rates.[21]

Charles still had to establish what portion of his whole estate was to be his own in the immediate future, prior to the time when his father's demise would bring it all to himself. This, too, had been well indicated in the records which his father had sent him. His father had bought Carrollton Manor in Frederick County with his son in mind. The extensive holding a few miles southwest of Frederick Town amounted to 10,000 acres. Another section, called "Addition," amounting to 2,700 acres yielded £250 sterling annually. Charles could also claim £400 sterling income a year from investments in the Baltimore Iron Works. This substantial source of income immediately available to Charles at his marriage should satisfy Louisa's requirement of the jointure, since it would yield the £3,500 annual income to her in the event of her husband's death. If there was any doubt about Charles' ability to assure the jointure from these sources, his father would add the 10,000 acres of Doughoregan and Chance Manors, where most of the Carroll slaves were located. The elder Carroll would bring this about at this time if necessary.[22]

Charles' father surely did not disguise his persistent desire that his son arrange a marriage of fortune, which he felt Louisa promised. Charles had entertained similar sentiments early in his courtship. As any gentlemen in such a situation, the Carrolls sought financial reciprocation for a generous jointure by winning a substantial dowry. Widowhood and the consequent jointure were contingent, but the dowry was certain of payment upon conclusion of the marriage. In view of this, it is understandable that Charles' father was impatient at not having adequate details of the Baker fortune and chided Charles for not giving him enough particulars. He was even anxious to learn if the recent visit to Bath had satisfied him on the state of the Baker wealth, and whether Baker had agreed to give his daughter to Charles in marriage.[23]

Charles now took all of these matters in his own hands without too much attention to paternal direction. As he went over the disappointing record of the Baker estate with his own handsome fortune before him, he became more demanding of the marriage than before. Suspecting Charles' disappointment at the Baker wealth and realizing his son's responsibility for the financial details, the father in his letters of February and April generously encouraged him in his independence and freedom. He was even displaying additional generosity by inviting Louisa's father to live with the Carrolls in Maryland, until he discovered that some of the Baker children were unmarried. "God will bless you in everything," he now assured his son, "which may contribute to your Temporal & Eternal walfare."[24] Charles need not be so financially demanding of the Bakers.

Temporalities were indeed only that. As Charles wrestled with all the other elements of the decision before him, he freely revealed the great distress which he experienced and how it had been affecting his health a month before he went to Bath. These complaints of Charles won his father's sympathy, even if a full understanding of them was wanting. "I hope they in a great measure proceed from the anxiety your passion for Miss Baker gives you," he wrote to his son. With simplicity, Charles showed that his own parental love complicated his distressed condition. "I should not choose to pursue my own happiness in opposition to any Parent's will," he said "nor wish to succeed if my succes should make that Parent [w]retched & unhappy."[25]

If Charles was thorough in estimating the financial factors which afflicted his courtship, he was no less so regarding the subtle human circumstances that tried his heart and his feelings for Louisa. By May, he was able to assess what some of these were. The visit to Bath had taught him much about Louisa's mother, which was also a lesson on her daughter. "The mother," he said, "could not bear to part with her daughter." This was a great disappointment, since he had counted on both parents to strengthen the daughter for a voyage to America. She may have been unable to bear her permanent departure from the household at her age, even if she stayed in England. Baker, Charles felt, became indifferent to the courtship at this time because of the mother's feelings. A friend told Charles that Baker even spoke slightingly of the Carroll fortune, thus showing the adverse influence of his wife. She was clearly the unattractive stamp of gentry which Charles found all too common in England. "Had I known the mother before I opened the affair," Charles now said with bitterness "I should have entirely dropped the thoughts of that marriage."[26]

In March, 1764, Charles again visited Paris. It was not a good time of the year for travel and the added cost as usual gave him concern. "I expect to be amply repaid the expense of that expedition," he explained to his father, "in the possession of a sensible, agreeable, & virtuous woman." There is much less in his letters to his father regarding his affection and devotion for Louisa than he expressed on the occasion of his previous visit. In the continuing negotiations with her father over the estate, many new circumstances and less romantic thoughts had entered into his relationship with her. Affection for her was still within him, but it had not grown as expected. As he returned from his visit, he became aware of this and noted the same dispositions in Louisa. For needed diversion, he occupied himself with making notes of his journey, from which a few months later he composed a journal for his father's benefit. He was also easily distracted by his accounts. Upon his return to London he found that his receipts did not match his expenses.[27]

Louisa's older sister was more unfavorable to Charles than was the mother. Closer to Charles' age, and more discerning of his manner as a gentleman, her criticism penetrated more deeply into Louisa's mind and feelings in a way that was crucial. Charles confided to Christopher Bird's aunt, Esther Bird Browne, that the sister was succeeding with her devious activity. The attraction and devotion which Louisa had once felt now began to fade. When Charles confessed to Esther that he experienced anguish at this, he was revealing that his own affection for Louisa was greater than he admitted to others. "At that time I would have given the . . . world," he said, for Louisa "to have entertained a better opinion of me." If Charles was not in love, he was not far from it. Yet, from this moment forward all was beyond hope, and it was natural that he found other reasons why the marriage did not seem suitable.[28]

Charles brooded on such thoughts through the spring and into the summer. "The young lady," he said of his misgivings about the future with Louisa, "has been bread [sic] up with very high notions not at all answerable to her fortune." He feared that the snobbery which he had found in the mother and sister had inevitably contaminated young Louisa. He left no doubt what they disliked in him. He had no appreciation for the town gentry of London and its milder counterpart in the counties of England and towns like Bath. His preference he now knew was for the simpler woman. "A domestic wife," he wrote in July, "not so fond of show and parade, who is not above the business of her family will best suit me." If the mother was not equal to the part, how would Louisa be? "The mother," he caustically remarked, "is a vain [,] empty woman,[;] who knows but the daughter may take after her? I do not choose to make the risk."[29]

The affection of Charles for Louisa led him to mitigate this dim forecast of the future lady. He confessed that he did not yet know her well enough for a sweeping judgment. As early as April, 1764, furthermore, he felt certain that he did not love her, even though he might one day reach that happy state, possibly after marriage. But that marriage could not take place in the immediate future, as was now very definite and he must soon return to Maryland. At such a distance any progress in their natural devotion was impossible. "I wish extremely well to [Louisa]," he said fondly after his decision to terminate the courtship, "& married to a man worthy of her."[30]

As the impasse of the courtship had developed, and before Charles had made his decision in April to decline further involvement, Louisa's father made a final gesture for his family. He proposed that Charles follow his desire to return to America in the near future. In a few years, he might return and resume the courtship. Louisa would then be twenty years of age and the family more prepared to accept her separation from them by marriage and even by a voyage to Maryland. Charles could now decline with grace. The Bakers would thus show no lack of esteem for devoted Charles, which an outright rejection by either of the couple at this time would have suggested. Baker's proposal itself, however, carried the meaning of rejection without any outward offense. Dissatisfaction with the arrangements of a marriage rather than with the families or their respective spouses was thus politely expressed.

The deference for genteel propriety only helped Charles understand himself and his personal circumstances at the conclusion of his legal studies and residence in England. He confessed to his belief that Louisa had much affection for him. "What certainty is there," he wondered, "that the lady will remain for 4 years of the same opinion? or rather how probable is it she will not? I do not care to entangle myself in any such engagement." Amid all his good wishes for Louisa as she went her separate way, he strove to go his own with courage. "I have dropt all thought of Miss Baker," he wrote to his father in an effort to encourage himself in his decision. He acted out of consideration for her as well as himself. Her ties of affection to Charles existed, but they were of slender thread. To ask her to maintain them for three or four years of absence was unfair. Perhaps if Louisa and Charles had known each other better and if the bonds had been thus firmer, such a requirement of long separation would have been possible in the genteel traditions of romance. As it was, Charles and Louisa were unsuited to such dramatic rôles.[31]

Charles now turned in the direction of America, much the way he was when he first travelled to Paris to court Louisa. Although a few years older, he was still a young gentleman and anxious to establish his household as soon as possible. He would set off for America a free man, with the sorrow behind and ahead the joy of seeking out a bride among new acquaintances in Maryland, just as Watty Hoxton and old friends from St. Omers had done. He was very conscious that they were a good deal ahead of him. "I should choose to [be] settled without loss of time"; he wrote in March, 1764, "the sooner the better." His courtship had begun in the wake of his mother's death. He was now more conscious than ever of the ebb of time. "The chances of my living so long, are against me," he brooded, "as I am of thin and amunic [anemic] puny habit of body." By leaving England now and marrying soon, he said hopefully, "I might live to bring up my children." Charles clearly had not come through his stormy courtship with Louisa without taking great treasure from it; he would bear it from the Old World to the New, as he revealed in these mature reflections. He was now as much ready to play the role of husband on the manor, as lawyer in the arena of Maryland politics.[32]

Chapter 8

A REVOLUTIONARY IN SPIRIT

The anxieties of his courtship left their mark upon Charles as he struggled to conclude his last two years of legal studies in London. "I apply to the Law," he complained, "but cannot apply with that assiduity I would wish." It was true that he did not have even average health and was put to a severe physical and psychological test. "No fatigue can be greater," he believed, "than the intense application of the mind to difficult and abstruse knowledge." Yet he had a penchant for the acquisition of such knowledge and would not give up the pursuit of law on the high plain upon which he had entered it in 1759.[1]

In addition to his personal problems, the circumstances in which he studied had not improved his third year in London. At this stage, he should have passed from greater emphasis upon book study to some experience in the preparation of actual cases and practice in court. By 1762, he had not yet discovered a method suitable to his special situation nor a satisfactory instructor. Fortunately Charles had the taste and the means for the diversion of travel and vacationing, which at this time took him to Margate for bathing and for that salubrious air frequently recommended by eighteenth-century physicians. He returned to London after two weeks there in July. In further concern for his health, he had taken up the practice of regular horseback riding which his physician had recommended. He incurred considerable expense in keeping horses which he had bought. It appeared that his father too needed some medical advice, and he sent him a volume entitled *Ward's Medicines*. He also sent him some dropsy powders to be taken with broth or gruel. "The less they drink the better," was his advice to those using such powders! Such preoccupations reflected the distressed soul of Charles, despondent from a troubled courtship and weary of his exile.[2]

In view of all this, it is understandable that he had wished to be in America by the fall of 1762. Only the courtship really demanded that he remain. His father, however, urged that he stay on for greater mastery of law, which was to be the crowning of his education in a truly "Liberal Profession." He had made his son aware of the practical details of a gentleman's life in Maryland, where knowledge of law was essential to maintaining a vast fortune. But Charles felt that he could do the reading of law which he was doing in London in Maryland just as well. The formal instruction in London was not necessarily of such high quality as to make it worthwhile. In Mary-

imposed, particularly upon his father's health. He recommended his own philosophizing as a means of quieting such feelings of hostility and aggressiveness. "Conscious innocence," he wrote to his father, "is secure from envy and suspicion and superior to the base hearts of malice. . . ." The recommendation revealed the personality of the son more than a solution for his father. Charles was temperamentally and intellectually capable of this control over vindictiveness by his cultivated esteem for a sense of integrity. His father and Dulany were less inclined to such values. A balance of such an attitude in a man of affairs made him prudent but above foolish docility. Charles had attained a valuable trait of mind and heart for a gentleman. He had consciously cultivated this mentality and was now testing it with increasing frequency in courtship, legal studies, litigation, and politics. He was striving to be a man of affairs as well as an intellectual.[11]

Fortunately, there were other less demanding occasions for the exercise of discretion than transactions with the brilliant lawyer from Maryland. They were important all the same in the making of a gentleman. Through his cousin Captain Henry Carroll, he met other worthy mariners like Kelty and Hanson, who carried Carroll letters as well as cargoes from the province to England. Charles reminded his father to entertain them upon their return to America, for they had done him acts of kindness and service. His own good offices with Sir Thomas Web in favor of his father's servant Ireland were not without personal embarrassment. He hoped that he would be relieved of this task with the recent passing of Sir Thomas, for his son John would not be so easily importuned for loans and efforts to acquire estate recognition for Ireland. However, now with the entrée which Charles had aided, Ireland was successful in getting further loans from Lady Web. Such patronage by Charles was only one occasion in a wide range of provincial associations which he had in his years in London. Thomas M. Lee of Maryland, for example, who was in London at this time, was from an important Maryland family which would give the State of Maryland one of its first governors; and Charles formed ties of friendship with him. While his father's report that Charles had dined with Thomas Jefferson, the future bright light of Virginia politics, was unfounded, Jefferson would have found young Charles a kindred revolutionary in spirit, had he met him in England at this time. Even in London, then,

Charles was involved in Maryland provincial society, so many of whose important gentlemen found their way into his company.[12]

He also grew in his sense of identity with his own Catholic counter-revolutionary society in these years. Through his reading at this time he grew in an understanding of the legal condition of the Roman Catholic element in the British Empire. He sent his father some of these books for Doughoregan library. New pamphlets on the Catholic case against the penal laws and statutes were among the growing collection. At this time, he also gave greater attention to Irish history, not merely to support his own claim to noble lineage in connection with his courtship of Louisa Baker, but to understand the effect of such laws where he felt they had their harshest effect. Warner's *History of Ireland* and *Dissertations on Irish History* were purchased. With great care, he pursued his own family's seventeenth-century experience of British discrimination. Father Anthony Carroll's sister assisted Charles in his quest for this information in 1762. Before the Protestant Revolution of 1688, he learned, Kean Carroll's brother, Charles, had enrolled for the study of law at Inner Temple, London. Following the revolution came a sad reversal of good fortune. Access to the legal profession became restricted. Records of land forfeiture were found for Kean Carroll, of whom Charles was a direct descendant. Charles studiously reconstructed this picture, copying down what information he had gained from Ireland. He enlisted the assistance of a man in England named Whitten, who had special knowledge of such matters. Whitten through an agent in Dublin investigated the records of the college there, which showed Charles to be descended from nobility in the line of Roger, Prince of Ely, who died in 1407. Useful books were collected and sent to Maryland. This interest was closely related to his continual concern with the growing political web to bring about the suppression of the Society of Jesus, which was the chief educational force for the intellectual survival of the Catholic gentry in the province as well as in the mother country. He gathered pamphlets and reports which described the Bourbon tyranny; it was not unlike the experience of his forebears for three generations at the hands of the English monarchy.[13]

It was with this mentality that Charles watched the progress of the Seven Years War. In 1762 he was optimistically awaiting an ultimate English victory. The peace would put an end to the excuse the Maryland Assembly had made of the war with Catholic France for the double-tax on its provincial Catholics. The reassurance which Charles had gained from Lord Baltimore and the proprietary party regarding mitigation of discrimination made Maryland far more a land of welcome as he now approached the time of his return to America.

While in Paris in 1758, he had followed the international conflict closely enough to foresee many of its developments. Prussia promised to be a determining force in the outcome. William Pitt, who had not been favorable to expenditures in Prussia's favor, realized in the last stages of the war the wisdom of reasonable subsidies. After Frederick II had established friendly relations with the new Russian ruler Peter III, the Prussians weakened the opposition to which Russia belonged by prior diplomacy. In the enlightened despot of Prussia, Charles saw the usefulness of the monarchy, especially in time of war. He thought Frederick nearly invincible. Pitt himself finally admitted that America was being won in Germany, for Prussia tied down the French forces on the continent, leaving the English superior in North America. Realizing that Prussia was the crucial factor in the last years of the war, Charles estimated that the aid of Denmark might be required for complete victory. The new shift in Prussian diplomacy might also complicate the English position in the war because Prussian interests in Italy might lead to demands for compensation there. All about him in England, he saw the last strenuous effort at victory, particularly in Parliament and the military departments. The French bombarded at Cassel had crossed over the Fulda River. "We wait with impatience the consequences of this event," he wrote on the 4th of July, 1762.[14]

When Charles visited France in 1763, he understood the vast naval superiority of England, possessing even Calais and Dunkirk, which he viewed as military enclaves. Here, ships of sixty guns, he estimated, could safely ride at anchor. Monarchies had their limitations; France, surely, and England too, even though constructed on the foundation of a constitution and Parliament. The blessings of the English monarchy, however, were not to be denied in 1763. Quebec had fallen. France, in spite of the family compact and her alliance with Spain in the last years of the war, was on her knees. William Pitt thought that a high price in territorial aggrandizement was possible if additional time were allowed for a crushing military victory. The ministry was willing to lower that price, however, in order to save the French nation's resources and avert future antagonisms by an early peace in 1763. As Charles already knew, Pitt's ambitions had been ruled out of the preliminary negotiations and the Peace of Paris in 1763 brought down the curtain on the long, bloody drama. While imperial-minded Englishmen might be displeased, Charles, the provincial Marylander, found it acceptable and very beneficial to his own future in America. Hysteria would now recede, and with it the anti-Catholic militancy in the Lower House of the Maryland Assembly.[15]

Charles always played the critic as he viewed the great national monarchies in action during these years of crisis. His father told him to observe the French government carefully as part of his education, and he continued the assignment in London. He had seen France deprived of constitutional means to protect civil liberty, which was no less the case with England. He now became personally involved in an instance verifying his analysis. While France silenced her guns and recalled her soldiers in 1763, she only heightened her warfare against the Jesuit Order. This demonstrated to Charles that her government was an enemy of religious as well as civil liberty. Indeed, it now appeared that liberty was indivisible. In February, 1763, he predicted that Jesuit revenues would be completely confiscated and not merely in particular provinces where the spoliation had already begun. They will ultimately be expelled, he sadly foretold.[16]

For some time Charles had been reading pamphlets on these morbid proceedings and was anxious to send them to his father. With his own family long a target of a harsh provincial parliament, it was not surprising that he turned his fierce criticism against the *Parlement* of Aix-la-Chapelle. Reflecting his reformer temperament, he made a hero of Monsieur d'Eguilles, President of the *Parlement,* who dared to stand in the way of the arbitrary action against the religious order, leading a minority of 27 against the 29 who passed the decree of condemnation. Charles had the president's pamphlet *Les Arrêts et Arrêtés de la Compagnie* at hand as he wrote to his father of the events. Such material had been suppressed and burned by the parlement. As a sequel to tyranny, Eguilles after a heavy fine was banished from the province. A clergyman friend was similarly fined. "I am told," Charles reported, "that the Parlement of Aix had made it a felony to correspond with a Jesuit." Charles himself had he been in France would have been under such a condemnation. Yet, he was not deterred from his visit to Paris after these events, nor from his loyalty to his devoted educators.[17]

Was there any recourse against such assemblies? What of the case of the Maryland Assembly? To what degradation an exalted institution of man could fall! "The decisions and proceedings of most assemblies," he wrote with the mordancy of Tacitus, "when once Passion or interest prevails, are more tyrannical and oppressive than the positive cruelty of a Lawless Tyrant." After some months, he had arrived at an analysis of the French monarchy and viewed the acts of the Aix-la-Chapelle and other *parlements* as acting with contempt for royal authority. The weakness of the crown opened the door to such precipitancy, injustice, and violence by the *parlements*. Charles was filled with disgust over the king for failing his obligations to French society. In the reasoning of Montesquieu, the monarch should be a restraint upon the *parlement,* especially in such instances of lawlessness as these. Intrigue similar to that of Pombal's in Portugal had undermined the French court. There was no hope for a government so corrupted in its royal chambers. Charles despised the policy of one who was weak in the face of such tyranny.[18]

In this case he did not excuse a certain Jesuit who had taken an oath that truckled to tyrannical forces in the government. Charles would "despise him for his servile compliance," as he said in the case of one who took such an oath, for it was "incompatible with his honour." Such an act would have been a disgrace to any Carroll generation; every one had been tried time and again. Charles felt great distress at such disloyalty to the faith in men who had been his educators, and he left no doubt that they also betrayed the liberal political principles which they had taught him. Those who resisted the infringement of freedom stood high in his regard, and France, rather than the Jesuits, was the tragic figure as they went into banishment. He still regarded "Jesuites men of republican principles who will not fail to inspire the youths with a love of liberty." Perhaps the lesson would be retained in France among those who had learned republican principles more profoundly through the experience of arbitrary government. Attachment to republicanism might come, for surely that was the answer to such arbitrary acts. This must be what Charles firmly grasped in these moments of deep emotion when he wrote: "Thus in 20 years time Loyalty to kings will be no more the characteristic of the French nation: the nobility will be patriots instead of Courtiers; from slaves to kings transformed to friends of liberty." There would be a French Revolution as a result of those ideas of republicanism which at Paris, Bourges, and London he had learned to cherish even under decadent monarchical regimes.[19]

Montesquieu, the French natural law philosopher whose *Spirit of the Laws* Charles had acquired before coming to London, disposed him to regard the British monarchy in a different light from that of France. He had an opportunity to study the government in London in action after study of the writings. The balance of authority between the king, parliament, and the courts was clear enough in theory. In his efforts to ameliorate conditions in Maryland, he had appealed to one authority against another with enough success to keep alive his hope of greater reform. This experience gave depth to his knowledge of the British imperial government. Charles also had the great advantage of personally knowing and visiting with the men who occupied positions at the very center of England's constitutional monarchy. The Barrington family, as a notable example, branched into the king's cabinet, Parliament, and the bench. He was on the most friendly terms with the Queen's Attorney General Hussey in 1764. Hussey was especially important in this capacity during the period of George III's illness when the queen served as regent. The attorney general was charmed by Charles' attachment to Maryland and welcomed his gift of choice beef from America. Charles was also acquainted with members of Parliament such as Bratt and Camphion. Long accustomed to reading written accounts of affairs of state, his conversations with men of importance brought him considerably greater understanding of the British Constitution at work in these years of crisis in Parliament and the cabinet.[20]

The Tory Party, with which the Carroll family was linked at the time of the Revolution of 1688, had experienced a transmutation by the middle of the eighteenth century. The Hanovers themselves, who owed their regal position in England to the Revolution of 1688 and the Whig Party, now found fault with the way in which the settlement in favor of parliamentary power was working out in the face of gigantic problems of imperial rule. Montesquieu himself had seen some validity in the old Tory criticism of the weakened condition of the king's authority. As president of his French provincial *parlement*, he had invited the Duke of Burwick, James II's grandson and pretender to the throne, to address that body. While the mid-century

Tory Party rejected any assumptions in favor of a Stuart restoration, they did not hesitate to hold that the Crown was too weak. Lord Bolingbroke, intellectual confrère of Montesquieu, was not above aligning himself with the Tories once again.[21]

When young George III came to power in 1760, he looked to this party for aid in a more vigorous reassertion of the royal authority than that allowed by the 1688 Constitution. William Pitt, riding high as a Whig favorite in Parliament, had taken power from George III's ministers at the crucial hour of the war and directed the war efforts toward ultimate victory. As he continued, however, his position left British administration in the ambiguous state which it experienced during the strong ministries of Walpole and Pelham. George III was determined to make the cabinet the king's ministers once again rather than the instrument of Parliament. After 1760, therefore, he looked to the Tory John Stuart, Lord of Bute, and his partisans. In this form of strengthened monarchy the counterweight to Parliament which Montesquieu and Carroll admired would become a fact. Lord Bute lost no time in demonstrating the efficacy of George's reform when he concluded the peace in 1763 over the opposition of William Pitt and the Whigs, who objected to concessions required by France. The ministry as a cabinet under these conditions was able to administer the British Government. At the same time Parliament could now legislate with the helpful enlightenment of a more independent cabinet. Charles seemed to understand the validity of this arrangement and so no harsh words for George were found in his writings at a time when he castigated the French king and court. His leniency with George III was reflected in the case of George Sackville. Charles took note of the court material brought against him after the Battle of Minden, but made no commentary on the king's action which reinstated Sackville. One day, Charles would find Sackville in the office of Secretary of State for the Colonies at the height of the American Revolution.[22]

Charles thus reflected the Tory criticism of Parliament before it became popular in America. The process of representation was viciously corrupted, as had long been known. In 1764, he deplored the extravagance of parliamentary partisans at their dinners and upon other occasions. He saw what he considered a corrupt minority harassing the ministry. "I am of the opinion," he wrote in July of 1764 a few months before departing for America, "they will oust the present ministry. . . ." No sympathizer with the purported popular will, or any pretense by Parliament that it represented it, he admired an independent-minded ministry even though at the moment it was unpopular. "It required great abilities in the ministry, if unpopular," he believed, "to stand his ground long in such a country as this." The checks and balances of authority in England were indeed precarious. Factious parties' interests, he believed, were the causes. These were the cardinal sins to which republicanism in the classical tradition had been a sworn enemy. Montesquieu had admitted that republicanism was the ideal form, even though it seemed beyond the reach of the European nations of his day. Charles, however, felt that republicanism was attainable, and was inclined to recommend it for England. It was his belief and hope at this early date that the great experiment of America would emerge in both independence and republicanism.[23]

Always inclined to see these philosophical principles in the dramatic events of the present, Charles was drawn to the case of John Wilkes, Member of Parliament from Aylesbury. The cry of "Wilkes and Liberty" caught his ear as it came from London mobs. The loose-living editor of the *North Briton,* given to scurrility in his manner of treating public questions, was a far cry from the civility and virtue (patriotism) required of a public-spirited gentleman according to Charles. Wilkes' case, all the same, involved the principle of free speech in Parliament, and the security of a minority against Star Chamber proceedings. The case was not altogether unlike the expulsion of Eguilles as an author defending a minority from the *Parlement d'Aix-la-Chapelle.* Wilkes was clearly with Pitt and other Whig dissenters to the peace arrangement made by Bute. If he were given to his accustomed extravagance, which his enemies so effectively used against him, he would have called the Treaty of Paris treason because of the concessions it made to the enemy. It was, Wilkes wrote less scurrilously in the historic Article No. 45 of *North Briton,* "the most abandoned instance of ministerial effrontery." The ministry soon issued writs for his arrest and that of other authors, printers, and publishers who had collaborated in his charges.[24]

Was Wilkes shielded by Parliamentary privilege from indictment for seditious libel? Was the Wilkes dissent of No. 45 such a crime? These questions which arose in Charles' mind were familiar ones drawn from the American experience of Peter Zenger's successful defense of free speech in 1735. The weapon used by the ministry against Parliament was portentous of the breakdown of Montesquieu's idealization of England's check and balance of authority, as Pitt and many Whigs were quick to see. Charles took the whole issue on its own terms and against his own adaptation of Montesquieu's political structure. He had expressed sympathy for the position of the ministry and its independent authority. But now the counterpoise of Parliamentary authority and independence was threatened. Parliament itself was unaware of this fact as it gathered support for the expulsion of Wilkes. Charles advocated neither the judicial condemnation of Wilkes by the court nor his expulsion from the House of Commons. By January of 1764, Wilkes had been acquitted by a lower court. Charles could now see that Parliament and the crown were set upon nullifying judicial authority, thereby corroding the system of checks and balances in the English Constitution.[25]

Charles realistically predicted that Wilkes would be expelled from Parliament and therefore would not return from France, where he had fled. Charles was better able to support Wilkes at this time because he found others more admirable who were under a similar condemnation for advocating the principle of free speech. It was evident from all sides that the British system was breaking down; the ministry was dominating Parliament, and both were effectively counteracting the court. Understandably, the Wilkes issue would linger on as a lever of politics and as the object of philosophical reflections about English political institutions. Even at a time when there were rumors of a proposed Stamp Act on the colonies, Charles understandably gave greater expression to the Wilkes controversy than others.[26]

By 1764, the Wilkes affair only confirmed Charles's willingness to reject the constitutional monarchy of England, especially as the origin of authority exercised in Maryland. In 1763, greatly impressed with the growth of Maryland, his ambitions for America's future had a vital awakening in the context of his critical observations on the center of the Empire's authority. "In time," he said of his country on November 12, 1763, "it will and must be independent." As the year went on, the form of that independence was undeniable in the face of his critique of the French and English monarchies. He took his stand for republicanism as idealized by Montesquieu. It could be fulfilled in America. Charles shrewdly fixed his attention on the crucial issue which would be at the heart of the controversy leading to rebellion—Parliament's restrictions on America. He had acquired published records on the votes of the House of Commons and in March of 1764 was arranging to send these to his father. In May, he sent a copy of the *American Act,* which made provision for the stamp tax on Americans. He had earlier been alert to the rumors of the Stamp Act and further legislation. He realized the role which the London merchants played in urging such a tax with Grenville. Since the previous year, he had followed the representations which Virginia had been making against the new pattern of legislation in Parliament.[27]

Charles Carroll's hostile criticism of England's monarchy and his growing impulse toward independence also originated in his own counter-revolutionary society. In April, he sent his father *Consideration on the Penal Laws against Roman Catholics.* The same Parliament which rode into power in 1688 had in these latter days also taxed and restricted Catholic religious dissenters. Religious freedom was therefore involved in the general movement toward independence from Parliament.[28]

As Charles summed up all of these aspirations in July of 1764, he made plans with Captain Walker to board the *Randolph* for passage to the James River in Virginia. He must soon go to see what destiny awaited him in America and to discover in what way it "must become independent." He declared prophetically: "America is a growing country: in time it will and must be independent."[29]

Chapter 9

HIS PROVINCIAL SOCIETY

The *Randolph* departed from Gravesend with Charles aboard in early July, 1764. Captain Walker steered a swift course southwestward to Bermuda. Rather than continue that course as the first Maryland settlers had done more than a century before on the *Ark* and the *Dove*, the *Randolph* veered westward by northwest and proceeded without benefit of a strong wind and ocean current. Recalling the log of his father's rapid eastward passage to England in 1757, Charles was discouraged, for the *Randolph* had covered only 350 miles in thirty days west of Bermuda. It was late September when he arrived at Hampton, Virginia, on the north bank of the James River estuary. He was relieved to pass Cape Henry, east of which his Uncle Henry had lost his life more than forty years before. Charles' plan was to proceed up the Chesapeake Bay by a sloop departing from Norfolk on the south shore of the James. Because it was late in docking, he had to await loading of cargoes before he could finally set sail about Christmastime.[1]

Progress up the Bay had hardly begun when the pilot ran the vessel aground. He was later no more effective with the contrary winds which caused frequent stops on the Eastern Shore of Maryland. Charles showed his usual resourcefulness in relieving the tedium. Colonel Matthew Tilghman, a prominent official of the provincial government, was a good friend of the Carrolls, and Charles felt free to call at their splendid manor of Wye House. The Blakes, Cookes, and other families gave further welcome to the long-suffering seafarer, who by now had abandoned the sloop and was proceeding by land to the Western Shore. In January he finally arrived at Baltimore and may have visited Doughoregan Manor, which was some fifteen miles to the west. When in a few days he came to Annapolis, it was a joyful moment for father and son, who had not seen each other for twelve years. He caught the warmth of the family life at the town mansion, which was due so much to Mrs. Rachel Darnall and her sixteen-year-old daughter Molly. After some leisurely days of affectionate conversation and exchanges of news, the whole household was busy with preparations for the formal social receptions of the young gentleman. The promises of Benjamin Tasker and others of splendid balls and other pageantry were now to be fulfilled. At his father's insistence Charles was getting out his ruffled shirts and other finery, which was not entirely to his own taste. The grand entry into Maryland society had taken place by February 14, 1765.[2]

As a young man of twenty-eight, possessed of the highest credentials of the academe and gentility, Charles was not to be denied public regard as a man of high standing. Nor was his father reluctant to pass on the family's patrimony to its rightful heir; but it would do his son no honor if he fully retired, as though there were only room for one of the family in the firmament of the provincial society. There was a vulgar rumor that the father had turned over £40,000 to his son upon his arrival. Charles resented both the insinuations and the error in fact. An orderly arrangement had been made with him while he was still in England. It granted him a separate manor southwest of Frederick City, which he called Carrollton. By the fall, he was legally connected with it as the source of his own particular identification among the various Charles Carrolls found in Maryland. While he did not intend any long residence in it, he informed everyone that he should be known and addressed henceforth as Charles Carroll of Carrollton. Having no family of his own, however, and at his father's encouragement, he resided at the Annapolis mansion and spent the summers at Doughoregan. While Charles had scotched the rumor of a large sterling grant from his father, he made it clear that he was destined for the entire Carroll fortune as only son and beneficiary under the law of primogeniture. For the present, a collaboration was sincerely desired by both father and son. "We wish to continue, on the best of terms," Charles told his English friend Graves. "Never Father and Son were on better."[3]

As a young man in Paris, Charles had acquainted himself with his father's fortune. He had advised and acted for him both there and in London. The detailed elements of that wealth were mastered by him at the time of his courtship of Louisa Baker. Out of deference to his father he did not meddle in those matters at this time, but awaited the proper moment which his father would determine. He tended to his own manor and gradually came to apply to its day-to-day needs the agricultural theory which he had learned in England with only occasional practical experience on county estates. By September of 1765 he was already able to tell Graves how the Englishman could acquire tobacco actually grown on Carrollton Manor. He took occasion to instruct his friend on the operation of the international market, concluding on a promotional note. Very soon, he was arranging for enlargement of his herds of livestock, leases for his mill, and contracts for building grist and saw mills. He learned the advantage of exacting payments in Pennsylvania dollars. His father as of yet did not require much assistance from him at Doughoregan and his other manors, but Charles let him feel that he was available.[4]

As a lawyer, he was a special object of pride in the eyes of his father. Here, the scope of his activity swung widest and provided the grand supplement which the father had long desired, having been denied an opportunity for those studies himself. Although as a Catholic, Charles could not appear with a client in court, his advisory rôle was not restricted. He could arrange court pleadings by other lawyers in his cases. His father was not slow to seek his son's legal assistance. Others also asked his advice, Catholic relatives seemingly taking special advantage of his distinctive position in the profession. Daniel Carroll Sr., father of John and Daniel his cousins, found the advice of Charles valuable, as did the Digges family. He was sensitive to his father's position in all of this success. "I cannot flatter myself [that] my pains and troubles," he wrote to Daniel, "will be so amply rewarded as my father's have been." He did not expect nor wish that his father should go into eclipse with the transit of the young provincial luminary of Roman, French, and English civil law.[5]

Indeed, there was no danger that this would happen in view of the elder Carroll's transactions for the Baltimore Iron Works at this time. He was still very much master of the ledger, and in many cases director of the corporation. As heir of the Carroll fortune Charles viewed this complex but lucrative element with respect and his father's long career in the pioneering enterprise with admiration. Nothing in his European education had approximated apprenticeship. His father inspired Charles to rise to the accomplishments of the province's eminent entrepreneur.

Toward the end of 1765 Charles collected his impressions of Maryland and its society. In the lingering warmth of his receptions he was more than kindly in what he said. It was clear that he was regarded as one who not only belonged to that society, but also as one who warmly embraced it. The alteration in mind and spirit over the past years had indeed been substantial. Several years before, upon his arrival in London, he had had only the impressions of Maryland which he had received from his father after the family's bitter contest with the double-tax. Marylanders were, he then said with bitterness, "an uncultivated, insolent rabble." Indeed, they composed a "barbarous Country." With the end of the war in 1763, the proprietary party and the other non-Catholic friends of the Carroll family resumed their former benign relationships. Charles sensed all of this in his father's letters, and in what he could learn from knowledgeable parties in London during the two years prior to his return to America. There had been, for example, conversations with Daniel Dulany the Younger, the Bladens, and other proprietary partisans in London who had firsthand reports from the province.[6]

Acquaintance with English gentry life had also played a part in favorably altering his view of Maryland society. Not always with adequate evidence, Charles came to believe that the better sort of Maryland folk more approximately approached the gentry ideals in contrast to those in England. With the assumptions of the Physiocrats in favor of an agricultural society, he believed that he would find in the province the simplicity and sincerity which his reforming spirit had sought in vain in England. His hopes were now singularly high. Come to Maryland, he told Bradshaw, and experience the wholesome life of society in the New World. Leave behind the dissolute life of the British Isles, whose Parliament only reflected the general decline of England's civilization. Even the climate and soil are superior to England. A Maryland November has the mildness of an English August. "I have heard," he says, "many that have travelled through the colonies give the preference to Maryland both in point of climate and the fertility of its soil and the sociability of its inhabitants." He was intent upon proving his colony's virtues as he sent Graves some native venison together with an appropriate Maryland recipe. Blessings of a higher order in America were especially noted. "Even the arts and sciences commence to flourish in these [parts], as in arms, the day, I hope, will come when America will be superior to all the world. Without prejudice or partiality, I do not believe the universe can show a finer country. . . ."[7]

His favorable views always tended to carry with them a judgment against the decadent mother country. Charles Carroll the Barrister and his wife had gone to England, and their experiences agreed with his own. "I was not surprised that she prefers the domestic amusements of Maryland to ye vanities of St. James' [Court of St. James]," he wrote. "The society of a few choice friends is worth all ye pomp & emptiness of a court. . . . The dissipation, the ambition, & vanity of ye great are more mortal enemies to the unity, ye source [and] basis of friendship. . . ." His Maryland relatives and friends were a delight to Charles and he once censured an English family of his own name for dealing shamefully with one of their own. With the zest of Juvenal, he attacked George III and his court. Funds for a magnificent collection of classical antiquity were refused by the king. "The money if not applied to the purpose, will be lavished on something more insignificant, or on some parasite, or whore, or phi[la]nderer," he commented. "His Majesty no doubt as a connoiseur [*sic*] in these matters will recommend the purchase to Parliament—particularly if there should be buttons amongst the antiquities. For I have heard his majesty is a great adept at making buttons." Apparently there were no buttons in the collection.[8]

In contrast to England's standards, Charles asserted his own notion of simplicity in the household. He took possession of the Annapolis mansion very much in the spirit of his father, who said: "Be Content with what is neat Clean & necessary." The mansion was all of this because it possessed the spaciousness which lent itself to elegance without grandeur. The restraint of the classical style of Roman times prevailed. "What is decent & convenient, you ought to Have," he told Charles. "Pride & Vanity are not to be indulged. . . . There is no end to a desire for finery of any sort. . . ." Charles did not think that grandeur was proper, even in England. "The affluence of individuals will support a thousand follies," he told Graves. Indulgence in imaginary wants opens the door to corruption in public figures, decline of patriotism in the citizen, and wantonness in women. Desire of unworthy objects inspires indifference to good and bad means to attain affluence. It was not a question of the liberal expenditure of money, but the object of the expense. Maryland promised an environment which would allow Charles to buy the better things—like books and art works, and what was genuinely useful. There was even restraint here, however, as seen in his efforts at securing a landscape painting suitable for a large wall in the Annapolis mansion. He first sought a work six feet in length by the London artist Marlow but reconsidered in favor of an Annapolis artist who was less expensive. The destructive effect of extravagance he well understood. He told the Countess Auzoüer in France that trace of her Butler kinsmen had been lost with the dissipation or decline of their wealth. "They are extinct, or so miserably reduced by poverty as to be unknown: in a commercial nation, the glory of illustrious progeniture will not screen their need . . . from obscurity & want." These expressions of his gentry idealism may not always have been imitated by Marylanders, but his countrymen admired any success Charles might have in pursuit of them. The Carrolls and their kinsmen, therefore, were always anxious to see their young gentlemen inclined toward moderation.[9]

For some years now, Charles had nurtured thoughts about the woman who one day with him would build up a household according to this taste. The inclination to extravagance had appeared too likely in Louisa, as in other English women. A provincial woman, while simpler in taste, might at the same time be easily given to frivolity, which was equally unpromising. "What more dreadful," he said, "than to be linked for life to a dull companion whose whole conversation is confined to the colors and fashion of her dress, the empty chit-chat of the tea table, or the talking of hogs." He knew too well "that the community of women in general neglect to improve their understanding by reflection, and reading, by the conversation of gentlemen." A woman who did not neglect these things might be a rarity in England. At least in Maryland, one might hope to find a woman who gave "attention to such duties as fall to the share of mistress of a family."[10]

Fortunately for Charles, his wealth as well as his personal qualities were more than able together to win him warm acceptance by the Maryland gentry society. In his first few years, however, he had to acquire the symbols of assurance by membership in the social clubs; he considered the expenditures required for this quite proper. The way into the Jockey Club he knew well enough before he left England. In London, he had bought creditable mares to provide him exercise, and he had the knowledge of breed expected by a society enthusiastic about such a diversion. Through Charles Digges he went about acquiring the best bay stallions and mares in Maryland. He gave enthusiastic accounts of Maryland races to Daniel Carroll who was visiting in England. Not satisfied with native breeds, he contacted Lockhart Gordon, brother of the Duke of Avoyme, a well-known sportsman and good friend from London days, in order to acquire English mares of the highest quality. Charles negotiated for more than a year in order to get these prizes, for he had trouble distracting the sportsman Gordon with such business. He finally succeeded, thanks to the prodding of Gordon by Graves and Jennings. Charles was not entirely satisfied with what he got since the mares were not bay colored, nor was their pedigree properly certified. As a first effort, however, he was successful enough, and in 1768 he was given membership in the Jockey Club. There were other diversions and superfluities to which he gave moderate attention in much the same spirit. Stylish liquors like Hermitage appealed to guests; so too imported clarets and burgundies. They were not always what pleased the Carrolls who hoped that their own vineyards would soon produce wine of equal quality without the reputation and expense of the fashionable brands. Charles was a critic of English sartorial display, but his friend Bird could be trusted to buy him clothes of superior quality in England which were according to his simplicity of taste. In one instance, it was thought proper to have a master craftsman in England make a handsome carriage.[11]

For all of his initiation into the sportsman's life in Maryland, Charles was still very often with his books. The flow of volumes into the Carroll library continued, and his good friend Graves in London saw to acquisitions of the latest editions. It was not surprising at this time that his old friend Colonel Ludwell in England provided in his will that Charles have a choice of the books in his library. Charles still preferred to have his books bound in England, where craftsmanship was far superior. An array of titles filled his letters. Dryden and Addison, the models for the gentleman's prose, were requested; Swift's latest volumes arrived. In addition to literary and philosophical works, he now had an opportunity to enlarge his scientific reading, stimulated by the New World environment. He explored botanical life at the gentleman's level of curiosity. At Doughoregan and Carrollton manors, he could experiment with hybrids of flowers and grains. He was even lured into biological science by the wild life of the province, sending an English friend a flying squirrel on one occasion. He believed, however, that plant life in America was the chief kind of scientific interest from which England could profit. His new books reflected this interest.[12]

His father drew Charles to an interest in scientific farming as an intellectual amusement as well as a practical employment. One of the great founders of scientific agriculture, Arthur Young, was producing books at this time that summed up his observations in England and on the continent. Graves tried to supply the Carrolls with the latest of these volumes. Other authors and titles on these topics are noted in Charles' correspondence at this time. From Young, the Carrolls learned how to make a turnip slicer and successfully experimented with feeding hogs chopped potatoes. The more challenging venture of a vineyard was undertaken with great care. "The Vineyard when Compleated will be a great Ornament to the Plantation," his father explained, "& I am in hopes the *Utile* [useful] will accompany the *dulce* [pleasant]." Thus, at a time when Charles was reading about Bering's discoveries of the North Pacific and similar amusements for a gentleman's mind, he was also at home with scientific discovery and experimentation of his own.[13]

Even without the advanced theatres of Paris and London, he made a noble effort at maintaining his aesthetic sense. The poetry of the classics and the vernacular played their usual rôle. As compensation for his provincial environment at this time he turned to drawing and painting. He earnestly asked Graves to send him Webb's treatise and to acquire the Paris edition of a French author's work. He was undoubtedly in need of considerable study, he confessed to Esther Browne, as his faulty executions plainly showed. Association with Charles Willson Peale undoubtedly encouraged him to his efforts. Yet, the theatre was not entirely out of his reach. New editions of plays were acquired and read. The new theatre at Annapolis produced Kelly's *Word for the Wise,* done in the style of the comedies of manners which he had seen in London.[14]

While Charles was always equal to the life of Diogenes, alone with his books and paintings, kindred souls were gathered together at the Homony Club and soon welcomed him to their circle. The life of a scholar and savant was necessary for him not merely as a humanist, but as a Catholic since he was kept from the arena of public affairs, and he could find satisfaction in some measure in the salon. In this, he had a special call to the Homony Club, even though discussion of religion and politics was taboo. He found here a tolerant and broadly humanistic group which promised to expand his somewhat straitened spirit. Beside the artist Peale, sat the articulate Anglican churchman Jonathan Boucher. Commerce need not stifle a liberal mind, as the merchant Anthony Stewart could show. Samuel Chase's father had inveighed against Catholics from St. Paul's pulpit some ten years before, but the son had the benefit of a legal education and the broader view of the layman. The kinsman of Charles' friend of London days, Edmund Jennings, Thomas Jennings, was among the other lawyers as well as William Paca. Lloyd Dulany, an associate in the Baltimore Iron Works, was there. William Eddis, the literate proprietary official, attended under a non-political title. The simplicity of the club was hardly offensive to Charles, who found no odious resemblance to the salons of Paris, Bourges, and London, which he had frequented several years before.[15]

Thus it was that Charles more than his father was on his way to identification with the Protestant gentry. This was a part of the new political context which was replacing his father's associations during the difficult times of militant hostility toward Catholics. The proprietary alliance had held up moderately well, but Charles was in reality building beyond it. In the new setting, the counter-revolutionary society did not disappear, certainly not as a self-conscious group; but its motif was undergoing a modification, so that it did not appear as a collection of beleaguered and belligerent dissidents. The Catholic gentry society still held a sense of cleavage with Maryland life, and Charles was affected by this fact. His social acceptance in other areas, however, mollified his resentment at disfranchisement and exclusion from public office. He believed that these disabilities had some advantages. The compulsory private character of the Catholic made it easier for him to be "honorable, honest, [and] independent." "Socrates [,] the wisest & most virtuous of the Heathens," he noted, "declined all office of State from persuasion that man cou'd not long be great & virtuous." While these thoughts occurred to him shortly before his return to America, they cast his situation in Maryland in a more optimistic light than his father was likely to appreciate. His European experiences and the storehouse of a "virtuous education" gave him a rewarding life apart from civic involvement. "So little is my ambition," he explained, "[my] bent to retirement so strong that I am determined leaving all ambitious pursuits to confine myself to the retirement recom[d]. [recommended] of my paternal ancestors." The material and cultural wealth of the Carrolls through three generations provided both strength and honor to the position of the exclusion which was the price of loyalty to their faith. This explains the sense of contentment with himself and his environment found in his writings during his first years at home again in Maryland.[16]

Mollified though his alienation was, he could not ignore the literature of gentility which called the gentleman to his highest rôle as servant of the public good. This promised the fruition of all his learning which was most impressive in reference to public questions.

While at this time he did not know how that rôle would be played, or if it would fall to him at all, his readiness was beyond question. Unknown to himself, the door of the Homony Club would provide him entry upon this scene. Here, men of affairs would see his potential for civic enterprises and for helping solve public questions. While he might not discuss politics at the club's sessions, the way was opened to settings outside its doors. So with a certain frustration from his exclusion from politics, there also went a clear hope of influence on public affairs. In such enlightened club members as Chase and Paca, moreover, the narrow dogmas that excluded him from full enjoyment of a gentleman's place in civic affairs were under attack. Perhaps with them a new era was in the making; and, if so, it would indeed be revolutionary. It would not be revolutionary if collaboration with these men required that he break his natural ties with his own Catholic society. And so he went on, enriching his associations with Father John Carroll and his family, the Cookes, and the many other Catholic aristocrats.[17]

In Maryland, the Catholic gentry were tied closely to Jesuit priests very much as they were in England. A chaplain resided at Doughoregan Manor, and ministered to Catholics of the neighborhood; the Annapolis mansion and its chapel were regularly visited by him. Charles could not help but be impressed by his father's great concern to keep the sacramental life of their faith vital under difficult conditions. He was reminded to attend to specific obligations such as his Easter Communion. In these days when the Bourbon Monarchies were dispersing the Jesuit Order, the Carrolls expressed a deep concern for their many friends like the brother of the Marylander, Father Moylan, who had been arrested at Cadiz. From Europe, Charles heard that his devoted tutor Father Crookshanks had been arrested by order of the *Parlement de Paris,* but fortunately, he was set free in time. In the face of these European conditions, Maryland for all of its restriction left the ministers of his faith relatively free to serve their Catholic community.[18]

This reasonable contentment with Maryland society did not put to rest the reforming spirit of Charles, nor leave him a bland observer of the passing scene. In time, he gave stringent interpretation to his ideal of simplicity in the outward life of the gentleman. "I am resolved to live as becomes a gentleman," he told an English friend, "to avoid every appearance of meanness, of prodigality and ostentation. I assure you I would not accept my Father's estate upon condition of consuming the annual profits in gaudy equipages, empty palmed and show and in company more empty than these." Such vices were semblances of the England that he had left. Full of resentment at England's oppression of the colonies, he resolved that America must become independent. He saw now that the gentry must set an example of frugality and industry to the common people. He would have a waistcoat without lace for the most impressive social occasions, regardless of what his father might want. The days of conflict with England might one day call for an end to even these modest imports.[19]

Charles reasserted his conviction that the gentleman of pleasure was a plague to himself as well as to his society, particularly in these times of crisis. Gordon might be excused in an English environment, but not in America. Gentility acquired by birth, as he noted in the case of this English nobleman, without any growth in an understanding of its obligations, left the fop and the sportsman. He told Bradshaw of Mrs. Lee, whom both had known in England, and who had brought her bad morals with her to America. She found her own kind in a man named Anderson. Their affair brought a scandalous pregnancy and miscarriage. As for the rake, it is not necessarily a woman of her kind that attracts him. The very modesty of a Rachel Cooke might give rise to the rake's schemes for a conventional marriage. "The luster of that virtue shines brighter in their view which they most want, for [modesty] secures to them a fidelity which their conduct may not deserve." Characteristically, Charles calls upon ancient and modern history to verify his sociological analysis of the rake's true nature and behavior. He was armed against his pattern of immorality in the context of proprietary patronage. While events might fall short of making a cuckold and a mistress of a gentry couple, a few instances of compromise might destroy family honor and self-respect. It may be that Charles was a bit too suspicious of society. He related to Daniel Barrington some gossip about John Morton Gordon, the recent beneficiary of an appointment in the colony. The lord proprietor's fondness for the pretty wife of Gordon, it was said, accounted for his patronage. Gossip logically had it that Gordon would go to America and his wife remain in England, thus satisfying the sixth Lord Baltimore, who had nothing left of his reputation by this time. Gordon's wife, however, accompanied him to America. The incident does reveal the climate of social feeling at least as Charles was experiencing it during his first years after his return to America. Furthermore, he was at an age of anticipating the choice of a wife; his observations about matches then in the making among friends and acquaintances took account of the difficulties the Maryland gentry experienced. Convenience in marriage, with or without love as a principle, had its inevitable results in one case which he noted at this time.[20]

The maintenance of one's wealth put another strain on the Maryland gentleman's fiber. While the Carroll fortune had been originally launched with proprietary patronage, it continued and grew without it in the days of Charles and his father. The Carrolls had a respect for law and took care in establishing their titles to wealth; they put high store on honesty in financial transactions. Their sense of honor passed beyond written contracts to the spoken word of promise among gentlemen. Charles had an experience which brought out his feelings about this form of honesty. A poor tenant had promised to sell him some wild turkeys for his friend Bird. His landlord, however, prevented him from honoring his promise. "Imagine this landlord!" Charles exclaimed; "[with his lack] of politeness or ye obligation of a promise." One would think that he was "never out of the wilds of America. Yet, he was educated in England & is now a member of our lower house of Assembly & styles himself a gentleman: but there are such natures which no education can mend alter or reform." He made a similar reflection in the case of Gordon, through whom he had arranged a purchase of mares and in whom for a time he suspected dishonesty. He feared that Gordon may have reached the sad state in which one has no shame over a dishonest act. The cause was clear enough. "How dangerous is the love of pleasure in all men! particularly in those whose means are so scanty and whose desires so unbounded—poverty and a strong propensity to pleasure in ye same person are incompatible with honesty." While Gordon ultimately paid out the money for the mares, what Charles described was not uncommon.[21]

Certain crass if humorous delinquencies of Marylanders caught his eye. His clerk William Deards was to pay some money to a William Steward, but Deards reported that the gentleman's condition might make this impossible. Steward was last seen stretched out on the highway between Annapolis and South River Ferry. He was "near being run over by Ladies in a Chaize," Deards explained. "We have reason to suppose that his stomach was neither overcharged with Bonny Clabber nor Scotch Cale, but rather with some of Mr. Dick's Claret to which he had paid very great respect." There were more distinguished performances, if less reprehensible, as in the case of Daniel Dulany's "spirited" wrestling match with Mr. DeButte at the governor's White Hall Manor. The excitement of the contest so upset the governor's wife that it led to a miscarriage.[22]

The vices and foibles of Maryland gentry society, Charles understood, derived fundamentally from a lack of the discipline of work which the maintaining of a great fortune required. The "habit of business," which he called this virtue, required that a gentleman assign a specific time each day to keeping his accounts; directing and planning the daily details of his manor, mansion, and business affairs. A handsome fortune kept intact was witness to the existence of this virtue in the one who possessed it and handed it on to his descendants. One who worked daily in this spirit was a great benefactor to his own immediate family and the next generation. Honor of the family name among his fellow gentlemen arose from these results of the habit of business. In outward appearance, the hardworking gentleman was not unlike the Puritan who saw idleness as the devil's workshop; but while the motif was different in Charles, the effect of discipline and order was similar. He understandably resented those in Maryland who did not appreciate this virtue and who sought devious ways to reap the rewards Charles enjoyed. "There is a mean below dirty envy," he told Jennings, "which cre[e]ps thro' all ranks and cannot suffer a man a superiority of fortune[,] of merit[,] or of understanding in a fellow citizen. . . ." Dishonesty entered into the life of a gentleman who was not equal to the habit of business and sought questionable means to wealth. "The common sort and indeed the better (be it spoken between friends)," he believed, "have not that same opinion of strict justice and integrity and do not pay that regard to it in their dealings which I did wish for their honor and for their advantage."[23]

There were other veins of criticism drawn from his ethic of work and wealth. Expenditures which produced vulgarities and ultimately ended in folly offended his sense of business. Seduction increased with thoughtless spending. The extravagant Lloyd mansion at Annapolis provided a lesson. How people would laugh one day at a magnificent dwelling when it would be occupied by poorly educated children, bereft of the genteel life of their forebears! He told the Countess Auzoüer how one without a sense of business might fail in the scheme of primogeniture. "The glory of illustrious progeniture will not screen from obscurity and want," he explained in reference to one of his kinsmen. Michael Macnemara, who recently died in a debtors' jail, had begun his reckless career long ago. While the penalty fell on him only in his last days, his two sons would bear the stigma of his failure for a whole lifetime. One was now a surgeon's mate and the other an apprentice. Charles held little hope for them, believing they would come by their father's vices instead of the fortune he once possessed. "Passion led him on to vice [,] to want," he explained, "& from want to ignominy." The ring of Charles' own motivation is unmistakable, and it explains why he possessed the discipline of a man with the habit of business.[24]

The study and use of law in Charles' case were closely related to the habit of business. In addition to contributing to a life of virile activity, law had an elevating influence on his mind, which was drawn to reflection on principles even in the midst of practical details. As a part of the Catholic counter-revolutionary society, the quest for higher law as a foundation for his freedom was an ennobling exercise. It was closely connected with his reasoning about the grievances of the province against the mother country. He fully appreciated the inner support which legal training gave to the true gentleman. When Bradshaw spoke of quitting Inner Temple, Charles warned him that without the tasks of a lawyer to occupy him he would surely be unduly absorbed in the role of sportsman. The effect on his honor, family, and fortune could be tragic. With law, he said, "you will be enabled to leave a splendid fortune to your son. . . ."[25]

The moral fiber of Charles belonged to a Christian gentleman who did not put aside his reform mentality in viewing his Church and religious life generally. To the pious but simple, he may not have appeared promising. His generous and tolerant relationships with Protestants under English colonial circumstances in this era were no small accomplishment and testified to his creativity. The pleasantness of his spirit was reflected in his humorous observation to a Protestant friend in which he notes a social affair planned for November 5. "It happens to be the [anniversary of the] Gunpowder Plot—but no wonder that a bloody minded papist should choose for feasting and merriment a day which had like (if you believe the story) to have proved so fatal to a Protestant King and Parliament." Again he is found to be the Catholic intellectual as he continues to read the literature of the Enlightenment and to confront an uneasy age. While he kept his deep sympathy for the Jesuits as victims of Bourbon tyranny, he realistically appraised what later historians of the Order would admit to be an unwholesome involvement in politics. On one occasion, he made a harsh criticism of Father Ashton, who had served as chaplain at Doughoregan. Men of his stamp, he said, "are troublesome animals in a family. . . ." As religious men, they were called to gentility according to the pattern of DeSales and Croiset. Their failings were serious, especially to Charles whose tutors and friends in the Order both in France and England stood so high by the standards of Christian gentility. Charles' father gives some impression of his idealization of the priest in the person of the Abbé L'Isle Dieu. "I loved him the moment I saw him," he once wrote to his son, "his Virtue is so Conspicuous [,] his manner so engaging th[a]t a man must be insensible not to Esteem him on the lightest acquaintance. . . .[;] these are the sentiments of my Heart th[a]t I love & Esteem him. . . ."[26]

The Ashton relationship is understood only in the aristocratic structure of the Church in the province, which put great demands on both the clergy and the laity. Charles' father paid Ashton a stipend for his residence at Doughoregan, and this matter came into controversy at the time a change of chaplains was made in 1773. Ashton had been Anthony Carroll's agent with power of attorney, and this too could have given rise to the strained feelings, since the elder Carroll was a party to this business. The blame was not all on one side, as his father told Charles. "Mr. Ashton has fretted His Guts to Fiddle strings about Mr. Lucas's pranks," he confessed. "We have teased Him not a little, Have Compassion on Him." Proximity of residence undoubtedly gave rise to these situations, since not all of the ministering clergy lived apart on their own manors. There were other difficult roles for the layman Charles. He and his father often acquired Irish Catholic servants for the province, thus adding to the Catholic population in the environs of their own manors. As aristocratic laymen, they were expected to see that these persons were cared for spiritually as well as materially. Good example was required of Charles, but so too a defense of their religious and other rights in the public forum. The religious literature in the Carroll libraries would benefit them. Charity required that he help some servants to rise in the social scale, in order that their faith receive the support of gentility. All of this was added to the great obligation of care for slaves owned by Charles and his father. As an educated and articulate layman, his views would affect important ecclesiastical policy, in the tradition of the Maryland Catholic gentry. Charles' father, for example, had collaborated with other laymen and with the Maryland clergy in petitioning a vicar apostolic for the province. They pointed out the inadvisability of anyone with full episcopal power, in view of the prevailing hostility to provincial bishops among Maryland Protestants. The challenge to Christian gentility to which Charles was responding thus opened wide before him.[27]

Chapter 10

A LADY FOR HIS MANOR

Charles was still without a lady for his manor. At the age of twenty-eight, the thought distressed him and deprived him of the full sense of security which he desired. He socialized with young couples, made friends with young women, and was open to all of the impressions that this life made upon him. Maryland women as a group he viewed critically, and spoke his mind. Individually there were those who appealed to him against the background of his own idealizations. Ever present were the lingering thoughts of his extended courtship of Louisa Baker. His sentiments of those days were not entirely at rest, but soon would be as he deepened his friendships with Marylanders.[1]

In his own household at Doughoregan and Annapolis, was his cousin Mary (Molly) Darnall, sixteen years of age and as yet only a pleasant curiosity. His close acquaintance with her as she came to womanhood, however, contributed to his understanding about a future wife. Older women claimed his more serious attention, especially when they were of his faith. Even though they might be near relatives, this did not necessarily pose an obstacle to a lasting relationship ending in marriage. The family of his young friend William Cooke held his special interest because Charles found pleasant company with his sisters, Nancy and Rachel. Because they lived only twenty-three miles from the Carrolls, they were considered neighbors as well as kinsmen; frequent visits by Charles were possible.[2]

By the fall of 1765, marriage was much on the mind of Charles, reluctant though he was to admit it. "Indeed I am uncertain whether I shall ever marry," he cautiously confides to Graves, "unless I meet with a lady of good sense." He protested too much that he would not be overridden merely by a desire to have an heir and that any union will rest on true affection for his spouse. It is not accurate for him to say that "matrimony is at present but little the subject of my thoughts," for there is too much of such talk in his letters. Christopher Bird had married, and Charles was curious to know the results of the experiment. "Tell me," he asks, "now the honeymoon is over (do not read this to your wife) what are your real sentiments of that sweet slavery [?]" "Write to me of all my acquaintances," he asked Bird, "and be particular as to one for whose happiness is equally near my heart with my own." These were his thoughts for Louisa, a little more than a year after he had said good-bye to her in England. Yet the memory of disappointment in Louisa made him hesitant. He transparently exaggerated the happiness of his present condition:

"The love of retirement grows upon me—even melancholy pleases."
He was reconciled to some bitterness in any station of life. Jennings
was now destined to marry a beautiful woman, but Charles was
suspicious. He would like to know "how it is beauty and other good
qualities seldom meet in the same person." Where will he find a
woman concerned about improving her understanding, a companion
in conversation, and one above the trivialities that obsess so many
women whom he sees? As his observations became as precise as this
by the end of 1765, Charles revealed that he was very much in quest
of a lady for his manor.[3]

Early in the following year, he found that his affections were
persistently drawn to Rachel Cooke. She was twenty-three years of
age and he was now twenty-nine. As a distant cousin, of course,
she had learned how Charles had broken off his courtship of Louisa
Baker, but she had evidence enough that this was as much his doing
as hers. Rachel might well consider herself better known to Charles
than Louisa had been, isolated as Louisa had been in her Parisian
convent school. Her feminine pride was further satisfied that she had
no fortune like Louisa's and that it was entirely herself that drew him.
Such attention from Charles testified that she possessed his much
spoken criterion of true womanhood. Her response to his esteem was
fullhearted. The close friendship of the two families apart from their
kinship enriched the mutual sentiment of the couple.[4]

Charles did not conceal the enchantment that had come to him.
His English friends could not misread it as a reaction to disenchant-
ment with Louisa, the music of whose name, he had once said, was
greater than the "sweetest lines of Pope." Harmoniously, he now
adjusted the two enchantments. "Now I can pronounce [it]," he said
of Louisa's name, "as indifferent as Nancy, Betsy, or any other name."
He explained that his heart and mind were better prepared for such
music of Pope than had been the case with Louisa. Yes, upon consideration Louisa had not satisfied the philosopher but only the
romanticist in Charles the reformer. "A greater commendation I cannot make of the young lady," he assures Bird of Rachel, "than by
pronouncing her no way inferior to Louisa. . . ." He delights in the
sweetness of her temper and other amiable qualities. She is also
"handsome enough." "A modesty that would charm a Rake," he
candidly tells a friend, is what he sees in her to complete what he
finds so desirable. Indeed, Rachel has found a maturity in him which

Louisa never knew and perhaps which Charles had not possessed until this second courtship.[5]

In late spring, Charles and Rachel planned July 8 as their wedding day. In May, he told his Maryland friends of the forthcoming event with enthusiasm and satisfaction. Since their kinship was sufficiently close some dispensations were necessary; but there was no elaborate arrangement for jointure and dowry, Rachel's family being of very modest means. Just when things were progressing smoothly, a severe fever afflicted Charles in the middle of June and continued into July, thereby necessitating postponement of the wedding. A despondency came over him that was greater than the fever. The thought of his weak constitution had tortured him from time to time, but now it was nearly mastering him. "If I do not recover my health and strength," he told Graves, "I will drop all thoughts of entering into that state [of matrimony]." The harsh specter of death again hovered close at hand, even though Charles sought to envelop it with philosophical reflections. "I am not so much attached to this life," he wrote heroically to Christopher Bird in July, "but that I can part with it without any great regrets, or so far afraid of death as to shrink away with fear and trembling at its near approach. If I do not deceive myself I could meet it even with composure." Morose thoughts of a troubled and complex spirit, now weakened in body, they were spoken in a Christian tradition, blended with Renaissance robustness and Classical Stoicism.[6]

Charles, the man of reason and optimism, however, soon asserted this other side of himself in the dialogue of comfort which he held with his friends and himself. As the fever abated, he was ready to take up again his grand but difficult project. "I really join with you in the opinion that every State has its thorns," he wrote to Bird, "and that the matrimonial one [,] if entered into with prudence, has the fewest." With this revived hope, he made plans for a fall wedding. "I cannot agree with Swift," he now triumphantly tells Bradshaw, "that no wise man ever married from good sense." He asks his friends and agents in Europe to assist in properly provisioning his future bride's wardrobe. In peace, he commends all to the prayers of Father Chapman in England. With the wedding date now set for November 5, Charles merrily tells of his complete compliance with Rachel the bride. Womanhood must be humored by all—philosophers, bishops, popes, and husbands—he tells Frances Bird Browne. "The sooner we poor wretches comply, our compliance has a better grace." "Pray do not shew this part to your brother," he says in reference to Christopher Bird, "he will say [,'] ah poor Carroll I thought it would come to this.' " He left a token of his loving subservience in this letter when he requested further wardrobe items for Rachel.[7]

On October 14, Charles and Rachel obtained the marriage license and the dispensation of the Church required for marriages of cousins. With their family and friends, they began to talk about the forthcoming happy event and make plans. Looking back on his illness of July, Charles felt that he had been snatched from death. Within a few days, however, Rachel suddenly became ill and was confined to bed for several days. Postponement of the wedding again became a disheartening possibility. She was not too sick to receive the solicitous visits of Charles. Even though the appointed day for the wedding passed with Rachel in her sick bed, he was not demoralized. Suddenly in the midst of his confidence and composure, death took Rachel from him on November 25. The shocking blow left his mind in complete distraction; for he had not known, nor possibly had Rachel's physician, the mortal force of her illness. What Charles could say in the household of Doughoregan or Annapolis—to his father, Mrs. Darnall, Molly and the Cooke family, would not come easily. In a few days, he did reveal the deep anguish which shrouded his profound spirit. "I loved her most sincerely," he wrote in simplicity to Graves, "and had all the reason to believe I was as sincerely loved. Judge my loss, and by it of what I now feel." "From our mutual affection," he told Jennings a little later, "I had the strongest assurance of happiness in the married state." He reminisced about those qualities of Rachel which he had proudly announced a year before: "the sweetness of her temper, her virtue and good sense. . . ."[8]

In March of 1767, Charles spoke the thoughts that strengthened a spirit now afflicted by another agony. They were cast in the simple and humble frame of his Christian gentility. "It has pleased God," he said, "to teach me by this severe visitation that no happiness but what results from virtue is permanent and secure. Happy is that man who makes a right use of such trials. . . [;] he can draw some consolation from the affliction itself."[9]

Charles had sadly experienced the ending of a courtship in England; now again, after the courtship had culminated in a permanent pledge of mutual love it was sealed with the finality of death. An even more obscure path now lay ahead as he turned from the grave of Rachel. He put a lock of her hair in a miniature portrait of his espoused and placed the loving memento in his secretary drawer. Like Louisa, Rachel would continue an element of his future life, which in his nobility of mind he could accept without prejudice to a love that might be ahead. In his sense of proportion, he could also reflect that death had nearly snatched his own life in July 1766 and with it these living memories. In gratitude, he accepted the life that remained to him and would reach out for any future enlargement of it, even in the manner of those two courtships. Thus, life was to be had in affliction as well as delight, as he had so often reminded his friends; there was expectation and hope in both experiences. Lesser folk might view him a tragic character, but Charles understood the drama of life, as well as literature, so well that he could distinguish dissonant notes from a rich pathetic chord. In another sense from what he once attributed to him, Pope was right. The names of Rachel and Louisa would always be music, but only as he would modulate and harmonize them.[10]

The undulation of joy, anxiety, and sorrow which marked the deeply personal experience of Rachel Cooke was complemented by Charles' other involvements in a full life. It was during these very years that he formed many complex relationships with Maryland society. He implicated himself in its growing debate with the mother country in the wake of the Stamp Act of 1765. His tenacious desire to see how America might become independent continually asserted itself. It led to an accelerated reading on the issues and the stages of alienation as they developed. His conversations and letters brilliantly reflected the intense concern of his mind and heart for the good of his country as the crisis yearly mounted. The day-to-day affairs affecting his manor and future patrimony did not distract him from the political realm to which his wealth was closely tied. These disciplined activities of mind and spirit by a man with a habit of business and his religious and philosophical reflection which flowed so richly from these intense personal and social experiences provided a saving balm to his heart bereft of Rachel.

In March, 1767, Charles came out of mourning and appeared with propriety at the wedding of his friend Jack Brice, four months after the day that his own marriage was to have taken place. It was good to see old friends again. He took notice once more of young Maryland women, no doubt with the candid thought that he was about to begin another courtship, should the blessed opportunity come to him after a reasonable effort. In the course of the year he was pleasantly surprised to learn that his hopes came to rest in one of his own household, Molly Darnall. During his three years in Maryland he had seen her progress to attractive young womanhood.[11]

At first glance, it was clear that the vivacity of her childhood and adolescence had not left her as she came to marriageable age. The complexity of her family background and its connections with Charles' father would on the eve of it seem forbidding and productive of other results. Strangely enough, Molly Darnall wore her somber family inheritance with an attractive style and a spirit that was striking and compelling to Charles. It seemed unlikely that he would respond with the first inclinations toward love for one whose family was marked by disgrace. By this time, Charles was aware of all the details that were missing at the time of his meeting with Henry Darnall III, the attorney general, in London, who was then seeking the office of secretary for the province. He now knew that Darnall had been indicted for embezzlement while serving as a customs official in Maryland. Charles' father had provided bond for Darnall, who ultimately fled to Europe. His son and Molly's father, Henry, Jr., or the Fourth, even while separated from his wife, Rachel Brooke Darnall, continued to bring grief to the family by his extravagance. Eventually court action was taken to protect what landed wealth was left for the support of Molly and Rachel. Like his father, Henry Jr. too left the province ultimately ending up in Newfoundland.[12]

It was at this depth of degradation that the love between the two families took hold and uplifted the life of Molly and her mother. The disgrace was thus transformed and left a noble luster about the young daughter, which Charles discerned as she arrived at womanhood. Doughoregan Manor and the Annapolis mansion were given over as a home to the virtual widow and her child through the generosity of Charles' father. The act of sacrifice by the Carrolls was more than reciprocated. It was Rachel Brooke Darnall who had nursed and cared for Charles' mother Elizabeth Brooke Carroll through the anguish-filled months that preceded her death. His father was consoled by Rachel and Molly in the days that followed. In the years after 1761, it was to them that he owed the feminine warmth which Charles himself found at Annapolis and Doughoregan upon his return to Maryland.[13]

Charles' father undoubtedly took on the rôle of Molly's tutor for the seven years prior to the return of his son. He had succeeded and pronounced her possessed of a "great share of good sense, a solid judgment", and she was "strictly virtuous & perfectly good natured." Charles could see that she was satisfactory by his own standards of womanhood, for she was well read and equal to the conversation of gentlemen. She was already a suitable companion at eighteen years of age and promised to become even more acceptable. The social recovery of Rachel Darnall and Molly was undeniable. Maryland society being more tolerant of the two Henry Darnalls than Charles was inclined to be, it was possible for the very proprietary connections of Molly's grandfather to benefit Molly and those who befriended her. Former Governor Samuel Ogle's daughter, Mary Ogle Rideout, delighted in the friendship of Molly. Her husband, as secretary to Governor Sharpe, was regarded as an eminent adviser of the proprietary government. Caroline Calvert Eden, wife of the next governor, was also charmed by the vivacious Molly. Neither Charles nor his father could move more graciously among the political establishment of the colony. The talk which she provided him and his father was not the chitchat of the tea table so much deplored by Charles in Maryland women; she was very much in the world of interests followed by both men. It was becoming clear to Charles, commentator on gentility's true scheme of womanhood, that women are individuals and that in Molly's case he was being carried away by that individuality. Her character was equal both to adversity and a zest for life. Indeed, authors of the literature on gentility would say that she was "sensible." Very clearly, she was neither Louisa nor Rachel, but very much herself with an individuality which made possible her own particular claim on the affections of Charles.[14]

For her part, Molly found the same love of life in Charles, subdued though it was by his high urbanity and recent experience of sorrow. His two courtships only confirmed her admiration, which removed any obstacles to her growing, mature affection. As for her feminine pride, she had been too young to compete with Rachel Cooke. Her view of Louisa on this score was not greatly different from Rachel's, which had been sensible. Molly had the further satisfaction that Charles was more thoroughly acquainted with her than his earlier loves. His father made no paternal intercession in her favor, unless it was the original act of charity which brought Molly and her mother to Doughoregan. "He had not the most distant hint from me," his father told Graves, "th[a]t Miss Darnall would make a good wife."[15]

Introspective and sensitive by nature, Charles needed greater assurance than most men that he was deeply fixed in the affections of the woman he loved. He had doubted that this was the case with Louisa. In contrast to his remarks about Louisa's love for him, there is not the least doubt found in what he says of Molly that would suggest a lack of confidence in her love for him. How else is it possible to explain what he told his greatest confidant, William Graves: "I prefer her to all the women I have even seen, even to Louisa"? Such love was shown quite simply by a clear but undemonstrative esteem for her as "blessed with every good quality." She must have heard unmistakably from him in many wonderful ways what he said so directly to Graves: "The young lady already has my heart. . . ." She herself was the only dowry and he was glad that there was no money complicating his motivation to the marriage. If his English friends were skeptical, Rachel Cooke's brother, William, who would soon be in London would assure them of his genuine love for Molly. While Charles said that he was like Caesar determined to cross the Rubicon into his new life, the delay with legal details of the marriage contract only revealed his strong desire for the marriage and the ardor of his love for Molly. "Particularly in love," he told Jennings, "a passion wh[ich]. must less suffer suspense, will hardly admit of delay. . . ."[16]

Characteristically, Charles must couple this disinterested love with the demands of honor for his family and of legal requirements by Church and state. He was obliged to see to the security of the patrimony which he would hand down to his heir or if he had none to see that it would remain in the Carroll family to whomever he named to receive his wealth. This was especially necessary at this time, since his father had established the details by which his fortune in real and personal property would be consigned to him. In this situation, Molly gave assurance that she could make no legal claim upon the Carroll fortune, particularly its landed wealth, in the event the demise of Charles preceded her own. Molly and her mother were agreeable to this and arranged to make a petition to the Maryland Assembly disclaiming any share of the Carroll inheritance. Because there was no Darnall estate of importance, Molly had no legal foundation for jointure. In lieu of this, the Carrolls agreed to assure her £300 annual income in the event of her widowhood, without specifying any real property from which it might derive.[17]

There was one obstacle to the conclusion of this arrangement. Molly was not yet of the legal age necessary for signing such a disclaimer. An additional action by the Maryland Assembly was necessary, in order to enable her to give force to such a document. What would have otherwise been a simple procedure was complicated by the hostility of Daniel Dulany, who obstructed passage of the bill. The year 1767 passed without any successful action.

Not trusting the assembly, Charles now hoped for protection in a special interpretation of English law, which, according to some, provided that real property could not be alienated from a family under any circumstances. Charles delved into Blackstone and hired a lawyer to verify this contention. He sought out a book on consanguinity and other topics related to the increasingly complicated marriage problem. He uncovered the legal risk that Carroll money loaned out at interest might conceivably be claimed by Molly and her family as a result of the marriage. The scholar Charles from some unlikely intellectual interest was soon able to compose a modest treatise on inheritance in English common law which traced the modifications developing in colonial legal rulings. Yet in the end, it seemed precarious to proceed without a special assembly act. By spring of 1768, the assembly had finally passed the act enabling Molly to make the disclaimer. Charles had to endure some crude, if humorous, lines in the *Maryland Gazette*, which adverted to the oddity of a gentleman requiring an enabling act on the eve of his nuptials. A few complications in the Church dispensations required additional attention. Bustle with lesser matters continued to the eve of the blessed day. The Brownes in England had finally provided the new suit which Charles sought for the occasion, "well made[,] genteel[,] but without any lace about it. . . ." On June 5, 1768, Charles Carroll of Carrollton married Molly Darnall in their Annapolis mansion.[18]

The young heir to the Carroll fortune and traditions settled down to married life in his ancestral abode which held the aura of great family episodes of the past. Charles' father and Molly's mother were often there, although they generally resided at Doughoregan, where the young couple spent their summer months. The son would now have full scope for developing his sense of business and responsibility;

and his father assured him that the collaboration would go along with Charles' enjoying £1000 sterling income a year in addition to his benefits from Carrollton Manor. Full title to the Annapolis mansion and its grounds were his. If anything further was needed beyond these sources of payments, his father would provide it ungrudgingly. The whole of Doughoregan Manor, it was agreed, should come to him as well as lesser ones. The many loans, their interest, and other personal property would soon pass under his jurisdiction. Charles was thus given the highest sense of dignity and security. "I think he should live so as to make a decent provision for younger children," his father said superfluously to Graves, "& to leave ye Estate to his eldest son Entier & in as good a Plight as I shall leave it to him. For although I see a large & independent Fortune will not make ye Possessor of it . . . independent, yet it must make him inexcusable if he be not so." No Maryland patriarch had greater reason for confidence in his heir. The father's thoughts were surely the son's. Indeed, Graves hastened to warn Charles against hoarding, as he pursued his refined notions of simplicity in his life of gentility. But neither Graves nor Charles' father, who had handed on the material substance of that life, would prevent him from elaborating the family patrimony according to his own distinctive spirit.[19]

The "puny constitution" of Charles always required attention. The distresses, joys, social exertions of the past few years, and his increased burden of work accounted for his illness of December, 1768. His father, the seasoned tutor, was at hand with a useful remedy at this stage of his son's development as a gentleman of great responsibility. Do one thing at a time, Charles was told, and work at it as though there were nothing else to do. Charles was always inclined to accept this kind of advice from such a hardy soul as the venerable patriarch. On one occasion, he heard that his father was ill, only to receive a letter a month later telling him that he was now recovered and equal to a walk of two miles. Although he was a man nearing the end of his days, his father inflicted no morose thoughts on his devoted son. "I shall see it," he said of death, "without sermon & with Resignation." Charles had imbibed this hardy Christian attitude which was no small aid in his own critical illness of a few years before. He quietly continued the practices learned in his years of study in France which were calculated to fortify the successful gentleman's health of mind and body. He rode horseback regularly. The lure of travel for him was not what it was to one who had not lived in France and England, but the curiosity of Charles about his own country, of which he was so proud, led him to visit other parts of the province.[20]

The year following their marriage Charles was overjoyed when he learned that Molly was to bear him a child. He hoped that it would be a boy, which would thus assure him that he now had an heir. Instead, a girl was born, and named Elizabeth after Charles' mother. In poor health, the child lingered on for six months, and before the year was over, in 1769 she died. Molly's anxiety and ensuing sorrow drew the loving concern of Charles. When spring arrived in 1770, he took her and her mother for a restful visit to the Eastern Shore, where they had many friends.[21]

In late summer, Molly was expecting another child. She gave no indication as she would later that that she was afflicted with "female complaint,"—that common lot of eighteenth-century women, the trial of having too many children over too brief a period of time. Charles and Molly, regardless of her condition and her father-in-law's criticisms, intended to enjoy the social season at Annapolis. Charles expected the child's delivery would take place before the racing season began. In the last week of August, however, Molly was off to the theatre while Charles was at Doughoregan. Her only embarrassment was at being overcome by the heat of the theatre, or so Charles' father diagnosed the case as part of his admonitions to the couple. On September 4 word was sent to Charles that Molly had again given birth to a baby daughter. The child was called Mary after the mother, and she soon had "Polly" as a name of endearment. Unlike the mother, Charles seemed to be something less than the adoring parent. His father wrote asking Molly to kiss little Polly for him, since Charles ignored such silly requests. The "little levities" of the baby annoyed Charles, but in time, he became more at ease as better conduct appeared.[22]

A year passed in the roles of dutiful parents to their first surviving child. Ever thoughtful of Molly's natural gaiety as well as her own "puny constitution," Charles planned in August of 1771 to visit Philadelphia and New York. They would first enjoy the racing season with all of its social adjuncts and invited their parents to join them. The contemplated departure for the north in October, however, did not materialize. Molly's exhausting social activity, according to her father-in-law, left her in poor health. Toward the end of

November, she began to feel better. Charles and Molly, together with her good friend Mary Ogle Rideout and her husband proceeded to Philadelphia, where they enjoyed the warm hospitality of their mutual friends. By December, they were in New York for more of the same social life, which probably was not as strenuous as the racing season at Annapolis. Charles had conversation pieces for his letter to Charles Carroll the Barrister, and Molly agreed with Charles' acceptance of Horace on the benefits of travel. But Charles, the disciple of Montesquieu, Doumat, and Hume, as well as Horace fed his mind on observations of provincial life in these parts. He reflected on the future of the region's two great cities. The many pamphlets and studies he had recently read on British colonial government were put in broader perspective. What he learned was now more important than his observations of the European scene some ten years before.[23]

In March of 1772, Charles revealed in a letter to Graves how his domestic life had its own burdens together with these pleasanter aspects. In reference to news of a mutual friend's approaching marriage, he took occasion to reflect on his own distress at not having a male heir to his family fortune. It would be a tragedy, he confessed, if it did not pass to a descendant of his own body. He reverted to a vein of reflection long familiar to friends like Graves. He was of puny constitution, and could not count on a long life like his father. His "grand climacteristic" might pass and with it, hope for an heir. But hope again returned when in the spring Molly was again preparing to give birth to a child. Alas, another daughter was born. "I am now the father not of many children, but of two girls," he says, jocosely veiling his disappointment. He makes a cynical reference to the Latin legal dictum, *pater est quem nuptiae demonstrant*, or, the wives establish who the father is. It was neither in sardonic humor, however, nor lightheartedness, that the couple named the child Louisa Rachel, two names identified with the father's romantic past. Certainly the gesture was one of assurance to Molly that there was nothing of suspicion or jealousy between the parents. It was not so unnatural for Charles had a courtly regard for womanhood and esteem for two persons who were part of his life's story.[24]

But these thoughts were short-lived; for in the early fall Louisa Rachel died, following the first child Elizabeth to the grave. The blow left Molly very depressed and Charles once more anxious. Would that they were free from all of the complexities of mind in patrician child-bearing and more like a simple yeoman farm couple! As gentry of the better sort, Charles and Molly had to carry on with this somber shadow frequently passing through a house without an heir. It would not be until 1774 that Charles would again express his hopes to Graves. His hopes were finally realized with the birth of Charles Carroll IV, to be known as Charles Carroll of Homewood, or Charles Jr.[25]

At the very time that Molly was grieving the loss of her child, another shock came to her—the last episode in the renegade career of her father took place. While reading a Newfoundland newspaper, Charles found an account of Henry Darnall's execution as a common criminal. Although he wished to keep the news of this from his wife, he had to write a letter to his father at Doughoregan, where Molly was visiting at this time, in order to reveal the contents of this news. "Without reflection I gave yr letter to me to Molly," his father wrote September 6 of his imprudence. "I am sorry for it Has the Acc[oun]t. of Her Fathers being Executed [. It has] made Her low spirited." While she was perhaps always prepared for the worst in regard to her father, the humiliation was great indeed, reviving recollections of earlier disgraces. The strong love between her and Charles had reckoned with such an eventuality, and again overcame one more trial in their life together. All of this is reflected in her solicitous expressions of distress at an illness Charles experienced at this very time. For a woman to be "sensible" in the midst of these trials of 1772 was indeed uncommon; and Molly won increased devotion from Charles for the spirit in which she bore them.[26]

Even during these times, she maintained her natural zest for the social life of Annapolis and played the very proper companion of Charles. While it was a congenial outlet for both, it was not without demands on their prudence. Charles' father was not always generous in understanding the young couple. "I hope y[ou]r debauch at the Govr. [Governor's Mansion]," he wrote in March, 1772, "has not Hurt you. . . ." His source of information on the party was Father Ashton, "not the most exact intelligencer." The "debauch" was an altercation between Dr. Steuart and Major Jennifer on a political topic. "I hope to hear . . . th[a]t Molly has got rid of Her Cold," he wrote after the sad events of the fall had passed and given way to the social life of the moment, "& recover'd from the fatigue of her Company & Rakeing." The censor did not even spare Molly's mother.

"I think she did not like to leave Mrs. Scots Rout," he wrote to Charles somewhat later. "This as entre nous." Even allowing for the milder eighteenth-century connotations of these uncomplimentary words—debauch, rakeing, rout—the old patriarch showed an aversion for euphemism in suggesting the conduct of these social affairs. The exuberant Molly and her more dignified Charles, he knew all the same, could come under no serious charge, even in difficult settings. There is evidence, for example, that the governor made improper advances toward Molly at a social affair in the early spring of 1773. She responded indignantly to his foolishness, from which he took offense. For a time thereafter Charles reciprocated the aloofness which the governor showed the couple. "Congratulate her on it," Charles' father said of Molly's conduct, "for I do not know th[a]t His smiles or intimacy have redounded to ye Credit of any Ladies on whom He has been pleased to bestow them." The continued presence of the two at state affairs indicates the high standing of their style of gentility.[27]

A special finesse was needed, indeed, to preserve the best results of their "virtuous education." It was urbane self-respect, rather than arrogance, that brought about the needed poise to Charles' display of honor; this in turn increased public acceptance and respect for his kinsmen. He had not been involved in any noisy Catholic issue like the double-tax controversy of his father, which important men had not yet forgotten. His honor was now great enough to secure respect for his wife, even though her father had only recently been executed as an outcast of the gentry society. The mark of familial piety must have borne such an authenticity in Charles that it would not be challenged with impunity. With his manor composed and his place in society established, Charles manfully maintained a good name as well as a good fortune for himself, his wife, and close members of his family.[28]

CHAPTER 11

HIS STYLE OF GENTLEMAN

Charles Carroll of Carrollton's style of gentility won him an eminent place in Maryland's gentry society. His many talents, education, and handsome family patrimony led to a creation of this style. In his own complicated mind, however, he was increasingly aware that in this province far more than in England one did not simply arrive at a gentleman's station and rest secure for his remaining days. The Bakers had probably viewed Charles as a planter gentleman much like the sort they had known in the Caribbean sugar islands; but he was something far more than this. The full life of business which he transacted in Annapolis demonstrated that the overseeing of a single crop like tobacco, while an impressive employment, was only a small portion of his constant concern. Not one plantation, but several came within his domain; not a single crop, but a variety of grains, livestock, orchards, gristing and cider mills, small factories for weaving cloth, and an array of crafts to keep the manors in good repair. All preyed upon the time of Charles Carroll and urged him to develop a style of life equal to fulfilling his place in society.

If these activities evoked the temper of an anxious proprietor and vigilant manager, there was yet more to be encountered. The marketing of Carroll products led Charles into the domestic and European trade. He became an entrepreneur and by his success increasingly involved himself in a highly developed provincial and imperial economy. Large profit could not be hoarded in a bank during this pre-industrial era. He ventured into the precarious world of land speculation. With more daring than most provincials, the Carrolls had passed even beyond this to putting out of loans to persons in the highest social and political positions in the colony. His father had also bequeathed him a role in a pioneering business enterprise, the Baltimore Iron Works. This brought further annual profits, which restlessly sought outlets in loans at favorable interest returns. The tempo of this life left by comparison the English gentleman and the seventeenth-century Virginia planter type innocent occupants of sinecures.

Charles was confronted with a magnificent challenge to his genius, but also with a most vexing assault on his studious disposition. Pervading this vast realm of his economic patrimony were the complicating political and social realities which extended from the Potomac to the Thames. Much like a medieval baron, he knew that the clashes in the larger princedoms sent reverberations into his own principality. He would constantly seek to control their effect in collaboration with his fellow provincial gentlemen. Here, his professional training as a lawyer and scholar provided him the means to deal with issues larger than land titles and debt collections. He bore, in addition, the unique task of fending off hostilities which might fall on his own Catholic counter-revolutionary society. Indeed, Charles wore a gentleman's mantle with many fabrics of honor and responsibility: planter, entrepreneur, statesman, and Catholic aristocrat. While he had for some years prepared in mind and heart for the rôle, the enactment now became a trial as well as a triumph for his great and sensitive spirit. Within a few years, he moved beyond his father's tutelage and by 1773 came to full stature, fashioned in his own distinctive style.

Although Charles resided at Annapolis after his marriage, his father continually wrote to him about details of Doughoregan and the other estates. The acquisition and use of both Negro slaves and white servants required constant attention. A white gardener and a Negro boy were sent from Doughoregan for service at the Annapolis mansion and its grounds; Charles saw to their training. The youngster was protected from bad companions and brought under the discipline of regular work. After a year, he was able to handle the tools and succeed with the demands of a gentleman's garden. The white servant was paid £3 a month, for which was exacted six days of work a week. In another instance, Charles consulted with his father about the construction of stone pillars with suitable capitals and sought out a craftsman capable of doing this kind of work, which was under way in 1770. The cider mill was enlarged shortly after this; so was the cloth factory, so that the plantation would not have to depend upon these goods coming from England. Special craftsmen such as carpenters and shoemakers were always needed in addition to the usual ones. The vineyards created further need along this line. The role of Charles as lord of the manor was seen in this context in 1773, when he was at Doughoregan directing all workers of whatever category in the common chore of the fall grape harvest.[1]

The relationship to his father during the first five years after Charles' return from Europe could not accurately be described as an apprenticeship. It was loftier and subtler than that. In the case of the large number of slaves in the Carroll patrimony, however, Charles was on very unfamiliar ground and had much more to learn. In 1773, his father listed 330 slaves, an increase of 57 during the preceding eight years. From his boyhood, he remembered the institution of slavery and accepted it. His studies abroad, concerned as they often were with human rights, left this slavery realm of social reform unexplored, at least as far as his writings indicate. On the other hand, there were no remarks in support or in rationalization of the institution; in keeping with his personality, he would have recorded them if they had had any hold on his mind. His expressed opposition on philosophical grounds later in his life also confirms this estimate. He therefore underwent induction into this perplexing world at the hands of his father and without any of the sureness seen in his approach to his other employments.[2]

He learned that the slave was a financial investment, whose security rested fundamentally on the safeguard of his health. The elder Carroll was intent upon averting any cases of smallpox and administered inoculations to more than 110 Negro children in 1770, a benefit Charles himself had not experienced when he was in London. He was asked to take care of this in the case of two children at Annapolis. Security and success rested upon discipline as well as health. He had to face the harsh aspect of his father, who believed in physical punishment as a means to discipline. Some of the slaves had stolen from a neighbor; his father tells him that he will seek them out and thoroughly whip them. He will be stern with others who had lost some items through carelessness. Charles reported the delinquency of a slave named Timothy, who had been working on some of his buildings. The slave penitently knelt before the elder Carroll and begged forgiveness. "Without punishment," he told his son in the case of another delinquent, "there is no keeping Servants of any Sort. His Chastisement may deter my other Servants from following His Example." The man in question was put in stocks.[3]

All of this was in an atmosphere of paternalism, where the slave never attained adulthood in the relationship. Yet it had its kindlier features. Charles' father, for example, was anxious to see that the young boy Giles spent some time with his mother, who worked at the Annapolis mansion. Charles was at the side of his Negro servant, Grace, in her last hours and wrote of her illness and death to his father. "Poor old creature," he said with sentiment, "I hope she is happy. . . ." The Church had put stern injunctions on the Catholic layman to see to the spiritual welfare of the slaves. Some Christian denominations had at one time withheld baptism from slaves on the assumption that the sacrament required their emancipation. Spanish theologians argued against any form of enslavement on the grounds of both Christian teaching and natural law. Neither of these traditions entered into Maryland Catholic culture as reflected in the writing of the Carrolls. The major burden of obligation on them was for the instruction and spiritual safeguard of the slaves and their family life. This was the message they most frequently had preached to them. On one occasion, however, Charles expressed concern that his father was not giving adequate care to his slaves. Sickness had been reported and criticism came to Charles. House Negroes, he had heard, lived far better than the others. "I can safely say," his father immediately reported, "no man in Maryland Can Shew in proportion to our number, such likely well looking slaves."[4]

The white indentured and free servants were both better off than the Negro slaves, even though they too were under a servile discipline. Unlike the Negro, they were not regarded as children or by implication congenitally inferior. Imperial and colonial laws protected them during the period of indentured servitude, which was about five years, and prescribed the details of passage to freedom. Of these, some stayed on and worked for wages. Yet both groups felt the rod of discipline. Charles was told by his father that he should deduct one worker's pay because of his absence from the premises. In another place, he is reminded of the natural rights of such servants, and at times outright charity was required of him, particularly in the case of the less fortunate. "Is it not a duty," his father explained, "to give such a man what Pleasure and Comfort we can." Some generosity is also seen in the three quarts of cider provided servants each day. It did not always satisfy some: two men were disciplined for neglecting a chore at Doughoregan after becoming thoroughly inebriated at Baltimore.[5]

The supply of servants was not easily maintained. Occasionally, a convict had to be transported from Europe. Skilled farmers and gardeners were sought out in England. The elder Carroll did not overlook his father's native land and arranged for transportation of whole families through agents in Cork. A special duty was levied in many cases where legislation existed for the exclusion of Irish Catholic immigrants. Some of these, as well as native servants, rose in the social scale after their period of service. Men like Riggs and Ireland proved able overseers and in time came to enlarge their own landholdings to a point where they were considered meaner or middling sort of gentlemen. There were instances where their children went abroad to school. Free servants by their acquired skill and knowledge transacted difficult and important matters for the masters of the manor. The seemingly trivial matter of recovering a pair of stolen horses from a Carroll manor involved two provincial governors as well as a Carroll servant as negotiator.[6]

Charles carried considerably more experience into the merchant-planter role than in that of master of servants and slaves. While in England, he had aided his father in the marketing of tobacco and other produce; now, as his father kept him informed of crop developments, he gave full scope to this at Annapolis. He also supervised foreign imports of wool, cotton, Madeira wine, claret, and a host of other products. Records show varied produce—corn, flour, potatoes; and the Carrolls served as agents for neighboring planters in marketing goods. The progress of grain deposits had to be watched from point to point in America and abroad. Father and son shrewdly estimated how long deposits of produce should be held off until a rise in prices took place. In some cases, they made advanced contracts with merchants for grain and other goods which they would receive from third parties in the demanding role of middleman. Complicated bookkeeping was inevitable; more and more of it was left to Charles, who had studied the Venetian method in London. The accounts of London agents were also in his hands and consultation about them with his father was often necessary.[7]

The sportsman's concern for acquiring fine mares, it is true, would go on, but without the great attention Charles had given to this the first few years of his residence at Annapolis. The sophisticated demand of his growing responsibilities is seen in what is required to market tobacco properly. His father tells him that he should not merely depend on local warehouses and their quotations of prices. This may be proper for a small seller, but his shippers should come to him. It is therefore essential that he follow and even anticipate the prices, bringing pressure to bear for higher quotations. In time, Charles collaborated with other merchant-planters to protect Maryland against the factors and other middlemen in England. It was decided that they would locate the Marylander Joshua Johnson and others in England who would serve as more reliable factors in the service of the Carrolls and other Maryland planters. An association of planters in a tobacco inspection system was tied in with this device. Charles Carroll thus became not merely a planter but a merchant gentleman of considerable stature.[8]

His father as a young man had venturesomely entered upon a career of land and manufacturing investment; and had soon become involved in outright speculation. Loans, of course, as a result of the profits that he made, continued to go out to relatives, the Catholic gentry, and prominent persons such as Ridgely and Dorsey. Charles now took up the role of entrepreneur with great vigor. The records of the Baltimore Iron Works show that he was deeply involved in the expansion taking place at this time. By 1770 pig iron production reaches seventy tons per month, and forge casting, two and a half tons per month. Playing an even more prominent part in the subsequent growth, Charles dealt directly with new iron factors in Scotland, strove to master the fluctuating price patterns of that foreign market. In 1772, he embarked upon a land venture which envisaged the acquisition of several thousand acres in the Ohio country with thirty other gentlemen. The younger Carroll was under scrutiny in these endeavors. His father found fault with his business sense where the acquisition of horses was concerned. Payment of $200 for a pair of horses, especially in Virginia currency, seemed foolish; but the father, it should be remembered, did not have his son's enthusiasm for horses, whether used for breeding or racing. Charles was praised, on the other hand, for his sound recommendations regarding the Carroll estates. Such thorny questions as land titles and rents were clearly better off in his hands. His father asked him to investigate one case which went back to the year 1660 in the rent rolls of the land office.[9]

The reputation of his father as a tightfisted financier was not a welcome legacy to the son. Yet not all of the evidence is favorable to this stereotype. "Poor Dilling," the elder Carroll tells his son in recommending indulgence on one occasion, "had got ye money ready last fall to pay me but broke his leg by a fall from his horse. He spent all ye money on doctors who at last cut off his leg. He proposes this fall to mortgage his land to me as a better security." Perhaps this is not a great show of mercy; but he could have exacted payment by force of the debtors' jail, or confiscation, which was not an unusual recourse in those days among creditors. Sharpness and shrewdness were necessary for survival in those who lived on the Carroll plane of business life, as Charles soon understood. In 1773, he quickly detected that a tobacco factor had confused the purchase records. He showed other signs of being wary in this same case. "The universal bad character of the man," Charles discovered, "is against him—but this entre nous."[10]

It became clear in time that he was not necessarily burdened with the legacy of his father's reputation when he came to have his own style of business. The father felt that his son was merely aiding a crony, when Charles retained a man named Deards as his clerk and assistant. He disregarded his father's view and, as time would tell, Deards proved an invaluable aid for many years to come. Charles crossed swords with his father on a very delicate point in 1769, when his father wanted him to resurvey certain land in the hope of enlarging the original holdings. He felt that there was no title to the parcel upon which the logic of the claim would have to rest. Perhaps, Charles was more sensitive than his father on such matters. By 1773, there were other clashes of opinion, the father finding negligence in his son's conduct of business. It became increasingly clear, however, that Charles was arriving at full stature as master of the Carroll fortunes. His father now graciously welcomed the day, and assumed a subordinate role. "If you have been Hitherto satisfied with my behaviour," the elder Carroll says with humility and affection, "I think I shall not alter it, but allways remaining y[ou]r well wisher. . . ." "He keeps my books," he told Graves, "& takes what money He pleases. . . . When I want money [,] I call on my son to supply me." "I am retired to a very Pleasant Healthy Seat in the Country," he wrote with a certain finality.[11]

Charles did not inherit his father's peculiar abrasiveness, as some were not above telling the elder Carroll. His suavity and reasonableness, however, carried a quiet forcefulness beneath the surface, appearing when the occasion required it. The genteel and benign lord of the manor at times played the exacting master of slaves and servants. "I wish you would order him a good whipping," he told his father regarding one slave; "there is nothing I detest more than bad head: it is a shame to spoil good wheat by mere negligence." The taste of rye was in the flour because the slave did not clean the grinding stones after processing the rye. "Two of them have been whipped," he tells his father regarding some recalcitrants, "& Will

shall have a severe whipping tomorrow—they are now quite quelled."
He became a taskmaster of those who were responsible for poorly
made shoes. On another occasion, he took up a legal fight in order
to acquire slaves to whom he claimed title by a long-standing mortgage. The other side of Charles as a disciple of the Enlightenment,
however, asserted itself on occasion. His father was intent upon
removing one slave guilty of adultery. "The crime of adultery is
certainly great," he instructed his father, but "the removal of Henry
will not prevent it."[12]

Charles sensed the growing power which his skill in law gave him.
His father thought that bluster might bring some debtors to payment.
The son knew better and was not afraid to take the more demanding
remedy in the courts. "Without bringing suit," he explained, "you
need not flatter yourself with being paid." He chided his father's less
vigorous style in other ways. The son says that tardy payments of debt
should be stopped and mortgages pressed. He was told that the iron
works could not be enlarged without passage of a Maryland Assembly
bill. Not satisfied with this rationalization of delay, he took the matter
up with George Plater, a high-ranking politician and lawyer. Somewhat symbolically of the rising power of the name of Carroll, Charles
became connected with Daniel Carroll's efforts at securing the incorporation of Carrollsburg in Prince George's County. Further encouragement to enlarge his own role with the Carroll fortunes came
from his father, who now confessed to the fatigue which he experienced in following the details of business at Doughoregan. There was
the suggestion in this that the full entry of Charles onto the center of
the stage had arrived.[13]

In such a position of wealth, honor, and power, Charles would have
to meet the challenges to all three of these enviable possessions from
other men of ambition. The countless dealings of such men with one
another in the provincial society gave rise to conflicts which in
eighteenth-century style quickly took on the appearance of personal
affront. A rapid triumph or an irreversible, tragic defeat was found in
the duel, to which the conflict often moved. This moment had arrived
for Charles Carroll of Carrollton, September 24, 1769.

He was at an Annapolis coffee house, when his clerk Deards approached his table and nervously handed him a few pieces of paper.
In the presence of friends Charles silently read the scurrilous lines that
came from the pen of Lloyd Dulany, brother of Daniel, the Attorney

General of Maryland. He became embarrassed in his silence. After glancing blows at Charles' self-respect, Dulany poured out his spleen on the elder Carroll, knowing that this would give the greatest insult and provocation. "As for that monster of Vice & profligacy," he said, "I will still Echo tht universal Voice of his Country, that he is the deepest stain on the times, and that the Laws have long scandalously slept, in not dragging him forth, as a sacrifice to public Justice." Dulany protested that these were not the "emanations of rancor & prejudice."[14]

Now in full command of Carroll affairs, Charles was able to reconstruct the collision of circumstances which had brought about this eruption between the two families. His father the past few years had applied heavy pressure on Lloyd Dulany and Walter, son of the Attorney General. The Dulanys now had charge of the accounts of the Baltimore Iron Works and the elder Carroll demanded that the books be balanced and reported the very first of the year. This carried the implication that there was dishonesty afoot and that court action was being contemplated by the Carrolls. The Dulanys, on the other hand, had a counterclaim against the Carrolls as creditors of the estate of James Heath, son-in-law of Daniel Dulany, and nephew of Lloyd. Compound interest, it was said, had been extracted from the Heaths in the course of this transaction. Somewhere in the exchange the idea was also given to Charles that his father was open to the charge of perjury, probably in connection with the Heath question.[15]

There may have been "emanations of rancor and prejudice" in Lloyd Dulany, but they did not destroy effective craftiness in his assault. Physically the larger man and experienced with guns, he calculated timidity in Charles of the "puny constitution," whose lack of experience deprived him of the advantage of youth. Perhaps Dulany had learned that Charles had theoretical disagreements with his father about the morality and legality of charging compound interest. At least he knew that the younger Carroll would be humiliated by a public scrutiny of his father in the role of moneylender. Dulany may also have given him credit for a sensitive conscience which was opposed to the folly of dueling. If Charles did not hold his father off from court action on the iron works litigation, Dulany calculated, he had no choice but to respond in writing to the scurrilous attack on the Carroll honor. This in turn would inevitably force Charles to a duel with pistols, from which he would naturally shrink. Conventional intervention by others would probably prevent the duel in any event, but Charles would then be open to a court indictment as the aggressor because of his anticipated letter of challenge.[16]

During the next few days, Charles wrestled with one of the greatest crises of his life. Even among professional soldiers of classical times, he could recall in plotting his course, ruse and surprise were the ingredients of a victorious battle. Self-possessed amidst his mounting anxiety, he threw an unexpected, diversionary attack at Dulany. A report had come to Dulany that Charles possessed evidence of the indentured servant status of Dulany's father, Daniel Dulany the Elder, during his first years in the colony. The Dulany family had tactfully kept this skeleton from public knowledge in recent times. In mockery, Charles menaced his opponent with a public revelation in retaliation against Dulany's charges. His move uncovered a sense of folly in Dulany's provocation, which sensible folk would recognize.[17]

Within four days of receiving Dulany's letter, Charles had drafted his response, which carefully left him free of any legal charge as an aggressor. This letter of September 29, a Friday, vindicated his courage and honor. In it, he instructed Dulany that he would proceed the following morning along an appointed route with Deards as his companion. If his enemy should threaten his life and honor, he would take the necessary means to defend both. "I look upon you as a bravo," he writes in a final taunt of this strategic letter, "egged on by another too dastardly to appear in defense of his own character." Daniel Dulany, not Lloyd, is the moving force behind the attack! This letter concluded, Charles then instructs Deards to compose a letter to his father setting forth the grounds for the impending encounter. The clerk is to bring the letter with all speed to Doughoregan and ask his father, in view of the danger, to come to Annapolis. Fortunately Molly was with his father at the ominous moment when he took from the cabinet her father's pistol, a morbid bequest from one who met violent death at the hands of the law.[18]

Later in the day Friday the 29th, as anxiety mounted, a messenger brought a letter from Lloyd Dulany. As Charles began to read its contents, the tension of fear relaxed for the first time in four days. "Tell me," Dulany wrote, veiling his defeat, "do you wait for my making such a palpable overture as will render me the aggressor[?]"

Charles immediately perceived that his enemy, as he had calculated, had hoped for a victory in court rather than on the field of honor, where he now made it clear he would not appear. Like Caesar among the barbarians of Gaul, or Fabian Cunctator harassing the Carthaginians, Charles reviewed with delight the success of his ruse and strategy of surprise. Dulany still reeled from the attack on his and his brother Daniel's ungenteel origin: "Why you silly puppy, how can you be such a fool as to insinuate that a certain person is afraid & —afraid of whom? I will not tell his [Daniel's] son out of regard for your Bones." It was not, after all, a dishonorable way to save one's bones from Walter Dulany. In the final analysis, he saw his own acumen and self-possession triumph, which as an intellectual, was his chief point of honor. Dulany, furthermore, even provided the satisfying picture of one protesting too much his own valor and the genteel standing of his family. Charles would not be pilloried as he deserved, Lloyd Dulany bleated, for attempting to "depreciate the sacred Character of a courteous, wise & good man—the cause of whose memory shall shortly be that of the public." There is a final protest that Daniel Dulany is not behind Lloyd's activities: "As for your Hint of my acting for another it is a Lie, spick & span from your jesuitical forge—." He protested too much, as all could see. The victory was in the pen, especially as it was guided by the mind and spirit of a greater man.[19]

Dulany's letter arrived before Deards, in preparation for his departure for Doughoregan, had concluded his own. He could now add the latest episode in his summary for Charles' father. He noted that the elder Carroll need not now come for the once impending trial or burial, which would have resulted had the case turned out for the worse. Charles had to add to the letter he composed for his father before hearing from Dulany. He wrote a postscript which explained how he avoided being legally considered an aggressor. "I hoped I should be justified before God & man," he said with gravity. "I will leave to you to judge from the above letters of our conduct. . . ." He had little trust in a jury of common folk to understand the sense of honor among gentlemen which could bring on such threats to human life. He had clearly anticipated the very real possibility of a formal duel, even if he had put no formal challenge in writing. The letter he had written could well have brought such a response. While the present crisis had passed, the victor did not deny the possibility of future threats. "I shall take no further notice of Lloyd," he concluded in his own emotional mood of bravado, "but shall go prepared to blow out his brains, if he should offer any insult to my person. . . ." Dulany will in time be chastised for his abusive remarks, but with more rational means.[20]

Trepidity continued the following days, as is clear from his instructions to Deards. The Darnall pistol was to be returned to Doughoregan; but a "pair of riding pistols under a foot long" were to be secured. Pocket pistols were preferable, but they are hard to obtain. Charles makes further reflections during the days following Friday the 29th, and in his letter to his father suggests that the matter is not entirely concluded, for Dulany "is engaged too deep to to retreat with honor." "Their silly pride is mortified," he says. "With all their assurance they cannot deny their Father was an indented serv[an]t." As for his own family's honor, he is disturbed at Lloyd Dulany's hints of perjury by Carroll's father, of which Daniel is undoubtedly the source. The soul of Charles the philosopher began to speak its part as the whole episode moves into perspective. "If such outrageous abuse should go unpunished," he reflects, "if the grossest insinuations are permitted to be thrown out ag[ains]t a gentleman's character by such scoundrels with impunity," then society is in an insane condition. The rationale of dueling is absurd. Some would say that the physically weaker man is given a fair chance, since he can resort to the equality of a contest with pistols. "But how unequal & hard is the injured man's fate," he reasons, "to be under the necessity of exposing his life to eminent danger, of submitting to the shame of being deemed a coward if he does not shew a proper spirit—Besides[,] the injured person may engage under great disadvantages—in the late instance had I been killed what dear connections should I have left behind me! & who would have grieved at Lloyd's death." Understandably, Charles wishes to consult with his father about this insane state of affairs.[21]

Although he continued through October and November without any new attack from the Dulanys, he and his father were much occupied with the charge against their moneylending activities. Charles composed a long document which his father used in preparing a response to his enemies on the question of compound interest. There were two questions: was it illegal and was it immoral? Charles developed his explanation along the lines of what ethical philosophers called the *penal law theory*. If there were specific laws against compound interest, his father could be fined or imprisoned for their violation. "In a legal sense; he explained, "usury means ye taking of a greater premium or sum for the loan of every hundered than what ye laws allows or has determinately fixed." The charge of usury and the meaning of the term, therefore, rested on the presence or absence of specific legislation. Legal violations of this kind, however, did not automatically bring one under moral guilt or sin, which arose only when one failed to pay the penalty.[22]

This was an important point, since the Dulanys had suggested that there was moral guilt in his father's financial dealings. Charles made it speculatively clear what would be required to show moral guilt. In general, the victimizing of another unjustly was morally wrong, even if no specific legislation outlawed the practice that produced such an effect. He then proceeded to reason beyond his father's case. If a law were drawn up against compound interest or similar practices, one would have to investigate its meaning and intent before one could say that it was immoral (and not merely illegal) to violate it. "The reason of the law must be inquired into," he told his father. The violation of a law is clearly immoral in the case where "the chief reason is to prevent rapacity on ye one hand, & to screen unthinking debtors from ruin on the other." This is not the verified intention in the case of many laws regulating interest. "Many illegal actions," he therefore was able to conclude, "contain no moral guilt." By instructing his father in this fashion, he seems to have passed beyond a more simplified view than that which he had expressed when in London and which gave rise to a disagreement with his father. Then, he had thought that all laws on usury had as their intent the prevention of victimizing a debtor; and he had erroneously assumed that Maryland had laws against compound interest. Now, he established that there were no such laws as would give color to the Dulany charge. He further demonstrated what would be necessary in a concrete case to show that his father had acted immorally apart from any specific law. In the economic circumstances of the Maryland gentry society, he was able to demonstrate the reasonableness and equity found in the interest-taking practice of men like his father. Normally, the borrower gains added wealth by the loan that helps him build or maintain an instrument of future profit; during the same period, the creditor is deprived of this opportunity, for which he asks compensation both in regular and in compound interest.[23]

Charles won the complete confidence of his father. "I submit my letter to D.D. [Daniel Dulany] to y[ou]r Correction in Point of Stile and thought," he wrote. The Elder Carroll explained how his son gave him valuable enlightenment on the crucial point of compound interest: "I have as you desired set forth the Distinction between Illegall & Immorall Acts & hope to y[ou]r Satisfaction." The conduct of his father with the assembly in past years had been touched upon by the Dulanys, but Charles thought that this matter could be put aside for the present since it would bring up discussion of other parties who might be alienated by such references. The long and carefully developed case reached the Dulanys and deterred them from any of the threats which Lloyd had made in September as a "bravo egged on" by the attorney general. The year drew to a close with the Carroll honor intact. In this magnificent style, Charles the lawyer, philosopher, and courageous gentleman rose to even greater stature in the eyes of his own family, its friends and foes, and of the whole Maryland gentry.[24]

He had hardly recovered from the encounter with his enemies in the fall of 1769, when a distressing contest with his kinsmen descended upon him. In April of 1770, Ignatius Digges brought suit against the Carrolls for a substantial amount of money. He had married Mary Carroll, first cousin of Charles. Her father, Daniel Carroll, had died prematurely and left the trusteeship of his estate to his brother, Charles' father. Stock of the Baltimore Iron Works was in the estate, a share of which fell to Mary Carroll Digges. All of the stockholders shared in the losses recently incurred by the organization, but Digges claimed that Charles' father as keeper of the company accounts was liable for the purported negligence which had caused the loss; it was said that he should have insured the company against such an eventuality. Digges also claimed that Charles' father should present vouchers to show records of small expenditures or stand under suspicion of misappropriation. A claim of £1800 was being made in favor of Digges. What probably encouraged him to provoke litigation of this matter was his own long-standing debt to the Carrolls. They had offered a compromise, but Digges spurned it, to the vexation of Charles' father. "If he thinks it a condescension unbecoming him," his father wrote, "we differ widely in opinion, indeed it might be an

avowall of his precipitate & preposterous behaviour." The Carrolls, on
the other hand, found the prospect of relatives at one another's
throats in a public court room utterly distasteful. The examination of
moneylender Carroll was again on the verge of public display. The
irony of the present case, as a sequel to the Dulany attack, was the
intention of Digges to charge compound interest on the money purportedly due him from readjustment of iron works accounts at the
expense of the Carrolls. After a year of discussion, the Carrolls suspected that others became parties to the Digges suit in the hope that
success with his claim might pave the way for their own, since they
were as iron works associates affected by the losses noted in the case.[25]

Charles was inevitably pulled into these murky waters. He chose to
have Thomas Johnson collaborate with him in the case, since he could
not as a Catholic and a defendant provide the pleading in court. The
choice was a happy one, as the court scene of April, 1771, showed. The
two men had done their book work during the months prior to the
trial. With the help of Daniel Carroll, brother of Mary Carroll Digges,
it was shown that Digges' lawyers' charges were false. The purchase
of slaves by Charles' father did not constitute a misappropriation in
the cost that was written off for this. Furthermore, records were
found of credit given for other legitimate expenses. Johnson made a
dramatic, final appeal to the jury which became a legend thereafter.
The court, however, entered upon a long period of deliberation.
Charles' father smarted under the trying proceedings. The court, he
believed, was blind to the significance of an earlier action of his by
which he turned over his trustee commission to Daniel Carroll. Digges
evidently expected this office to come to himself; he was now plainly
offended and spiteful. There was ill feeling on the Carroll side as well.
"I am sure [you] allways will prefer an unblemished Reputation to
any sordid gain," the elder Carroll wrote disconsolately to his son,
Charles, "but learn from what has happened to me th[a]t the most
upright Conduct Cannot secure ag[ains]t the most foul mouthed
virulent Abuse." The son made an effort at reassuring his father, but
further adverse conditions intervened. Daniel Carroll had learned
from the governor that an unfavorable decision was imminent. Charles
feared that the whole case would be settled by political compromise
rather than by legal evidence and reasoning.[26]

While Charles was at White Hall consulting the governor's adviser,
Haywood, Eden himself approached him and urged that he give

over to Digges the Negro slaves or others of similar value, which was the transaction now at issue in the court. Charles explained how this gesture might impugn his family's honor and asked that he have time to consider such a compromise. His father was not well disposed to this political tampering, even though the governor was understandably seeking peace in the gentry community. He invited the governor to Doughoregan for further discussion. He advised his son, however, that some kind of public explanation would be necessary in the event of an unfavorable court decision. It would seem that this would also be required in any compromise of the governor's making. The appearance of confessing dishonest transactions had to be removed from any of these actions. Negotiations continued for another year after this, further revealing the shadowy elements in the financial litigation. The creditors of Digges, it now appeared, were debtors of the Carrolls; they were thus anxious to profit by a decision in favor of Digges, for whom they were willing to use their influence. James Brooke was called in at this time to examine the Digges books and play the role of peacemaker in the rapidly deteriorating condition between the two families. Charles and his father experienced the most unpleasant feelings in the face of their affection for Mary Carroll Digges and the declining health of Digges himself. It was not until 1773, however, that a resolution of the controversy came about. Charles brought his father to accept an arrangement for reimbursement of Digges to the amount of about £1500; allowance was made for interest due since 1752. Possession of slaves did not change from Carroll to Digges, as the latter had requested. The Carrolls further saved face in the provision for sterling payment to be made by a third party who held a bond to that amount over Digges, but who also was indebted to the Carrolls. The bond was thus cancelled. So it was that Charles ultimately saw the tortured and twisted affair through to a smooth pacification. Feelings were not so badly wounded that they would not heal under his future, gracious diplomacy. "It really gives me great Pleasure & satisfaction," his father wrote to him in tribute. "You are so thorough a Master."[27]

The galling thing about this whole episode was that an inconclusive sequel of the duel chapter went on at the same time. Charles' father was still pressing the Dulanys, particularly the attorney general's son Walter, to desist from their practice of belated reports on the iron company. Charles was urged to draw up a court indictment in order to bring a remedy to this and to recover money due to the Carrolls which had some connection with the company accounts. "I do not file a Bill ag[ains]t Him to expose Him," his father wrote in September, 1771, "But to Recover a debt wh[ich] I am Convinced Cannot be got by any other means. . . . Can anything but a bill put an end to His Evasient delays?" Daniel and Walter Dulany in response to this bill threatened to press against the Carrolls for their transaction of a debt held over the James Heath estate. The elder Carroll was not intimidated. "I think it will appear by my Books," he told his son, "th[a]t all the Compound interest was discounted when Ja[me]s Heath past his Bond for His father's Debt." Charles therefore found the prospects good for a favorable settlement of his father's claim, and for a successful defense of his father's reputation in loan practices.[28]

In time, he became equal to the tedium of patiently attending to such matters as these over a long period of time, avoiding precipitous action which might destroy his good name as well as his fortune. To develop such a style was not easy to one given to intellectual precision and decisive formulation of opinions. The harmonizing of these two movements of his personality brought about a high achievement in the ideals of gentility.

However, as he surveyed his vast inheritance and his success in the role of its master, Charles was not entirely content with himself. His father in the family tradition of managing affairs, it was true, had succeeded very well. "A long life has answered his expectations," his son wrote, "and has made him the richest individual in the province without ye favour of government[,] even in opposition to it, & in spite of ye many injustices suffered thro[ugh] ye envy of private & public persons." James Carroll, the guardian of Charles' father and his great uncle, had moulded the elder Carroll in this traditional role, which had brought a rich harvest. With greater subtlety, Charles feared that the same success might spoil him and his own more refined notion of gentility. He struggled to maintain the simplicity and frugality of life which had inspired him in Europe in the face of a corrupt gentry society there. The gambling and card playing which he deplored at Bourges was now inevitably part of his own social life; and he hardly reflected on its impropriety. His father now made a charge of prodigality against Molly, which fell equally on his son. "Can fine furniture [,] Cloaths &c be put in competition, with a provision for Children," he asks. "Pride & Vanity are not to be indulged at their Expense, nor are you to be fools because many are so. . . ."[29]

A frequent ambivalence understandably annoyed Charles. In purchasing items for Molly, he asked English merchants that "ye things be bought at ye best rate:—but at ye same [time] handsome & genteel." Where is the mean of his classical notion of virtue; the path between the middling sort of man and the dissipated gentry of London? "I approve of the Additions to the Coach House," his father writes, only to confuse the issue; "money layed out in usefull & lasting improvements is well layed out. When it is layed out in things of shew it is flung away." Perhaps a landscape scene by a London artist is mere show; Charles, therefore, commissions a provincial artist. He asks a higher grade of grain for his favorite horses. "Pamper my Horses & pinch my slaves," his father says in a sarcastic censuring of his son. Already Charles is beginning to worry about the dowries of his two baby daughters. Their independence brought by handsome dowries might make them ungrateful and disobedient. There was little danger, all the same, that Charles as a man of independent fortune would lose his independence to the gentry environment, which did not entirely share his idealism of simplicity. Mostly he wrestled with determining the proper expression of these ideals, not with the ideals themselves. Suitability in his material surroundings was measured by taste rather than the shilling. His style was fixed here and Molly read it very clearly. He was tolerant of her and his environment, however, making the proper indulgence as good taste suggested. He ultimately prevailed with a simplicity supported by taste, which was his ideal.[30]

It was his friend Graves who reminded him of the more serious challenge to his ideal of gentility. "I used to caution your son against too much economy," he wrote to Charles' father disarmingly. "I would like to see him spend more money on his estate and living than in outlays of money for profit." Graves would have Charles exclusively a landed gentleman, standing apart from the harassment of commerce and finance. His horseback riding would then be in leisure fashion, rather than as a "potion" taken by a town gentleman escaping from the oppression of his counting house. Was not the description by Graves what Charles himself envisaged as a true gentle-man's environment, one similar to Christopher Bird settled on his county estate in England? Indeed, he had no little agitation of mind over this very issue. His "pains and troubles" with legal litigation hardly promised to reward his desire for peace of mind; nor com-merce, his habit of studiousness. "I think you are too impatient," his father tells him of his precipitous marketing activities. Here was a symptom of his unrest and there were others: Charles wants busi-ness concluded without much delay. "You hate to stir from home." "You want business over from an aversion to trouble." "A man to have His Business done well must do it himself." Why does he not check out land titles himself, his father again nags. "I know you do not like such Work or Turn over old Papers even in y[ou]r owne house, but Property must be sacrificed or the necessary trouble & means taken in defence of it." "Wallace may be indolent," his father says tartly, "are you not more so in not constantly pressing Him. . . ." Shorten your leisurely letters and give me the facts of business, his father says.[31]

All of this tells of an inner struggle of Charles to adapt his ideals. He had brought an oversimplified concept of the gentleman from England, because he had not been concerned with the multitude of details about living it which now besieged him. As it turns out, how-ever, he is succeeding very well with these details and without sac-rificing his image; it is creatively translated into a more richly variegated setting than the stereotypes against which he originally discovered it. The bustle of commerce and finance had driven the voice of culture to silence in the lives of countless gentlemen who were caught up in it; but Charles had the "habit of business" and a colossal capacity for work. His orderly life enabled him to dispatch work without total absorption. It would be proven that too much business leads to bad business, and too much work to a sterility which destroys the capacity for work. This all made him capable of finding time for the things of the mind. It is here that the richness of Charles' life sustained him along the high plain he courageously chose to walk; for that richness supplied his spirit a full measure each day, drawn from his life as scholar, litterateur, and wise beneficiary of the good life.

The warmth of friendships was at once the pediment and the

capstone to his edifice of gentility. To his life of the spirit and to his hope in the midst of great trials, this source of energy flowed. His deepening love for Molly, even his courtships of Louisa and Rachel, were of the highest order in contributing to the inspiration which his life required. Other women, too, if in a different way, touched his outlook on life with an effect that is exclusively a feminine gift. Esther Bird Browne revealed in her relationship to Charles his openness to such influence. "Between you and me," he confided to her nephew, Christopher Bird, "I think her one of the most amiable women I ever knew, my poor mother excepted. I never loved any of her sex so well with that sort of affection which goes by ye name of friendship, and is ever found in esteem resulting from the endearing qualities of mind and heart, sweetness and evenness of temper, sincerity, unaffected piety and benevolence." This was as much a revelation of Charles as of Esther. He had a warm admiration and friendship for younger women such as the wife of Charles Carroll the Barrister. He tells Jennings of her attractive shyness, which will give way to a worthy object of friendship, "then a goodness of her heart will charm you." While he had no occasion to write of similar cases, there surely must have been other women favored by such friendship. The faithful gestures of Rachel Darnall in letters at the time of his mother's death were a priceless support. His richly spoken sympathy for her in her own personal tragedy left a lasting tie. The Carroll family relationships were wide indeed, and so there were other cases. Family solidarity fostered affection, and a disciplined propriety safeguarded the bonds.[32]

Charles seems to have composed his own version of Cicero's treatise on friendship [*De Amicitia*]. The remarks about Esther Browne reflect that classic. His friendships were constructed so carefully, that they lived on and on, even though miles of Maryland and even the Atlantic Ocean itself separated him from those who merited this gift of his. As a litterateur he had a special advantage in accomplishing this, since the composing of his letters was a pleasure and a work of art. "A kind of continued conversation is preserved," he tells Graves of their letter exchanges, "and we answer his questions as if present, and we are at liberty to propose our own in turn." He is not cynical about gifts and services among friends. "They contribute to keep alive & nourish friendship, display a generous spirit and a

turn of mind truly amiable. . . ." He sends a portrait of himself and
Molly done by Charles Willson Peale to Christopher Bird as a
special kind of gift. The friends tie him to their relatives. He wanted
Daniel Barrington to call on Bird and reports his conversations with
Barrington's relatives in Maryland He wanted Bird to compliment
three of his friends and congratulated their mutual friend Huddleston
on his marriage. His correspondence with Jennings and Bradshaw
was in a similar vein. With a few of these friends, he shared his
intimate reflections on his courtship of Louisa Baker, and in Esther
Bird Browne, he had a special confidant during these troubled days
of the heart. With childlike candor, he spoke to them of Rachel and
Molly, which testified to his confidence in their friendship.[33]

There was not as great need for letters to Marylanders, but enough
remain to show that there were enduring provincial friendships as
well. The Hoxtons and Brents, who as boys ventured forth with him
to St. Omers, were still close to him. There were warm letters to his
distant kinsmen, Charles Carroll the Barrister and Daniel Carroll.
In maintaining all of these ties, he told Jennings, he will stake out
time to leave his mind free from "ye serious trifles of this busy
scene." The reward was indeed great in the truly cosmopolitan and
deeply personal extension of himself that resulted. So it finally
appeared; Sir Joshua Reynolds had captured in a limited way and
at a premature moment, a painting of the Christian gentleman and
humanist which Charles now became in his own creative style.[34]

Chapter 12

REVOLUTIONARY CAST OF MIND

From early adolescence, Charles was motivated to submit to the ordeal of becoming an intellectual. A demanding regimen of work and activity alone made it possible for him to develop a cast of mind that was highly creative. Upon his return to America, he intensified this motivation and broadened his regimen, impelled by the trying personal experiences of composing a manor and becoming its master. The revolutionary cast of mind which began to form at the College of Louis the Great had undergone continuous growth at Bourges, Paris, and London. In the new setting of provincial life, it enlarged its scope and took on many subtle features. Maryland was a challenging and extensive laboratory, furnished with many unknown ingredients and uncluttered by the English environment which was so heavily freighted with fixed customs and traditions.

By 1772, Charles thoroughly understood himself as an intellectual. He had an insight into his own personality and behavior which helped him toward this ideal. "Notwithstanding matrimony & need of the climate," he humorously tells Graves of his trials as an intellectual, "my poor little carcas, and my spirits are kept up as you have guessed, by a variety of employments, business, exercise, and study: in short I never allow myself time to be idle, or the spleen to prey upon me." All of this activity is placed at one side of the fulcrum of his personality because of what he is at the other where his mind and spirit are given to deep reflection on himself and his experiences. He confesses the results are happy. "To this perpetual occupation I ascribe the really equal flow of spirits, which I cannot [ascribe to] my constitution, being naturally of melancholy & contemplative cast." What biological determinism: a puny constitution drives him to melancholy and contemplation, both of which seek an outlet in the multiplicity of his life! Where the complement lay was in contemplation. Without it, the activity would be sterile and chaotic, an aggravation rather than a remedy for melancholy. His behavior thus stands explained, at least to himself. His achievements come both as a result, and as a proof of his being right.[1]

The true philosopher is an older man. Charles told Graves that the time had arrived for both of them. To his own somewhat metaphysical style of thought, the powers of mind and spirit were compelling objects of philosophical reflection. He was thirty-five years of age in 1772, as he writes of this topic, and his friend a few years older. Poor Graves, his memory was slipping. "Read more & your memory will grow stronger," he is told. The trouble with Graves is his indolence. "Your age, is the fittest season for reading," Charles explains; "the Judgement is then matured, a knowledge and greater experience of the world enables a man of 40 or 50 to read with more benefits to himself, than men under that age usually reap from books." This was the fittest time for the improvement of their understanding. The multiplicity of duties and the indolence natural to the older person were no greater obstacles than those faced in their buoyant days as younger men. "Ye passions of youth, its giddiness, & dissipation are equal if not greater enemies to study." The life of the imagination depended on the memory; sustain the one by study and the other retained its vigor. Voltaire gave a good example of his contention. At the same time Charles was reminded that memory and imagination, while influencing each other toward maintaining vitality in later years, are yet distinct. Each has its own quality, as he himself had observed. "I have known myself several of very retentive memories," he noted, "and of imagination as cool as the frozen sea, as sluggish as the canals of Holland." The imagination is not here what it should be; it is too much like the memory, which is properly a "sober, cool & still operation." He saw the vivacious goddess of imagination in poetic contrast to the personality of memory, the subdued virgin. "The glowing blushes of that goddess disconcert ye virgin modesty of memory & put her out of countenance."[2]

As contemplative, it is clear, he was both poet and philosopher. While he spoke of what he observed in others, he assumed that others knew that his reflections on the mind and its powers came more from his own experience of himself than from others. It was this felicitous movement of his philosophizing mind to the poetic and to personal experience which led him to reflect on the visual after the manner of the scientist. He told Jennings that the squirrels and mocking birds which he requested were curiosities for children and women. The multitude of plants native to America promised much more. "[They] afford you some pleasure as a florist, or matter of thought & speculation as a naturalist, or Philosopher."

It is not surprising that Charles became a great reader of stories which reported new discoveries of strange parts of the world, as Byron did of South America at this time. The remote past as well as the remote places of the present engrossed his imagination and philosophical reflection much the same way. He never tired of Roman history and sought out Hooker's recent volume. Robertson's *History of Charles II*, Lord Clarendon's *History of the Rebellion*, Littleton's *History of Henry II*, and other such titles were on his library list. Gazettes from Maryland to Newfoundland, and the *Gentleman's Magazine* and others from England brought him closer to the changing face of history all about him. It was true that all of this was a fascinating exercise of memory and imagination, but it was science as well. The nature of man and his society were under microscopic analysis as the unfolding of past and present history took place before him. History consequently continued to be the matrix of his grasp of law. While he studied Blackstone's *Commentaries on the British Constitution*, he did not content himself until he found the original of the universal history from which the great constitutionalist quoted.[3]

The mature literary strokes so evident in the letters of Charles revealed the artist and the littérateur. It was natural that the bright prose of Voltaire drew his initial interest, just as he was repelled by a "barbarous & uncouth" translation of Machiavelli by Farnesworth. As it was, the poetic strands of metaphysical and scientific reflection that led him on, were joined by the *philosophes* with literary gifts who commanded his attention on a subject of philosophical reflection. At the same time, the orderly assimilation of years of reading and study made his mind come to bear critically on the most celebrated conversation pieces of the day. The most controversial and even blasphemous discussions came under his critical eye. If the philosophers moved with intelligence, wit, and style, he would follow, enlarging all the time beyond the scope of the author. In this manner he continued associations with Voltaire, Raynal, and Bolingbroke, whom he had read in France and England.[4]

Voltaire was at this time enlarging his assault on Christianity, and Charles entered into a dialogue of the mind with him, as though he were at his side in some Parisian salon. A year after his return from England, he was looking for the recently published letters of Voltaire. *Les Erreurs*, written by a critic of Voltaire, he found to have been answered by the master of the *philosophes* in his wide-ranging observations on North America. Voltaire's *Les Questionnes sur l'Encyclopédie*, Charles said, "abounds with wit & humour interspersed with the most judicious & Philosophical reflections." *L'Evangile du Jour*, on the other hand, "scarcely merits the appellation of a new publication, being rather a collection of his former detached pieces brought together into one view, placed in a new light, and animated with older coloring." Holwell has often been quoted by Voltaire, and Charles had finally secured a copy of his writings out of curiosity; he wanted to learn what substance there was behind Voltaire's representation of the Brahmin and religion generally in India. "The author of ye essays on crimes and punishments," he again commented on Voltaire, "has displayed a great fund of humanity in his little work, interspersed with many facts and judicious observations. The comment is plainly ye product of Voltaire's pen: his sarcastic wit and humour are so peculiar and original that ye [they] easily distinguish his works." The author's message on tolerance and justice was best received.[5]

While in Europe, Charles had thought through the earlier spoken case of Voltaire against Christianity, and what now came forth he considered warmed-over considerations, liable to the same criticism made earlier by the Marylander. Voltaire's brief for the failure of Christianity still stood a failure in Charles' eyes. A more romantic voice carrying the same theme but with different harmony left him no more impressed and even less interested. The controversy was becoming sterile, even in the new rendering of Jean-Jacques Rousseau. "I read no controversy," he explained. "The title of the book on miracles raised my curiosity and hath not satisfied it. By this time [,] Jean-Jacques Rousseau, I doubt not, is tired of ye wilds of Derbyshire: that restless, fantastical philosopher cannot live long in any place. I should not be surprised at his writing a satire upon ye government on purpose to draw upon himself a persecution." In Rousseau, the *philosophes* were becoming not only tedious but demented. With a surprise that few would appreciate, Charles told Graves that Gehegan's *History of Ireland* in his "bold & free style" set him above effective attack from those having as Rousseau and Voltaire vogue in France. If these critics would uproot their prejudices, he believed, they would come to see that they had no replacement for the Christianity they condemned.[6]

The signs were clear indeed. A young intellectual had crossed the threshold of his thirtieth year in such free-swinging criticism and he appeared clearly bent upon his own philosophizing. Because he had his own independent cast of mind drawn from wide reading, he promised to be creative and original. The books of others must give way to his own; their thoughts and writings to his. His urgency came less from dissatisfaction with the classics of the times than from hopeful prospects of the young provincial society of which he is part in a highly formative period. His thoughts were of progressive independence, and he must as a true revolutionary posit the goals and seek the paths that lead to them. Metaphysical and religious principles were fairly well established in his mind; it was time to discover a social philosophy which was organically rooted in his principles and the Maryland environment.

Charles was always aware that he lived in a society with an established religion. Far more than his father, he bore an urbane manner in accepting this fact of Maryland life. None doubted, however, that his critical mind cast devastating reflections on its validity. In England, he had conducted a dialogue with his Protestant friends Jennings and Graves on this very topic. They were sensitive to his dignified restiveness under the restrictions establishment imposed on his religious spirit. The dialogue continued in letters upon his return to America. After joking with Jennings about the Gunpowder Plot on one occasion in 1766, he turned the traditional English approach to tolerance along an entirely different and enlightening line of thought. Locke had made much of the political intent of Roman Catholicism, Charles knew, in disqualifying its adherents from an active part in public life. Discreetly shunning particulars which might offend an adherent of the Established Church, he said that in these schemes religion was always belabored for political advantage. The true purpose of religion would forever be distorted by a condition of establishment. "Ye savage wars, ye cruel massacres, ye deliberate murders commited by law, under ye sanction of Religion," he explained, "have not reformed ye morals of men. They have indeed answered ye purposes of ambition, they have abetted ye Revenge of an enraged Party and sometimes too they have served ye cravings of Lust." Jennings knew that Bloody Mary, or Bloody Elizabeth could have fit the reference; Catholic Spain, or Protestant England.

More sharply, however, Charles held a realistic hope that religion and policy of state might be separated, even though a moral society could not be separated from religion. "I could wish and I believe you wish with me," he exhorts Jennings, "that ye unhappy differences and disputes on speculative points of Theology had been confined to divines; or that the happiness of mankind had been ye object of these disputes." True, men in this enlightened age were not likely to be led into new chapters drawn from the era of the Wars of Religion; but potential leaders were at hand for this, should the general mood change. A letter from Jennings the following year tells of an instance of this when the Bishop of London ordered the closing of Catholic chapels. The animus of bigotry spews forth in the press of the "two most enlightened nations in Europe"—France and England. He would agree that Locke himself, with his reservations on tolerance in the case of Catholics, was another example from the ill effects of the "late Revolution" of 1688.[7]

The revolutionary cast of Charles' mind never left at rest his own disfranchisement for faith. At this very time, he still studied the statute laws which supported this discrimination. Barrington, whose brother wrote a theoretical treatise on obsolete statutes, further enlightened Charles by letter. Jonathan Swift gave a detailed examination of this topic, and Charles asked Graves to send him a copy of *Reasons Offered to the Parliament of Ireland for Repealing the Sacramental Test in Favor of the Catholics*. With his usual scholarly cast of mind Charles asked for the whole three-volume set of Swift in which this treatise was included. In 1767, he was prepared to make a moderate demand in revising establishment, which by the oath had kept Catholics from voting and sitting in the assembly. "If none but those who professed ye established religion were admitted to positions of profit and trust," he proposed, "and ye exclusion of all others made ye sole punishment of their dissenting from ye established mode of faith, this measure might probably make more proselytes thereto [to the Established Church], than even ye rigorous execution of penal laws." A seat in the assembly was not considered a position of profit and trust. The atmosphere which this would create would certainly relax the social tensions which Charles, for all of his aristocratic self-respect, felt implicitly. "Were an unlimited toleration allowed and men of all sects were to converse freely with each other, their aversion from a difference of religious principles would soon wear away." With their experience of Charles as evidence, Jennings and Graves surely accepted the validity of such a proposal.[8]

This was indeed a measured pace at which his mind moved against establishment, but he was also true to his revolutionary cast of mind. By 1772, a crescendo of this desire for disestablishment seems to have developed in one who had in such a short time attained eminence as a man of independent fortune and recognized knowledge regarding public questions. Instead of politely dodging the old cant that emanated from the "Black Legend" in English books, he made a different response. He felt that the times as well as his own convictions called for it. What does he think of Bowers' *History of the Popes?* "I have always understood it to be a katch penny," he stated quite bluntly, "wrote with great virulence & consequently abounding in falsehoods. I have as little veneration for bad popes as Mr. Bowers or anyone else, but even bad ones should not be caluminated & misrepresented. Bowers forgot Cicero's advice, *ne quid falsi dicere audeat, ne quid veri non audeat* [do not dare to speak a falsehood, do not hesitate to speak the truth]—he is not the only historian by whom that admirable maxim has been entirely disregarded."⁹

Two years later, as he moved closer to the role of a gentleman in public life, he attained a louder volume in his remarks against establishment of religion and its oppression of religious freedom. Charles pleasantly believed that in one of his letters Graves is trying to convert him; but it is not out of religious zeal that he urges Charles to join the established faith of his countrymen. In the eyes of the Creator, according to Graves, all religions are indifferent and hence he finds Charles hard to understand in his stubborn resistance to conformity. "Do you advise me to quit a false religion," Charles asks sarcastically in response, "& to adopt any false belief; & this merely to honor & humor the prejudices of fools or to be on a footing with knaves. I have too much sincerity & too much pride to do either, even if filial love did not restrain me—for I can truly say *nequeo lachrymas perferre parentis* [I am unable to bear the tears of a parent]." He had never thus brought his friends so far into his inner spirit as it labored under the disabilities of the English system. He continued relentlessly once this emotional display was made: "I am a warm friend of toleration, I execrate ye intolerating thirst of ye Church of Rome, and of other Churches—for she is not singular in that designing." All covenant states were under attack, and he was unable to conceal what was in his craw. "Selfish men invented the religious tests to exclude from posts of profit & trust their weaker or more conscientious fellow subjects; thus to secure to themselves all ye emoluments of government: Wharton's saying was a true as well as a witty one—[']The oaths of govern[men]t. were so framed as to damn one part of ye nation & shame the other.[']" Thus carried away, he confessed to his great desire to stand with dignity in the civil forum of eminent gentlemen. "If my countrymen judge me incapable of serving them in public station for believing ye moon to be made of green cheese, in this respect their conduct (if not wicked) is not less absurd than my belief. . . ." So it is out at last, but in his own commanding style, cast in the philosophical support which his church-state ideas provided. He chose to bind up the notion of separation of politics from religion with that of a state free of establishment. The rich feeling and the dramatic context in which he thus spoke his thoughts told the depth at which his reading and personal experience had interacted. He now saw the goal of religious freedom emerging into view, and he was near discovery of the road that led to it.[10]

In the realm of political theory and practice, Charles was even more creative. From his readings and reflections on the times within European civilization and the British Empire, he formed a general mould of revolutionary thought which would take on new creative lines of reform drawn from his provincial experience. The process could accurately be described as tending toward a sociological science based on historical analysis. His manner of further elaborating it by seeing its relevance to his provincial society was truly philosophical; and this reflection on the political order was similar to his analysis of church establishment and religious freedom. Under the influence of Montesquieu, he had arrived at a point of creativity. He attached himself to the republican form of society; not merely in theory, but as attainable in practice. What was the relation of this republicanism to the empire and the precise political form in the province? This was an important question because it conditioned his recommendations for reform at both levels. A broad speculative plateau provided his vantage point for surveying the problem; it was distinct but related to the republicanism portrayed by Montesquieu. Very clearly, a cyclical theory of history had taken root in his mind even before his return to America. It unmistakably instructed him that the decline of civilization in Europe could give rise to republicanism in America, given wise statesmanship. The major works which he studied provided detail to this plateau of cyclical history, to which only general reference is made in his views of imperial and provincial problems. In writing to Daines Barrington, the author of the volume on English statutes, he understands that his society is set in a happier era than in past times. At the same time, his great interest and reading in ancient history led him to the idea of growth and decline as seen in the civilization of Rome, to which he found a parallel in his own era. While there was growth in evidence, it must be decided where it is strongest with a promise for the future and how progress would be brought about. He thus creatively passed beyond the vision of his authors.[11]

Many writers in the early part of the eighteenth century with whom Charles was familiar had put the cyclical notion in vogue, and some speculated about the questions which concerned the young Marylander. Lord Bolingbroke in the 1730's was among the first. Buffon and Raynal examined the idea of cycles in the primitive corruption of North America, which was a reverse interpretation as far as Charles was concerned. Hume, whose volumes on English history he possessed and read, believed society to be in the process of progressive enlightenment coming from growth of a philosophical religion. He logically stressed historical figures who came under the influence of this principle of progress; and the idea that it was through law that liberty increasingly emerged with such leadership. While all of this was not necessarily a framework of cyclical history, Hume became cyclical at least in one repsect where he despondently treated the lot of English politics in the 1750's and 1760's. The Whigs and Tories by their dereliction of leadership were not attending to wise laws, Hume believed. Liberty was stifled as a result. In this situation, an impersonal event or a fortuitous turn of historical circumstances promised to bring deliverance, provided leadership responded properly. His dominant preoccupation with the British Empire and its trials rather than the broader trend of Western civilization, clearly placed him close to the thoughts of Charles, his reader. Hume did not, by what he said, view Europe as another version of a decaying Roman Empire, nor did he see decline in England on so grand a cyclical scale. Charles undoubtedly did and it is here that he showed his characteristic cast of mind, which was to pass beyond the conclusions of his classic texts and make his own elaborations. It may be that the philosophical religion in Hume was in Charles' view akin to Montesquieu's virtue or patriotism. Charles saw that together, they expressed the spirit which would guide the republic of the future. He creatively idealized this republic, as the term of the cyclical process, emerging in provincial America.[12]

In this scheme of thought, Voltaire was not a congenial force. Besides being out of sympathy with republicanism and virtue as the spirit of its laws, any cyclical theme in his writings was cast on the broader scene of European civilization as composed of several ages. His determinism by appeal to insignificant events as turning points was at work in explaining the springs that moved society. This put him out of sorts with Montesquieu and his Maryland disciple. Both men saw history in the hands of those equal to holding its destinies. In following the cyclical enactment, therefore, Charles saw the progressive decay of England and the rising advancement of the province. He would be a critic of ministers, parliamentarians, and kings as agents of a corrupt destiny; he would be eulogist of the provincial republic's patriots. The young provincial philosopher of history left his mark on his father and Graves. Wealth had begotten luxury, and vice in turn, the Englishman commented in 1770; tax gatherers and placemen swarm the countryside. "What must be the end of this shameless long Continued Want of Honour[,] publick spirit & Patriotism," Charles' father asks Graves rhetorically. It will end in "Anarchy & destruction." "All states labouring under the same Vices Have met with the fate which will be y[ou]r lot: That fate is impending[,] it Cannot be far off. . . ." "The period of the English Constitution is hastening to its final period of dissolution," he wrote with finality in November, 1765. "The symptoms of general decay are but too visible. . . ."[13]

Upon his return to America, Charles continued to study the British Empire thus in decline at its center, but rising in its province of Maryland. He not only ranged across its whole history, but he acquired books which gave account of imperial policy and affairs in the Far East as well as in the Western Hemisphere. In 1771, however, in a lengthy letter to Jennings, he spoke of a complete case which established her corruption and decline. Following his scientific methodology, he fixed an exact parallel to these times in those of the reign of the Roman emperor Caligula. Details were merely added during these years to what he had noted in 1768 of this trend in English civilization. Pitt's elevation to peerage was a sign of the endemic corruption, even though he appeared a worthy man at the moment. "Doubtless ye original intent of bestowing such honors," Charles explained, "was to reward conscious merit; how often they have been conferred with this view, it does not belong to me to say."

As he continued to study party politics in England, he was confirmed in his pessimism regarding "ye secret springs & workings of party." "The genuine Principles of either Whigism or Toryism are equally dangerous to our Constitution," he believed. "The power of the King and Lords would be annihilated by the former [Whigism]; by the latter [Toryism] the liberty of ye subject would be taken away and despotism established in its stead." The House of Lords will probably preside as a judicial body over the controverted will of Lord Baltimore. "Political considerations will no doubt . . . influence the determination." Blackstone might well enough say that the king could do no wrong: "The prerogative of the crown extends not to any injury; for being created for the benefit of the people, it cannot be exerted to their prejudice. . . ." But the ministers set policy and were answerable for it. Even a good king, if surrounded by corrupt ministers, can do little good.[14]

All of this was only new phraseology for observations made in London a few years before. What now takes place in a new and creative vein of thought was the concern of Charles for reform, not in England where corruption was too advanced, but in his own province. Here an unwholesome growth had sprung up, spawned by the mother country. To some extent, the original transplant to America accounted for this unhealthy condition. The revolutionary cast of Charles' mind was bent upon a full-scale examination which took into account foundations for healthy growth as well as dangerous tendencies which had recently developed. To Countess Auzoüer, he wrote of the tradition of freedom found in the Maryland Charter and early ordinances; these were the foundations which support the citizen's rights. He reminded his father that "Individuals have a right under the English govern[men]t. to censure the conduct of their rulers & representatives. . . ." From a comparative study of Blackstone and the laws of Maryland, he noted the wholesome modification of common law as it had developed in America. Yet, he reckons with the "commanding & omnipotent power of ye legislature to cut the gordian knot," when some need of the citizen is not met by established law both common and statutory. As far as provincials are concerned however, such a stroke did not come from Parliament, but from their own assembly, which was the counterpart of Parliament.[15]

Since it is fealty to the king, and not to Parliament, which binds the Marylander to the mother country, royal ministers have some role in the interpretation and elaboration of that fealty. Charles was fearful, however, that their superintending rôle over affairs in England might lead them to exercise power at the expense of freedom in the colonies. If the two are *"res dissociabiles,* incompatible, I am sorry for it," he tells Graves, "but let us retain our liberty whatever becomes of the honour" which power brings. He attacked the increasing efforts of the ministry "to render ye governors and chief officers of ye civil department independent of ye people [in the colonies]." He sees recent legislation for the operation of customs commissioners in the same light. Such a quest for power through these provincial puppets of the ministry sacrifices liberty and cannot but provoke rebellion. With the sarcasm of Voltaire, he suggests that the ministry hasten to reduce the strength of the provinces by putting an end to the influx of migrants to America. "I submit to ye wisdom of higher powers," he says, "a judgment whether this will prevent rebellion."[16]

Charles shrewdly saw that the governor and his council as members of the upper house of the assembly were captives of the Crown and the proprietor's ministers. Inevitably, the traditional right of appeal to London against this provincial establishment in a given instance would be uninformed and ineffective. In this setting, the creative mind of Charles saw the need for a revolutionary emancipation of the upper house, so that it became a true spokesman for the people. True, the assembly was the counterpart of Parliament, which was composed of two houses. "The peculiar and distinct powers" of the upper and lower houses, however, were not parallel to the Lords and Commons. It is not a colonial House of Lords they should have been, but representatives of the people in the spirit of the Commons. Originally at the colony's founding, he seems to imply, only one house made up the assembly, and it truly represented the people. The upper house had drifted too far away from this inspiration and had become in turn the tool of the governor, the proprietor, and the royal ministers. "I am inclined to think that a seat in a certain assembly," he wrote to Graves, "may be as fatal to private friendships, as dangerous to public liberty—why it should be so[,] I will not pretend to say. Perhaps the mind being totally absorbed in schemes of ambition becomes indifferent...."[17]

Absorption in this problem led Charles to study Montesquieu further and read an application to the Island of Jamaica that was made of him by an anonymous author in 1766. *The Privileges of the*

Island of Jamaica states Charles' case succinctly and forcefully: "If the Assembly do not hold their Privileges upon the same independent terms with the house of Commons, the people of this colony have no defence against the assaults of arbitrary power, no security for their lives, their liberties, or their properties." While the king in England could not exercise judicial power, the author notes in reference to Montesquieu's balance of powers notion, the governor was actually doing so in Jamaica. Coming to America did not deprive Jamaicans of these rights and securities; but now Jamaica might decline in freedom to that sad state that Ireland experienced, he wrote elsewhere. Charles, in his usual critical style, rejects the author's acquiescence in some kind of claim to provincial jurisdiction by Parliament. The Charter of the First Lord Baltimore had freed Maryland from this dependence on Parliament, and he believed that "the Revolutionists [of 1688] usurped [Baltimore's] government" and abrogated its ancient privileges. The author on Jamaica therefore did not settle the problem of the upper house. It is here, that Charles again entered upon a creative vein of speculation, full of importance for the future of Maryland. While the lower house assemblymen would represent the people who elect them in one way, he believed, the upper house would do so in a way which would be in striking contrast to its present condition of subservience to the governor, proprietor, and Crown.[18]

The heavy stamp of classical antiquity rested on his reflections as he came to see the upper house as the counterpart, not of the House of Peers but of the ancient Roman Senate—the admirable *senatus populusque Romani* so revered by Cicero. Very clearly the "better sort" of gentlemen must sit here, leaving the lower house to men of another quality. They would be the "Honest & well meaning men [who] generally entertained the same sentiments of public measures— *idem velle ac sentire de republica* [to wish and feel the same way about the republic], Tully says somewhere. . . ." "None but honest men," he explains of this type of Maryland senator, "will think alike or at least publically express their sentiments on the political parties and disputes which may happen to divide & distract their country." Elected patriots will not lose their popularity, as has happened to some in Maryland, because they change their language and opinions in the environment of a corrupt upper house or assembly. A remarkable vision was indeed beginning to take shape as he wrote thusly in 1770. There was little doubt that he aspired to the senatorial rôle, although three years before he had had no inclination openly to express it, let alone hope to attain it. "As individuals having an Interest in ye welfare of our country," he then wrote to Jennings, "we can not but wish well to it: but such is our situation in life[—] at least mine, that we can do but little more—Providence has placed us at too great a remove from those stations where the example of disinterestedness & publick spirit . . . has influence on ye actions of ye great. . . ."[19]

What emerged from his reflections, then, was a Maryland Senate which bore the hope of succeeding in the manner of the *senatus populusque Romanus*. It was plain that it would be elective, but occupied by the better sort of people, and would distinguish itself from the lower house by being above factionalism and meanness. He generously conceded to Daniel Barrington in England that the House of Peers had its finer moments in Parliament: "Th[e] Wisdom of the English Senate hath been much applauded—and times of faction and tumult excepted, equally famed for equity and moderation." But he could not forget the multiplicity of occasions when "the heat of party and private, interested views" prevailed against "cool reasoning and good policy." He was able to speak more frankly of the corruption beyond remedy in the mother country's institutions which was so clear at the moment of the Stamp Act. He would have excised factionalism from Maryland's upper house before the infection of the mother country in the colonial transplant had advanced to such a hopeless state as that one found in Parliament. "They seem to me," he satirically tells Jennings of the Parliamentary diseases in Maryland's upper house, "to spring from the same sources from which your factions have theirs: the want of a sufficient number of lucrative offices to gratify the avarice of the ambition of the 'Outs'." He was somewhat relieved that the common cause against an arbitrary Parliament removes factionalism for the moment from Maryland's Assembly. But, he also knew that the upper house, as an object of royal and proprietary patronage through the governor, could not long maintain a healthy independence; and so he urged his creative reform policy. It had to be elective and free from proprietary patronage.[20]

The most revolutionary stroke in Charles' design for the provinces within the empire was found in his view of the Maryland Charter. He believed this document decisively removed Parliament from jurisdiction over Marylanders, leaving only fealty to the king as the province's tie to the mother country. His emphasis was unique and radical as compared to the trend among his fellow provincials, and he stated it immediately upon his arrival in the colony. It was William Graves, who in 1766 grasped Charles' radical view. Graves had earlier contended that all colonial charters had subjected their respective provinces to Parliament. But Charles responded that only the Pennsylvania Charter provided any foundation for such a view. All of the other charters, and certainly Maryland's, freed their respective provinces from the jurisdiction of Parliament. Here was the source of his hope for Maryland's future. "England can never be enslaved but by a corrupt Parliament," he believed. Maryland by its charter was cut off from the corrupting power of Parliament. At the same time, his own parliamentary assembly had been tainted by its genetic origins; but a cure was possible, as he showed in his recommendation for reform of the upper house. He made it clear that he was not caught in the dilemma which faced the vast majority of Americans who had embraced the Glorious Revolution of 1688 and its principle of Parliamentary supremacy. It was that event which had led Marylanders to forget the freedom from the domination of Parliament which they possessed in their charter and other fundamental provincial law. Charles was bent upon restoring the tradition of the counter-revolutionary society, which made so much of this "Maryland Constitution."[21]

It was in the midst of these reflections and philosophical attachments that he confronted the power of Parliament in the Stamp Act, which defied everything he held on Maryland freedom. More than other provincials, he believed that this assumption of power by Parliament, and other similar instances that soon followed, called for the gravest concern. He had heard of preparations for a new tax on America during his last year in London. Instinctively, he sensed a radical attack on Maryland liberty. When he arrived at Annapolis, plans for its implementation were under way. Alienation from England grew; independence might be required, he thought. The challenge of Parliament was dissolving local factionalism in Maryland, for the Stamp Act extended the long grasp of Parliament into the pockets of Marylanders high and low. On every newspaper, public document, and certain items of everyday use, a levy was placed, raising the price the colonial would pay for these daily needs. The response was explosive. In September, 1765, Charles wrote to Daniel Carroll telling how the tax collector Flood's house was pulled down by the mob. Shortly after this, a scuffle occurred with British troops from the sloop *Hornet*. The stamp tax collector Hood, arriving from England, landed secretly when he heard that he was being burned in effigy. He soon fled to New York after the provincial officials refused his resignation. Even assembly tax levies were now resisted by the growing hostility of the people.[22]

Charles discussed these events with other friends in England, to whom he wrote many letters during these years of crisis. Jennings was especially involved in the Stamp Act controversy as it affected the American provinces, where he had once lived as a Marylander. While the legislation was forming in Parliament, he had written a pamphlet arguing against the wisdom of the Stamp Act. He was now embarrassed with Marylanders because Hood the stamp collector had made much of his purported connections with Jennings. Pleased with these writings as Carroll, Bordley, Brice, and other Marylanders were, they could not believe that Hood had Jennings' sympathy. "He only made use of your name to palliate his crime," Charles wrote to his friend. While he was grateful for the support of Jennings, Graves, and others in England, he was bitter about the apathy of the merchants who had previously deterred the ministry from such legislation, but failed to do so on this occasion.[23]

All the same, he spoke optimistically of the American response to the crisis. "The Americans are jealous of their privileges and resolved to maintain them," he wrote in December, 1765. This was the measure of vitality. "They are not yet corrupt enough to undervalue Liberty, they are truly sensible of its blessings, and not only talk of them as they do somewhere else, but really wish their continuance." The Sons of Liberty, he narrated, have organized and made a public protest. The colonists planned a non-importation association against English goods and he hoped for a united front by the colonies. Even though the economy had been in a recession since 1763, action was now vigorously taken. He told Daniel Barrington about the assembly scheme to float paper money to the amount of £10,000, with the prospect of having £97,000 available in ten years. Factionalism resulting from a pursuit of patronage faded for the moment. Charles hoped for "deliverance from the jaws of death." "I mean of political death," he explained to Bradshaw, "which poverty and slavery, the companions of the Stamp Act, will infallibly bring. . . ." America was clearly under a test for survival. "How long we may linger under our disease will depend upon the constitutional strength of our body—but linger we must and perhaps so long that our emaciated carcass when drained of all its vital moisture, its marrow and its blood by harpies *id est* stamp men, excise men, ministerial men, etc. will perfectly resemble the description of famine in Church-hill."[24]

As a man deeply involved in the career of a merchant, Charles sees the most forceful deterrence to Britain in commercial pressure, rather than in the violence of the crowd. "Our inability, while loaded with oppressive taxes to purchase your manufactures," he tells Graves, "will oblige us to manufacture for ourselves: the worse of evils this, that can possibly befall England. . . ." Of course, the loss of liberty in England would be even worse for her, and he suspected that this had already befallen her citizens there. Unlike many Americans, Charles feels that the colonists should never have acquiesced to the English restrictions on colonial trade by import and export duties, which took away a measure of freedom. This was an extreme position, which few Americans took at this time. "I can only say with Portius," he says prophetically to Bird, "the dawn is overcast, the warning lowers and heavily brings on the day with the fate of Liberty." The trade and property restrictions, increased by the legislation of 1765, would draw a fateful response. "Nothing but an armed force can execute the worse Laws." The details of the Stamp Act were ominous of tyranny, as its enforcement bore down hard against trial by jury and other fundamental English liberties. "The period of the English Constitution is hastening to a final period of dissolution," he warned Bradshaw. "I advise you to sell the estate in England and to purchase land in this province for liberty will maintain her empire. . . ." America was the last fair hope, if her citizens would but bestir themselves.[25]

Many Americans had better hopes from England than this. They did not, as Charles did, foresee that America must become independent. They found in the voice of William Pitt, Whig leader of Parliament, and others, the prospect of compromise after 1765. Charles held no such hope or desire. Grievances from the Stamp Act Congress in Boston, to which Maryland delegates were sent, did bring

Parliament to revise its thinking and repeal the Stamp Act. Pitt's voice was heard with some growing support; and so too, Edmund Burke's. Charles found unpromising Pitt's speech in favor of repeal, and his general colonial policy; it had "fine sallies in it mixed with absurdities." But even more, major surgery was required on the empire, and this Pitt did not understand. "Our wounds are deep," Charles noted, and still there was no promise of competent surgeons. Well enough to say, as Pitt did, that Parliament was not in all respects supreme over America. "Supposing what he advances to be true that the . . . legislature of G:B: [Great Britain] is supreme in all other instances but that of taxation," he explained to Jennings in March of 1767, "the Americans are exposed to an evil if not greater danger of slavery and oppression." If England was supreme in any respect, Charles maintained, liberty was doomed and tyranny assured. Maryland has lost her birthright of her charter, emancipation from Parliament.[26]

Pitt was intent upon continuing the control of commerce between the colonies and the mother country by Parliament. It was here that Charles found the flaw in Pitt's construction of the constitutional nature of Parliament's authority. Pitt probably saw the inconsistency of this principle of control with the rest of his system. "He did not speak his real sentiments," Charles believed, but spoke in this way *ad captandum vulgus*—to gain popularity with merchants and artisans as well as the general populace in England. If the authority of Parliament extended as a true legislative body to America, it would have had to embrace power over internal taxes in each province. By taking such power of taxation from Parliament, as Pitt professed to do, it no longer remained a true legislative body. Charles had the realistic fear that the power foregone for the moment would be taken up again, in spite of Pitt's plea to the contrary. As long as Parliament claimed supreme authority over the colonies, this was inevitable. "The distinction," Charles logically concluded, "between an absolute legislative authority, [and a legislature] divested of ye power of taxation, appear to me a contraditcion *in terminis*." "How can a legislature be absolute and supreme, when destitute of a power, which is the very soul and essence: and without which every legislature must be acknowledged incompleat, and inadequate to ye ends of government[?]"[27]

His case against Pitt now became truly dramatic. Parliament was a supreme legislature for the Isle of Britain, where it could levy internal taxes on her counties. Let Parliament be so confined. As for regulating the commerce of the colonies with the mother country, that too was taxation according to Charles; yet Pitt did not deny Parliament such power. Pitt did not explicitly admit this regulation to be a tax, but implicitly, he did. To cover up his inconsistency and uphold his notion of the supremacy of Parliament over the colonies in this form of commercial control, he considered the notion of the colonist's representation in Parliament. Such representation may not have been actual, according to Pitt, but it was virtual. This distinction to Charles was no more than a "mathematical line existing only in idea." Actual representation was real and only the citizens of the Isle of Britain were really represented in Parliament. "Ye doctrine of virtual representation is quite exploded," he concluded. That is why Pitt's attempt to fit the colonies under Parliament's supreme authority as an authentic legislative body is "mathematical . . . existing only in idea." The province fit realistically only under its own assembly, which played in America the rôle which Parliament held on the Isle of Britain. No, Pitt could not logically support Parliament's claim to control over colonial commerce and at the same time honor Maryland's Provincial Assembly.[28]

Charles highly esteemed the independence of American commerce and manufactures. This again reflected a radical, revolutionary cast of mind which did not rest at internal taxation with representation through the provincial assembly. He wanted control of external taxes on commerce as well. Pitt was earnest in pleading the general good with Americans and in getting them to comply with external taxation through control of commerce by Parliament. "No stretch of the Prerogative of the general good," Charles retorted, "will ever endanger our constitutions." Indeed Pitt was guilty of an "awkward and bungling attack." Thus, Charles went on to broaden his attack on the moderates and friends of America in England. What voice of freedom and of the people did Pitt possess in a House of Commons, so nefariously unrepresentative and subject to veto by the House of Lords? The queen's attorney Hussey was a good friend and, because of his kind words for America, deserved the Maryland bear hams, which Charles sent through Graves. But Hussey should have read more American pamphlets and understood the nature of colonial rights. Maryland's Assembly represented him not Parliament. Hussey aside, the less said of British ministers and other elements that lacked Pitt's friendship for America, the better; for they were a time-serving lot.[29]

In 1767, Charles continued immovable in his views. New British restrictions on commerce and manufactures were tolerantly viewed by friends of America like Pitt, but "Americans put them in their true light as the premiums upon their own manufactures." The following year the British Ministry through Parliament rescinded the Stamp Act, in line with what Graves called "Prudence & Policy." But when it appended the Declaratory Act in the process, it confirmed Charles' predictions of what to expect from the mother country. This act, while it accompanied the repeal of the Stamp Act, said that Parliament actually had the power to tax according to the measure of 1765. It categorically professed control over both internal and external taxes in the colonies, which included the most extensive restrictions on commerce. The response of the Carrolls to this new situation was clear from his father's letter to Graves. Parliament might well be proceeding according to "Prudence & Policy" in the repeal. This was hardly true, however, in the case of the Declaratory Act. The Act justified the continuance and enlargement of restrictions on American commerce. England courted great danger in this, for America was responding. The market for English manufactures in America would decline in retaliation, as the senior Carroll himself could show by manufacturing his own clothing for plantation slaves. America would not follow a "stupid passive obedience to unconstitutional measures. . . ." She would make commercial friends of powers who were rivals of England. America would not choose violent revolution, it was true, but there was another road—"a steady & determined Resolution to manifest our Rights. . . ." Indeed, England was hardly following a policy of "Prudence & Policy." A chapter of military oppression was about to unfold with the Boston Massacre and Tea Party. Charles' radical stand against internal and external taxes appeared by contrast more sound a course of "Prudence & Policy."[30]

Charles took the Declaratory Act of 1768 as darkly ominous. He was implacable in requiring a disavowal by Parliament of power over external as well as internal taxation of the colonies. Pitt had acquiesced in the spirit of the Declaratory Act, as Charles could have foretold: and so there was little hope in support of this kind. He nevertheless continued with an open mind to those in England who were sympathetic to America. He followed the texts of various laws under consideration by Parliament. He asked Graves to edit one pro-American pamphlet for him. "I am more interested than you imagine," he said, "in your political parties and disputes." The domestic scene in England, he understood, clearly affected colonial policy. Nonetheless, America must maintain her own firm stand. Of great importance was the kind of American posture in defense of liberty which occurred in the confrontation with the mother country.[31]

While Charles was heartened by American pamphlets which presented the grounds for grievances against the mother country, he was critical of them against the background of his own more radical view of the empire and provincial rights. He wanted Graves to consider the famous case for freedom from internal taxes in Maryland made by Daniel Dulany, *Consideration on the Propriety of Imposing Taxes in the British Colonies.* "It is written with the strength and solidity of argument," he wrote with generosity, "as must convince the understanding of all the unprejudiced." He even praised Dulany's presentation, which possessed a "beauty of style as cannot fail pleasing good men of taste. . . ." This was indeed high praise for the man whom he had found so vain when he conversed with him in London but a few years before. This was a strong cause that would bring the Dulanys and Carrolls together! Although Dulany was suitable fare and moderate enough for Americans and Englishmen, he was still not in the style of Charles, for Dulany would not support colonial freedom from external taxes.[32]

Two years later, John Dickinson of Pennsylvania published his famous *Letters from a Farmer in Pennsylvania to the Inhabitants of the British Colonies,* in which the Parliamentary claim to external taxation was denied. It won Charles' warmest praise, and he told his friend Graves of it. The *Letters* successfully stated the inadequate distinction between internal and external taxes, a distinction that was essential to the moderates in their efforts at living with the Declaratory Act. But again, Dickinson, as well as Dulany, fell short of Charles' restrictions on Parliamentary authority. Parliament, according to Dickinson, had a right to regulate and even suppress commerce and industry. Such a view was intolerable to Charles, who made a point of continually focusing his attack on this notion. Could it be that he had a gratuitous assumption that "America must become free and independent," and that he proceeded to rationalize to the point of irrelevance all English claims to colonial authority? This was hardly the case. He continued to read extensively on the legal and theoretical aspects of this issue. By 1768, he already had four volumes of Machen's abridgment of English statutes and sought the fifth one from Graves. More decisive, however, than anything else in the crucial decade before Independence were the authors he had read before 1765; the men who had made him a revolutionary in spirit in London— Montesquieu, Doumat, and Locke, all of whom he had read while he keenly observed the English parliamentary monarchy in action. He now integrated this intellectual ingredient into his experience of life under the Maryland constitution.[33]

In her ancient charter, first of all, he found common cause with Dickinson, and to some extent Dulany, against taxation by Parliament. "Not all the eloquence of a Mansfield," he told Graves, "can persuade us that Englishmen by leaving their country to settle these parts thereby lose the privileges of Englishmen. . . . Common Law . . . [the] most favorable to liberty we claim the invaluable privilege, that distinguishing Characteristic of the English Constitution of the taxes by our own representatives. . . ." Marylanders brought with them their assembly, which was for them what Parliament was for England. The colonies must judge for themselves; and there is no doubt that their assemblies are the last coercive force in the political structure, the final court of decision. If the ultimate authority rested in Parliament, as most Americans, and even friends of America in England held, the consequences brought tyranny. "They may go on *ad infinitum,*" he said of the ultimate logic that allowed the Stamp Act and Declaratory Act. "Allowing this unbounded power is a set of men at so great a distance so little acquainted with our circumstances, and not immediately affected with ye taxes laid upon us, what security remains for our property." The character of Parliament's membership gave little security, in any event, and the American attitude of "Prudence & Policy" toward England by moderates did not merit his support. "Men who have been so profuse and lavish with their constituent's money—will they be sparing of ours and better managers for strangers?" Even beyond these evils of property infringements, Parliament dealt carelessly with the right of trial by jury, freedom of press, and the right of petition. As for the king's ministers, Americans "would be at the mercy of every rapacious minister."[34]

This flow of radical rhetoric overwhelmed poor Graves. What

extreme liberty these Carrolls claim for their America! "America is no part of the British dominions," he said in desperation in 1770, "any more than Hanover." No, Charles would say. Dominion was possible. Maryland was bound to the king by fealty still, even if the Revolution of 1688 had created confusion in the king's position by Parliamentary usurpation. In Maryland, the majesty of the people was in their dominion according to a republican form. England by the mongrelization of 1688 had left neither monarchy nor republic. Parliamentary power had expanded in the unnatural vacuum that had resulted. British policy had drifted ever onward with increasing oppression coming upon America. Boards of customs were now established in America, in order to see that new levies were collected more effectively than previously. Writs of assistance empowered officials to draft the aid of colonists in carrying out collections. The new Townshend revenue acts were on the books and colonial protests rose against them. Again, the hopes of Americans were disappointed, as they had been with the repeal of the Stamp Act, for the new acts were repealed only to leave an abominable levy on tea. This tax proved to be the aggravation to Charles that the Declaratory Act had been as a sequel to the repeal of the Stamp Act. The Boston Massacre took place as armed enforcement by England grew: farther down the road to rebellion stood the Boston Tea Party.[35]

The explanation of America's plight to his English friends was the same for Charles: "The only dispute between us & England is whether England can take our money from us without our consent. . . ." He was able to visit the Eastern Shore of Maryland, Pennsylvania, and New York, where he sensed the general trend of unrest. The tobacco market was declining in England, although the prices rose somewhat for what shipments were made; but grain was able to command a wider market in Ireland, Portugal, and Spain, only to see a future clouded by the prospects of Parliamentary restrictions. His foreman Riggs told him of conscription in western Maryland, where England was unwilling to meet its needs even for military defenses, added to the burden of Maryland's tax contributions to the mother country. Not without vengeance, was Charles pleased with the progress of the American associations for preventing the importation of goods from England. When the *Good Intent* was turned back from Annapolis Harbor, he still had hopes that England by this economic pressure would come to her senses. When the Sons of Liberty took action at the time of passage of the Stamp Act, he was somewhat restrained, not agreeing with the harassment in which even Dulany engaged.[36]

He had his own mind about how the mob might join in the efforts at pressure on England without leaving the door open to loss of leadership by the better sort of folk. The economic boycott was best suited to the ordinary citizen's condition, since they felt the pressure as well as officials and merchants in England. The arguments for reform found in his letters to English friends were above the mob, but the boycott was levelled at its pocketbook. Appeal to their purse would win the majority's support of arguments for revising imperial policy. There was no other way. "The clamor of the People out of doors," he explained, "proceeds from their ignorance, prejudice, and passion[;] it is very difficult to get the better of these by reasoning. . . ." If America must become independent, it should do so without violence, insofar as America could choose. This was the essential mould of the revolutionary mind of the gentleman Charles Carroll of Carrollton in 1770.[37]

Chapter 13

COMPATRIOT OF REFORMERS

Before the Stamp Act, the Carroll family aligned itself with the proprietary party and the upper house of the assembly. The old Catholic counter-revolutionary society had a natural kinship with them as aristocrats, but also on ideological grounds. It was to this party that the Catholics had looked since the Revolution of 1688. Ten years before the Stamp Act, it was a fact that any mitigation of Maryland legislation against Catholics came from their efforts. The lower house, on the other hand, was controlled by their enemies. Now, however, a realignment was rapidly developing. The fresh young leadership of the lower house in the hands of Thomas Johnson, Jr., reflected a line of liberal thought which naturally attracted the sympathy of Charles Carroll of Carrollton. In political as well as religious principles he found here a compelling new alliance. He would gradually collaborate with these young liberals in private and ultimately would emerge in the public forum leading one of their attacks.

From Parliamentary tyranny as a target, he would turn to a similar infection which was developing in the Maryland branch of imperial political life. With prudent regard for the old proprietary party, he would at the same time strive to isolate its councilmen of the upper house; for they carried on a political policy which was hostile to the people's interests and to Carroll's own principles as now gaining acceptance in the lower house. So completely had Carroll been formed in his own tradition of gentility, that he could not long resist the urge to be a formative influence on his times as the ethos of his class required. He was about to find a gentleman's highest fulfillment, which was to take up a public role in the service of his provincial society.

Thomas Johnson, who was only five years older than Carroll, was not unlike him in political background. His family's coat-of-arms originated from the Restoration Era of the Stuarts, in Yarmouth, England, where his grandfather's adventure began. James Johnson, by marrying a ward of chancery, was forced to flee with his wife, Mary Baker, to St. Leonard's Creek, Maryland, in 1689. Like the Carroll Founder, he was soon in trouble with the new government, which he opposed. "All the people are rogues to the Government," he was charged with saying, "and I will never swear to any king but King James." Under these conditions he was forced to flee again, but this time without his wife. It was not until 1714 that he returned to

Maryland only to die a short time later, but not without leaving a son, Thomas, future father of Thomas Johnson, Jr. Some honor finally came to the family in this son of James, when he found a place in the lower house of the assembly and sponsored legislation in favor of better education. Thomas Johnson, Jr., was destined to bring even greater luster to the family name, but more in the rebel role of his grandfather. Thomas' father had married Dorcas Sedwick, daughter of a New England dissenting Puritan family, which had migrated to Maryland. She gave birth to Thomas on November 4, 1732. With such an energetic family background, and a tradition of aggressiveness, Johnson understandably ambitioned a place in the sun of Maryland social and political life. He was fortunate in finding a place in the law offices of Stephen Bordley, who had at one time been attorney general for the colony. In time, he came to serve as legal adviser to the most prominent gentlemen, among them the Carrolls. Particularly in the Carroll-Digges case, he collaborated with young Charles Carroll in the final settlement that was so long in coming.

When the Stamp Act was passed, Johnson, at the age of thirty-three, was in the lower house of the assembly. He served as chairman of the committee which was to respond to the governor's proclamation of the Act. His denunciation on this occasion was tempered by his role in preventing the danger of violence from the discontented western part of the province. Other young men of like mind were with him in the lower house at this time: William Paca, John Hall, and Charles Carroll the Barrister, who was the son of Dr. Charles Carroll, leader of the double-tax legislation.[1]

Hardly had the cry "no taxation without representation" died down after the repeal of the Stamp Act, when a similar arbitrary measure was contrived by the governor and the upper house. He established the amount of fees by proclamation. These fees were taxes, Johnson responded, as Lord Coke had clearly shown. The right of the lower house was therefore violated by the governor's action. The chamber looked to the leadership of Johnson, and his speech served as a remonstrance to be delivered to the governor in its name. In addition to allies from the time of the Stamp Act controversy, he now counted other young men, notably Samuel Chase, son of the rector of St. Paul's Church, Baltimore, who had inveighed against Catholics at the time of the double-tax legislation. "This act of power," the remonstrance stated, "is founded on the destruction of constitutional security." It was a far greater threat than Parliament's recent action, striking as it did at the very heart of provincial life. When Johnson concluded his speech on November 23, 1771, no legislative counter-move against the fee proclamation was possible because the governor prorogued the assembly.[2]

The governor rightly feared the young insurgents. They were brilliant in their oratory, but also profound in the issues they chose to make and the ground upon which they argued them. "I have frequently heard subjects debated," William Eddis, a high official of the governor, observed, "with great power of eloquence and force of reason; and the utmost regularity and propriety distinguished the whole of their proceedings." Johnson, Paca, Chase, and their associates were gentlemen dressed in the style of Carroll's revolutionary thought and civility. For all of his intensity of conviction and oratory, a friend found Johnson "a most social, joyous, companionable man." His law office was an open caucus to the young patriots. The same observer's overwrought doggerel still managed to convey the portrait of an intellectual not unlike Carroll:

> Seldom he smiles, and smiles in such a sort
> As if he mock'd himself, and scorn'd his spirit,
> That cou'd be mov'd to smile at anything.[3]

The anonymous observer and writer in the *Maryland Gazette* saw Carroll united in spirit and action with the others whom he identified as a group and described individually. "The transparency of his ideas, the brilliancy of his fancy, the graceful flow of his elocution," he says of William Paca, made all look forward to his "caper . . . on our political theatre." His politeness and tolerance appealed to Carroll as well as the background which had created both of these traits. He seems to have been from a family of Italian origin, which came to America in the latter part of the seventeenth century. After a time in Bordley's law offices, about the time that Johnson was there, he went to Inner Temple, London, and returned a year before Carroll, who may have met him among his fellow provincial law students. He came to the lower house in 1768. His marriage to Henrietta Maria Lloyd Chew brought him into the first families of Maryland society. Paca was a frequent visitor to Doughoregan Manor and socialized with Carroll at Annapolis.[4]

"Both of us were brought up in revolution principles," the *Gazette* observer noted of Samuel Chase, another member of Carroll's patriot group. This attachment was undoubtedly due to instructions in the classics of ancient Greece and Rome under his father, Reverend Thomas Chase, rector of St. Paul's Church, Baltimore. The law offices of Hammond and Hall gave him his legal education as well as a useful entrée to politics. John Hammond had succeeded to the leadership of the lower house after Charles Carroll had passed from the scene. Chase was perhaps not as suitable a companion for Carroll as were Paca and Johnson. "We were early cronies," the *Gazette* observer explains on this point. "Many a game have we played at five corns, an exercise ominous of our future enterprises." Carroll was only tolerant of card-playing, which tended to take him from his books and more refined conversation. From the viewpoint of the mayor and aldermen of Annapolis, in another setting, Chase was seen "as a busy, restless incendiary, a ringleader of mobs, a foul-mouthed and inflaming son of discord." Carroll might well have found this side of Chase's personality reminiscent of the relentlessly hostile Anglican preacher of St. Paul's; but there is no reason to believe his judgment so harsh as the mayor's. Chase viewed such critics as the mayor to be "despicable tools of power, emerged from obscurity and basking in proprietary sunshine." His remarkable talent and energy were recognized and esteemed by Carroll, who probably saw that a share in the sun of civic life would mollify a harsh element in his character. The Carrolls understood, too, that Chase was not blessed with a fortune as a parson's son by his marriage to Anne Baldwin. Although from his defensive posture he was given to display beyond his means, as shown in the case of his Annapolis mansion which he was forced to sell, the Carrolls considered him responsible and promising enough to loan him money needed in his various financial crises. Perhaps the elder Carroll was initially pried loose of a loan by a game of "five corns" with Chase.[5]

The question of tax for the support of the clergy ironically fell to Chase and Paca as one of the targets singled out by these young insurgent friends of Carroll. Chase and his associates were bent upon reducing his father's annual salary. The controversy, which began shortly after the Stamp Act crisis, went beyond the question of removing the 40 per poll [pound per citizen] tobacco tax for the support of the clergy. The whole nature and justification of the

Established Church came under examination. The clergy and the upper house responded by *ad hominem* arguments, charging that Paca and Chase were being led astray by their Romish associate Carroll. Fundamental stands on the nature and practices of religious freedom ultimately took place. But here, as in the fee case, the patriots sought with some success to isolate the governor from the upper house partisans and the clergy.[6]

As early as 1767, Reverend Jonathan Boucher, sensing the militant mood of the lower house, urged Governor Sharpe to petition a bishop for Maryland. However, Hammersley, the governor's chief adviser, believed that this action would lead to a form of establishment which was contrary to the Maryland Charter of 1632. The response of Chase and Paca, as well as that of the lower house, was immediate. The following year, they proposed that the power of supervision and removal of clergy be given to the lower house. Although they ultimately succeeded in passing this measure into law, it was never enforced. The Anglican clergy hastened to make their case against the legislation on the grounds of early Maryland law which provided for the privileges of "Holy Mother Church." It was contended that the phrase meant only the Church of England in its exact form as found in the mother country. The laws passed under William and Mary strove to fix more exactly ecclesiastical structures in Maryland in this spirit. They were favored by Boucher: but were declared by some to be invalid, since they were actually passed by Parliament after the end of this reign. The same was true, it was said, with regard to the 40 per poll tax which the clergy had enjoyed. Defenders of the *status quo* attacked the Paca and Chase group as advocates of anarchy and "Gentlemen of the New Regulation."[7]

Boucher and his partisans appealed to the governor for support. They fully realized that he was besieged by the lay gentry, who sought in the aid of the lower house protection and expansion of their power as vestrymen. Action to lower the clergy tax, on the other hand, was a token of this enlarged role of the lay vestry. In November, 1771, Boucher understandably complained to the governor of this turn of events, especially since the upper house, out of interest in lay vestry power and contrary to its traditional alignment, supported the policy of Paca and Chase in the lower house. "Former gov[erno]rs used to Place the Councill [upper house] as a Screen between themselves & the People," Boucher complained, "The case is [now] reversed." The acquisition of a bishop was clearly out of the question, it is true, but there was sentiment in favor of the 40 per poll tax that should have prevailed, at least with the governor and upper house. Carroll's father, and possibly Carroll himself, considered the cut of the clergy's salary imprudent, particularly in view of the harsh language generated by the legislation. "We may publickly disapprove," the elder Carroll said of Boucher's stronger church establishment, "but not in such harsh language, because it may be prejudiciall to us without answering any good End. . . ." The conclusion of this controversy as well as the fee question was not within sight as far as Carroll was concerned in 1771. Common principles, however, now bound him to Chase and Paca and to the corporate leadership of the patriots, who had to forge ahead according to their own lights. Paca and Chase in 1772 made it clear that the laity's notion of the Maryland Church differed radically from that of Boucher. The difference moved them far closer to the view of Maryland law and establishment which had been the tradition of the Catholic counter-revolutionary society, as well as Maryland society in general before the Revolution of 1688. There is little reason to doubt that Carroll and the patriots were undergoing a process of mutual enlightenment.[8]

Carroll's patriot group, then, gave focus to the two fundamental issues of freedom in the turmoil of Maryland politics following the Stamp Act. Their intelligence and conviction drew a wide following among the gentry. Of the younger men, two distant cousins of Carroll were more immediately under his influence—Charles Carroll the Barrister and Daniel Carroll. The role of Carroll's father in the trusteeship of the Barrister's estate during his minority smoothed over the relationships of the two families, which had become alienated at the time of the double-tax controversy of the 1750's. The developing liberal atmosphere after 1765 brought Carroll and the Barrister even closer together. The latter had served on the committee of the lower house which acted against the Stamp Act. In 1771, he was in England and exchanged letters with Carroll which revealed the growing unity of mind of the young patriots. The Barrister's estimate of the Wilkes case, which Carroll himself followed in its earliest chapter of 1764-1765 while he was in London, had agreed with Carroll's. The arbitrary way in which Parliament dealt with Wilkes, the Barrister now reported, showed "subversion of liberty [to be] an easy task. . . ." This experience of England in 1771 would make him a formidable ally of Carroll, who had an even fuller knowledge of the deteriorating conditions of England. Daniel Carroll, who was also in England at this time, became one of the more influential members of the Catholic gentry. He was also a great admirer of Johnson and present at his defense of the Carroll case with Digges of a few years before. Carroll spoke freely to Daniel as well as to the Barrister about his republican principles, confident of their strong common bond.[9]

There was political congeniality and hospitality shared with others on the stage of the rapidly moving drama in Maryland. Robert Goldsborough from the Eastern Shore was often invited to Doughoregan Manor. John Hall of Annapolis was another young friend in the lower house. Johnson, on occasion, brought other men like Tilghman with him on his visits to the Carroll "country retreat." Carroll's father had long-standing ties of friendship and political interest with older men in Maryland politics as well, and Carroll fell heir to their sympathetic hearing. Most important of these was John Hammond, who proved closest to the young patriots. He was far more temperate, however, than Paca in his differences over the Established Church and its clergy. The anonymous observer writing in the *Gazette*, he said, went too far in describing his opposition. The facetious speech attributed to him was fictitious. His wit would never lead him, as was falsely reported, to say that the clergy would be limited not only to a lower tobacco tax but to a restricted quota of three children in their families. Nor did he threaten them with Romish celibacy as an extreme penalty. In 1771 and 1772, Carroll's father did not put much reliance on the collaboration of Major Henry Ridgely, who had defaulted on a promise to attend a fee inspection caucus. Major Daniel of St. Thomas Jennifer always remained a long and fast friend of the Carrolls, but his sentiments generally rested with the upper house. His support, however, might easily shift the scales at a crucial moment because of his eminence among the gentry in politics.[10]

Never for a moment did the patriot group view itself as a faction or party. Their detestation of that epithet stemmed from its embodiment in the corrupt politics of Parliament. The mainspring of their concern for the public good was well defined in their defense of the lower house's privileges as the protector and voice of the people. This was, after all, the foundation of the British Constitution, as Carroll so often said. Faction reared its head only where selfish interest of men and groups was found. It is for this reason that the beneficiaries of fees from patronage and the established clergy from the per poll tax came under attack as an odious party faction. Interest with its evil connotation arose from taking these benefits, with ultimate harm to the people's welfare. Distortion of the constitution and usurpation of authority, in order to bring such benefits, were the clear sign of the man of interest. The debate as a result of these assumptions by the patriots combined the two elements of legal reasoning and rhetorical invective. The opponents of the patriots could and did respond in kind. On the score of interest, it had to be shown that one or another of the patriots was disappointed in his pursuit of interest, particularly as it derived from proprietary appointments. Except for Chase, it was not plausible to argue that the patriots constituted an underprivileged group, bent upon more favorable tax arrangements for their class by means of assembly action. From this standpoint, therefore, the contest on the two provincial issues of clergy tax and fees by proclamation stood on purer motivation than the complaints against the tax and commercial restrictions by Parliament.

Nothing revealed this subtlety of notions about faction and interest more than the great care Carroll and the patriots took to respect the proprietary leadership of the governor, while they attacked defenders of the fee and clergy bills. For Carroll, consideration of the governor was even more paramount than for the other patriots. His own Catholic counter-revolutionary tradition made him see that defense of his religious freedom had been accomplished in the past through the governor and his councilmen in the upper house in the face of mob influence on the lower house. He did not want to subvert this feature of the constitution's checks and balances while more fully establishing the authority of the lower house as the representative of the people. What made the task doubly difficult for Carroll was the position of Dulany in reference to the governor and the principles at issue in the debate. In the Stamp Act controversy, Dulany's pamphlet embodied the patriots' case to a large extent. Shortly after this, however, he defended the governor's right to duties on exports of tobacco. Yet he did not appear a man of interest and faction until after 1770, when he sought patronage and supported the governor's fee proclamation. His pursuit of influence with the governor and proprietor was extremely visible; but, under Governor Eden, his acceptability with both declined. Carroll, on the other hand, was emerging from a personal vendetta with the Dulanys, which had sprung from a business conflict within the Baltimore Iron Works. It was not easy to leave the governor above reproach in his attack on Dulany. The latter's anti-patriot stand after 1770 only added to Carroll's hostility. In view of Carroll's distress at the governor's imprudence with regard to Molly Carroll, he found it difficult to prevent his attack on Dulany from adding to the alienation.[11]

Nevertheless, with public spirit, Carroll proceeded to make his way through this maze. In May of 1770, he felt free to go directly to Governor Eden for sound information in the wake of rumors regarding the death of Lord Baltimore. Carroll concurred, although reluctantly, with Eden's desire to discuss the Digges case while it was pending in court. Such a mingling of the executive with the judicial was not wholly consistent with Carroll's position; but his father urged him to use the occasion to bring out the value of Johnson's plea for the Carrolls, which the governor apparently had not yet appreciated. Carroll was not necessarily an exception among the patriots by the way the governor freely approached him on such matters in the middle of 1771. Always more insistent on civility than even the governor and those closest to him were, he still found it a trial to be at the social affairs provided by the governor and his wife at White Hall. Carroll had to view Dulany wrestling with DeButte in a "drunken frolic," which was a diversion from Dulany's more dangerous intentions toward the Carrolls and the patriots. "He is perhaps brooding schemes of mischieve and Plans of crooked policy," Carroll said of him at the time the brawl took place. Mrs. Eden's miscarriage from the excitement of Dulany's frolic was even more distressing to Molly, who was one of her best friends. The annoyances between Carroll and the governor, however, were often mitigated by the affection of Mrs. Eden for the family. The hospitality of Doughoregan was often proffered in 1771 and 1772. If the governor and his brother cannot come, the senior Carroll would urge, let Mrs. Eden feel free to come.[12]

To his friends, Carroll did not conceal the tedium of maintaining this difficult relationship with Eden. "I think our politicians," he told Carroll the Barrister regarding Eden's court, "are as contemptible, & more pernicious than those in England." It was they who had egged Eden into the proclamation on fees. He did not want to put all of the blame on Eden himself. "War is now declared between Governm[en]t. & People," he explained, "or rather between a few placemen the real enemies to Governm[en]t. & all the inhabitants of this province." These men, however, were a danger because of the "fickle behaviour" of the governor. Understandably, Carroll needed encouragement to endure such company and traffic. His father was at hand with the familiar reflections which he had once offered to the young law scholar of Bourges and London: "You may Resolve to live in a desert if you will not generally Associate with the foolish Ficle mean spirited Men." Mere passivity was not recommended. Personal insult or denial of rights had to be courageously opposed, even under such trying circumstances. Only a man who was above faction and interest would have heeded such advice. Carroll, as a master of civility in the best traditions of gentility, was able to meet these demands with poise and prudence. Small wonder that the patriots honored such leadership![13]

Carroll moved among the various groups in conflict over the fee and clergy questions. In the Homony Club, at the Jockey Club during the racing season, and at other social occasions, he freely expressed his views according to the circumstances. He was gradually moving toward a decision as to how much more he should do in promoting the policies of the patriots. Before 1773, he was clearly under the influence of his father in this matter. Carroll esteemed him as a man possessed of a "spirit of youth & understanding of a man of 40." "He is the comfort of my life," he said. The elder Carroll was intensely interested in the fee and related questions, taking a public stand on these matters. In the fall of 1770, the *Maryland Gazette* took critical note of the tobacco fees of £1000 to £1500 that annually went to the provincial secretary. The clerk of the land office made profits as much as £1800. When the governor's proclamation called for fees of £600 for some offices, the elder Carroll believed that they would be taken for £300. Consequently, he had nothing but praise for the patriots, who attacked this fee structure. From other sources, he learned that more exorbitant fee returns were gained by others, relatives of the proprietor among them. In October of 1770, he took a dim view of the lower house's hope of reforming the fee structure as established by the proclamation.[14]

The assembly very likely would not probe into the conditions of sale connected with clerkships which had claims on fees: All feared Dulany, who would make reprisals on the leaders of such an inquiry. Carroll, his father believed, had the public spirit to expose this condition, perhaps spurred by his personal contempt for Dulany and resentment at his obstructive role. "It would not become you to promote it," Carroll's father told him, however, cautious in the face of Dulany's power. Father and son, often meeting at Doughoregan, weighed decisions in this and related matters. Exchanging English magazines, they continued to keep abreast of conditions in England that were similar to those they decried in Maryland. Ministers in England were the counterpart of the Maryland placemen of Dulany. "In my opinion," Carroll's father wrote to his son, "an Honest man Can hardly be found among any of them." The upper house was so corrupt that they thought the whole assembly like themselves. They were "Insolent in presuming th[a]t the Representatives of the People would demean themselves so much as to Enter into any treaty with them" on the fee proclamation.[15]

While the elder Carroll urged his son to refrain from public involvement in the fee questions and related matters, he did not follow such advice in his own case. In 1771, he collaborated in an extra-legal gathering which was to supply a voluntary system of regulating tobacco fees in view of the assembly's inability to arrive at a tobacco inspection bill for this purpose. In April, a meeting was planned for his own neighborhood at Elk Ridge outside Baltimore. The elder Carroll was urged by people of the area to attend. Similar meetings had already taken place elsewhere in the province, and he was enthusiastic about these endeavors at preventing arbitrary action by the governor and council. He believed that the influential Major Henry Ridgely was in sympathy with this kind of pressure and won an initial promise from him to attend the Elk Ridge meeting, although he was ultimately disappointed. The meeting of about forty gentlemen, which ultimately took place in the middle of the month, proved a failure. "Had I not seen it," he reported to his son, "I Could not have Believed the People Here to be so indifferent about a matter which so much concerns th[e]m."[16]

Carroll did not agree with his father's interpretation of Ridgely's conduct or the lack of determination in those attending the meeting. The device, not the people involved, was to blame. He had earlier observed a similar meeting at East River and found it unpromising. There was reason to believe that he wrote against such an extra-legal device in the *Maryland Gazette* in early March. At least he himself accepted the opinion expressed there. Such a voluntary convention to fix tobacco prices and fees had the "Force of club law." Maryland's legal structure called for reform by action within it; for her society and political form were fundamentally sound, unlike the condition of England. The present case was entirely different from the voluntary associations formed to resist restrictions on provincial commerce by the corrupt mother country. "Frequent associations of individuals," it was written in the *Gazette,* "are critical symbols of a sick commonweal. . . ." So Voltaire himself had observed. They were not appropriate to Maryland, therefore, and they might well turn the reform movement down the wrong road. This reasoning rested on Carroll's cyclical theory of history. While the mother country was in a state of decay, Maryland by contrast was on an upward course. If left sufficiently independent of the mother country, it would come to an even healthier republican condition. An enlightened and public-spirited elite, above factionalism and interest, could lead Maryland to such a reform; and do so without such an extra-legal device as the tobacco inspection meeting. By the end of the year, Carroll's father agreed with him that a legal tobacco inspection bill with fees established by the assembly of the people was what the colony needed and could get.[17]

This measure and the clergy legislation were all getting the continued attention of Johnson, Chase, and Paca in the political arena, at whose edge young Carroll stood as a frequent adviser. At the close of 1772, he was fully aware of this rôle; and so was his father. Although Carroll might overlook a meeting of the governor's grand council, he never forgot the grand councils of the patriots. Their deliberations and articulations must now pass beyond stated concern for principles to their effect in reforming the Maryland Assembly. Only then would the assembly become truly the servant of the people and the guardian of their liberty. Carroll now became more sensitive and penetrating in his diagnosis of the tensions between the upper and lower houses simply because he was increasingly involved in the political ferment which arose from these tensions. In 1773, he was destined to move from the edge of the political arena to its very center, there to lead the patriots and general public in the reform movement.[18]

Daniel Dulany, his own fortunes in decline with the governor and proprietor, suffered further deterioration from the fee proclamation controversy since he was considered its author. In January of 1773, he was, therefore, determined to make a public defense of the proclamation of fees. On the face of it he was defending the upper house; in reality he was defending himself as ministerial adviser of the governor who proclaimed the law. On January 7 the *Maryland Gazette* carried his dialogue between two citizens. With legal reasoning the objections of "First Citizen" to the fee proclamation were pedantically answered by "Second Citizen." The fixing of fees by proclamation, he argued, removed the danger of arbitrary action by governmental officials. The courts could now readily adjudicate any injustices from officers in their collections. The good of the people would therefore be safeguarded. Beginning in England in the seventeenth century, there were adequate precedents for proclamations of this kind. The patriot critics by their irresponsible attacks thus impugned the dignity of the governor and the upper house and threatened to subvert the order of the province. No sound legal grounds supported their pernicious attacks.[19]

There was an understandable urgency in the plea of Dulany, for the assembly was due to convene in February. Supporters of the clergy 40 per poll tax were in the same position. "A Freeholder" from St. Anne's Parish at Annapolis had already taken issue with the reasoning of Chase and Paca the previous year. How could the power of the vestry be vindicated by the force of custom, as the patriots claimed, since seventeenth-century Maryland law never even authorized the existence of vestries, let alone indicated how they should function in the province. The law of 1702 purportedly establishing them was invalid. On February 4, 1773, Boucher himself without pseudonym fired another salvo at the patriots. What kind of meaning was given to force of law by custom? The censuring of Maryland clergy by the patriots, furthermore, was redolent of anticlericalism. Respect for the priesthood, Boucher argued, carried with it acceptance of the office of bishop, which he now advocated for the province.[20]

The strategy of the patriots at this juncture was predictable, except for one maneuver which proved crucial. It was not wise to enlist Paca and Chase as respondents to Dulany; for this would load the fee proclamation question with the liabilities of the clergy controversy, which had now been fixed on Chase and Paca by Boucher and his partisans. Thomas Johnson, on the other hand, had already spoken and written against the fee proclamation. A new voice, supported by the same degree of learning and literacy, was needed; and the one to whom it belonged would have to demonstrate by his conduct of debate that he was not infected with factionalism and interest. Some tolerance of him by the governor, at least initially, was also required. He must have the sense of civility and propriety which would make him equal to isolating Dulany from the governor and allow a respectable demise of the fee measure.

Carroll did not need any formal caucus to understand the opening into public discussion which now came before him. Nor did the patriots fail to sense that Carroll's hour had arrived. From his conversations with Johnson, Chase, and Paca individually, he was made to understand, as he already saw, that he must move into the arena with the patriots. His father, furthermore, provided him further understanding of the sophisticated political situation which confronted him, for he had occasions to consult with these men, often as a group. Carroll's highly refined sense of civility in this situation was predictable against the background of his writings and well established expressions of gentility. He saw that he was called to civic leadership at last. It was therefore no surprise when the February 4 issue of the *Gazette,* which carried Boucher's irritated letter, also contained a longer one from Carroll under a pseudonym. The scope which it gave to his learning and literacy left no doubt as he rose to the occasion that "First Citizen" was Charles Carroll of Carrollton. Dulany's dialogue had provided Carroll's pseudonym as well as an outlet for his long maturing reflections carried in a highly developed literary style and taste.

In keeping with his own intellectual background and reforming instinct, Carroll delivered an incisive stroke at the principal behind the fee proclamation. Misled by his minister Dulany and the council, Carroll charged, Governor Eden had usurped the legislative and tax power of the people as reposing in the lower house. Eden had believed, on the other hand, that courts would according to his plan give the citizen the necessary safeguards for his fee system. But the judges as the governor's appointees were poor promise of an independent judicial authority when they sat before officers similarly appointed and now claiming fees. Tacitus in ancient times, Carroll explained, had shown that government to be effective need not destroy liberty; but it surely would if the executive was not divided from the judicial and legislative authorities, as in the present arrangement of fees by proclamation. The advising minister, however, and not the governor, should have borne the blame for the present mischief. Somewhat by analogy to the legal dictum "the king can do no wrong," the minister from whom the fee proclamation came was guilty, not the governor whom he advised. Carroll's attack, therefore, fell on Dulany. Carroll must make his charge from civic duty, for the life of the constitution was threatened by the present disruption in an essential balance of power. There can be little doubt, furthermore, that the fees were truly taxes; and therefore they should have originated in the lower house, rather than in a governor's proclamation. Using the historian Hume, whose volumes he had possessed and read for some time, he cited historical vindication of this power of taxation in the assembly of the people. It is the counterpart of Parliament, which had once defended its authority against attempted abridgments by the Stuart kings. Neither Lord Camden, nor any other authors Dulany might have cared to quote could subvert such an essential, constitutional principle as the right of taxation by the assembly representatives alone. "They have declared that to be legal," Carroll said sardonically of Dulany's authorities, "which the minister for the time being has deemed to be expedient."[21]

The following week, in the February 11 issue of the *Gazette,* the patriots under the name of Independent Whigs commended "First Citizen" for his urbane and penetrating treatment of the fee question. The patriots now had a name. In the eyes of their adversaries and the public in general, Carroll was a compatriot in the ranks of the Independent Whigs. "Junius" in the same publication complimented Carroll while he deplored the scurrility of Dulany. "An honest man," he wrote of Carroll, "like the true religion, appeals to the understanding, or modestly confides in the internal evidence of his conscience." Elsewhere in the issue, Johnson defended the reasoning of Chase and Paca in their interpretation of precedent and custom against Boucher's reasoning. While the vestry was not found in seventeenth-century Maryland, the province legitimately adapted it from long usage in the mother country. Paca, writing under his own name, further clarified his argument for the legality of the vestry from custom and noted that both Johnson and Robert Goldsborough approved of his view. He would also demonstrate with letters that he was not motivated by interest: for some had said that he was spiteful at having been denied an office of profit and trust by the proprietary government. It was now clear that the patriots had the name of Independent Whigs and could claim Carroll for their ranks.[22]

To no one's surprise, Dulany soon came back in response to "First Citizen" and to other pressure by the Whigs. He became further mired when he reasoned about precedence for fees by proclamation. By trying to deny fees to be in reality a tax on the people and therefore under assembly jurisdiction, he only intensified popular concern over the case which Carroll was making. He tried to insinuate that Carroll was secretly in sympathy with the Stuarts, even where Carroll criticized them for their arbitrary tax of ship money and dealing with the Church of England. Dulany obviously had to move on to new ground, mucky though it might be. Carroll was tied up with the Independent Whigs and their case against the clergy, Dulany would now say.

The Whigs trafficked with a son of Saint Omers, "the best seminary in the universe of the champions of civil and religious liberty. . . ." The result would be disestablishment of religion, accomplished with a papist's connivance. The Whigs should know the consequences which the career of Carroll's father less than two decades ago would show. He then "nearly brought on a relentless persecution against all of the same religious profession." The collaboration of the Catholic counter-revolutionary society of Carroll with the Independent Whigs, Dulany may have realized, took place in a far different setting of sentiment and principle from that which prevailed in the 1750's for his father. It was as "champion of civil and religious liberty," as Dulany with unknowing prophecy brought out, that the Whigs joined Carroll, while Carroll's role was with the fee question. Dulany was right in seeing Carroll satisfied with the alliance grounded on these principles and the subtly distinct roles of the other Whigs and Carroll. Dulany's reckless attack ultimately threw favorable light on the relationship as far as the public was concerned. As events proved, the public, like the Whigs, had shed much of the religious narrowness of their forebears.[23]

"Protestant Whig," writing in the *Gazette* at this time, unwittingly revealed that the Dulany faction was losing the argument. At the same time, he too turned to sarcasm and scurrility to keep others from supporting the Whigs. "The Holy inquisition of Jesuits and Independent Whigs," he said, "have so put the question that to speak in the words of Friar Bernard Deliciasi on a like subject, 'even St.

Peter and St. Paul, if they were now alive, if inquisition were made against them, according to the manner used by these inquisitors, could not defend themselves from heresy.[']" The turn to *ad hominem* arguments was inevitable, as Dulany's case proved more and more unpopular. He grasped at an obvious handle which was the legal incapacity of Carroll as a Catholic to have such an influence on a public question. The risk in Dulany's procedure was a backlash similar to what occurred when Boucher revealed his ambitions for a bishop. The "Antilon"-"First Citizen" controversy was testing the public depth of tolerance as well as sentiment against civil disabilities for religious reasons. When Paca and Chase in the March 11 issue of the *Gazette* put further pressure against Boucher's case for a stricter establishment of religion, Carroll's position as a tolerated Catholic was strengthened; so too his right to speak on public questions. Paca and Chase now had the official petition for a bishop published. In rather harsh terms the seven clergymen who signed it along with Boucher inveighed against Presbyterians in the Anglican parishes for complicity in this Whig maneuver. This antagonized important gentlemen of the vestries and also awakened active opposition among Presbyterians, Baptists, and other "sectaries" who feared that the spirit of intolerance for Catholics by some Anglicans would now soon fall on themselves as well. Paca in this issue wrote an explanation of his dissent from Boucher, saying that it was not founded on anti-clericalism as charged. Rather, a liberal sense of religious and civil liberty inspired him. Interaction of these issues, therefore, with Carroll's fee case continued to deepen the bond of principles and personalities among the Independent Whigs.[25]

Carroll responded to Dulany in the same March 11 issue of the *Gazette*. He was not distracted by Dulany's personal invective, but was anxious to strengthen and clarify his claim that the Maryland Assembly by the fee proclamation was being twisted further out of its natural shape as a representative of the people. Dulany had challenged the authority of Carroll to delve into such advanced political theory. The upper house, Carroll now explained, was not a true replica of Parliament in the province; but only the lower house truly represented the people, which is the fundamental intent of the English constitution for Parliament. (He put aside consideration of defects in the House of Lords, which would have made his parallel reasoning clearer.) On the other hand, the lower house was now obstructed in its proper role. "The legislature of this province," he explained, "wants [lacks] in its two first branches (from the independent condition of the Governor and the council [who compose the upper house]) a good deal of the freedom which is necessary to the legislature of a free country, and on this account, our constitution is defective in point of the legislature." Carroll said that the writings of an anonymous author on the Jamaican Assembly had led him to understand these defects, which he saw in his own provincial constitution at the present time. Because of this condition in the assembly, the balance of power between the executive, legislature, and judiciary had been overturned. The fee proclamation was the most striking revelation of these evils. One needed only to consult Montesquieu, as Carroll and the Jamaican author had done, to see the dangerous consequences of this imbalance. "There is no liberty," Carroll said in a quotation from Montesquieu, "if the power of judging be not separated from the legislative and executive powers." These were the good authorities for whom Dulany had asked; and he could have discerned them beneath the lines of Carroll's reasoning, if he had grasped them.[26]

In the polemical style which the debate naturally took, Carroll defended his father with poetic piety drawn from Alexander Pope. While Carroll's writings were his own, and not his father's or the Independent Whigs', he was not ashamed of his parental ties, contrary to Dulany's view of them. He then took up some of the technicalities of legal history and showed Dulany's misinterpretations of them or of the use Carroll has made of them. In various places throughout his letter, there was found abrasive rhetoric. The image of himself as a knight wounded by foul play was also employed. It was apparent that he did not think that Dulany would carry his invective into another installment, giving him credit for good judgment on how far one might go with such polemics. The central issue could bear nothing new from further exchanges. Only repetition and quibbling over technicalities in their respective erudition would result.[27]

There is an unmistakable air of satisfaction and sureness in this second letter of Carroll. His aspirations as a gentleman who had found an honorable, if precarious, rôle in the improvement of society seemed to have reached initial fulfillment. The two installments of "First Citizen" gave tribute to the many years of study, reflection, and cultivation of a highly literate sense of expression. His revolutionary thought had led him to discover a course leading around the parliamentary morass in which England was mired. The stump of the English Constitution was rotted, it was true; but the transplanted branch of the once vigorous tree in Maryland might yet be set upon an upright growth. The nurturing hands of the public-spirited men with whom he now collaborated as Independent Whigs were zealously at the task.

Chapter 14

EMERGING REVOLUTIONARY LEADER

If Dulany had been riding high in proprietary favor, the conflict with Carroll in the *Gazette* would not have continued. As things were, he had nothing to lose in his effort at discrediting Carroll by the questionable means common to political polemics. Second class citizen Carroll, playing the rôle of "First Citizen," continued to provide the only target available to his opponent. Dulany hoped to win public favor by attacking Carroll as a Catholic in compensation for his declining fortune in the fee debate itself. Through Carroll he would discredit his associates, the Independent Whigs. The Catholic would inevitably appear the leader of the Whig movement, or at least stand as an unworthy and insidious influence on it. Those who were losing ground in their support of the clergy per poll tax and in their quest for a bishop wanted to see Dulany succeed in discrediting Carroll. This would damage the popularity of his fellow Whigs, Paca and Chase, the authors of the anti-clergy legislation as well. Dulany would then salvage some favor with the governor and the proprietary party, who otherwise had a right to think he had sold them a bill of goods in the fees by proclamation measure. The accuracy of these predictions remained to be determined by the outcome of further debate with Carroll, which Dulany decided to take up once again.

It was not strange that at this juncture the forces of Carroll formed even closer bonds. By March 17, Carroll had sent questions to Paca and Chase and was awaiting their advice on the next phase of the controversy. They were expected at Doughoregan for dinner on their way back to Annapolis from Frederick. Both were about to publish another installment of their own controversy with Boucher and wanted his advice as well. Johnson, Chase, and Tilghman had dined at Doughoregan a few days before and discussed "First Citizen's" most recent letter, which won their unqualified approbation. Another meeting was held a few days later. James Howard was another caller. He told of the great impact Carroll made by his reasoning and peroration. Howard believed that many were ready to come over to Carroll's side in the future who were at the moment fearful of openly favoring his case. "First Citizen," however, found the greatest satisfaction in his father's praise. His gentlemanly restraint in the face of Dulany's abusive remarks was admirable. "I cannot shew my Approbation of y[ou]r Piece better," he said, "than by wishing that you may with good Health live to see a Son think as you do & express His thoughts with y[ou]r force[,] Elegance and Ease, shou[l]d that Happen to you[, you] will be sensible of the Pleasure I feel."[1]

Carroll clearly understood that his alliances complicated his own role. The Independent Whigs continued to write, as Paca and Chase, under their own names took up their counterattack against Boucher. They now founded the right to vestry on natural law, derived as it was from common law and the assembly as the representatives of the people. "Plain Truth" in veiled terms made indirect criticism of Carroll in the *Gazette;* although Boucher, writing in the same March 18 issue, did not make reference to him. A week later, however, "Clericus" combined the clergy and fee controversy, and poured bitter invective on Carroll. "It is quite consistent too, as you observe, for the confederacy [Independent Whigs] to maintain a chaplain of this same holy order of Jesus [Jesuits], as well as for the good of their country, as their own ghostly consolation. . . . He may furnish them with many important hints, toward the furtherance of their grand work, or rooting out the protestant establishment of this priest-ridden province." The "patriotic nursling" of St. Omers did not go without mention.[2]

The Carrolls were much disturbed by this turn in the controversy, inevitable as it seemed to be. Paca continued his arguments in these issues and Boucher finally made a mild reference to Carroll where "First Citizen" spoke of the tyranny of King James II in dealing with the Church of England. All of this was enough to implicate Carroll in the establishment controversy. The Carrolls were now exasperated with Boucher; for they learned that he had obtained confidential information from a person who attended the conversation of the governor with Chase and Paca. The series of miscellaneous writers at this time revealed the broadening effect of the controversy Carroll had chosen to precipitate out of a sense of public spirit. His response to the growing conflict was to lay in more ammunition for the predictable battle ahead—books, magazines, and advice from his Whig friends. He was, at the same time, assured by the favorable reaction of the general public to his argumentation in the *Gazette.* Jennifer, Rideout, Cook, and others gave him encouragement; and "First Citizen" was discussed with open admiration at the county court session.[3]

In spite of the embroilment with the governor's fee proclamation, the Carrolls strove to maintain their connections with him and the proprietary party in general. Daniel of St. Thomas Jennifer, an old friend, stood high in influence with the proprietary party, the governor, and even the council and upper house membership. He thus continued to hold a safe entering point into this official circle. "Antillon will be totally eclipsed by the Shield of the man with the long name," Jennifer wrote in praise of Carroll's Second Letter. "Your Son is a most flaming Patriot, and a red hot politician," he told Carroll's father. He frankly confessed, however, that he had strong reservations on the son's policy. Jennifer was more interested in the appointment of Americans to provincial offices and wanted legislation to that effect. While the exaction of fees was often unjust, he did not think that the maneuver of Carroll and the Whigs was advisable. Carroll's father observed that Jennifer was too interested in protecting a few officers whom he felt were not guilty of abuse. Jennifer, at least, was not clearly on the side of Dulany and this was a hopeful situation.[4]

Carroll personally communicated and visited with the governor during the period after his Second Letter. In the fluctuating atmosphere it was a tedious, if necessary, activity. Information on the rumored death of Lord Baltimore and other occasions might be used to keep up contact. It was in this way that he could estimate the effect of the controversy on Governor Eden. Carroll's father believed Eden to be a "Courtier." "Yet he would follow His owne opinion if His officials did not determin[e] him to follow ye opinion of others." It was in this situation that Jennifer was to be of help by showing Eden letters from the Carrolls which represented their view of matters beyond what was taken up in the *Gazette*. Shortly after publication of the Second Letter, Carroll made an attempt at visiting the governor alone. In the normal social life of Annapolis, he had other opportunities to visit with him, even if briefly, this in spite of the near crisis which his impropriety with Molly Carroll had created. There was even some evidence now that the governor was looking for a compromise. Dulany was studying the possibility of revising the legislation on fees in the face of the attack by the lower house and the growing unpopularity of his case. The violent opposition recently awakened on the Eastern Shore by the *Gazette* controversy was a clear sign to read, if he was not stubborn. Perhaps time would allow for the repair of Dulany, now regarded by the elder Carroll as a calumniator.[5]

About April 1, Carroll, the "First Citizen," rode to Dulany Mansion to meet Antilon. Old Dulany looked hardy and spoke of plans to go to Canada. He was glad the controversy was over, he said deviously. Carroll shrewdly doubted any retreat by Dulany either in reference to

Canada or the *Gazette*. It took only a short time to learn in what sense Dulany was glad that the controversy was dropped. On April 8, Carroll opened the *Gazette* to survey the secondary crossfire from less important outposts in the current controversies. He found that "Antilon" himself had mounted the central battery, and his guns were roaring once again. The hardiness and temper Carroll observed in the man on the occasion of the recent visit should have led him to expect the event; but apparently he did not. Unlike his father, Carroll could not assuage his temper by calling Dulany a liar and calumniator. "First Citizen" was compelled to man the fort once again, distasteful though it was for him.[6]

Dulany seemed aware that the process of legal reasoning about his case had run its course with his second letter. He therefore pressed a critique of Carroll's presentation along this line, which was heavily weighted with the historical development of law. He tried to turn attention away from this more effective genetic mode of Carroll's legal reasoning. He did so by quibbling about particular historical episodes and Carroll's treatment of them. Again he sought to enmesh Carroll in the establishment of religion question, which chiefly had concerned his colleagues Chase and Paca. With additional cleverness, he said that his adversary's father and fellow Catholics were maliciously attacked by the lower house in the 1750's. The governor and his council were now in a similar defensive situation, and Carroll was with his former persecutors in the lower house. He also showed contempt for Carroll's political theorizing, but dealt with only one instance to demonstrate this. The assembly function, which "First Citizen" recommended as distinct from the judiciary, hardly made it a counterpart of Parliament. The king as well as the House of Lords always had jurisdiction in certain judicial matters. Again, his adversary's dictum that the king could do no wrong smacked of Stuart divine right rule.[7]

While Dulany did not provide any advanced legal and political theory, he still gave further impulse to Maryland politics by his conservative challenge. Carroll was therefore unavoidably pulled ever more deeply into the political mainstream of discussion so long as his conviction as a public-spirited gentleman persisted. The conflicting currents were not all favorable to his emerging leadership of the Independent Whigs. Boucher's letter in the same issue which carried "Antilon's" piece made it clear that many had "swallowed the bait, which Mrr.[Misters] Chase and Paca threw out. . . ." This was said in the face of the strong and outspoken opposition to a bishop that was coming from Presbyterians. Boucher had tried desperately to show that a bishop would not change the degree of freedom dissenters enjoyed in Maryland. There was, however, none of the sarcasm and scurrility for Catholics here that was presented at length by "Clericus" in the same issue. But Carroll's fear that such writing would soon flow from the pen of "Antilon" was well founded.[8]

Men like Dorsey, Jennings, and Henry Howard, on the other hand, were vexed by Dulany's publication, especially by his further appeal to scurrility. As for Jennifer, Carroll had little hope that he would become actively involved on the side of "First Citizen." This seemed to be indicated by Jennifer's failure to answer the letters Carroll's father had sent him on the fee question. The growing demands by Dulany on Carroll's scholarship in support of his case could eventually discredit him, even though the majority sided with his view against fees by proclamation. Carroll was glad to know that Thomas Johnson stood at hand ready to help him with this problem. While Carroll's father was not a trained lawyer, he was a seasoned veteran of political combat in the rugged form of public life that Marylanders of his generation experienced. He wisely advised his son to shun such words as "knave" in standing as the intellectual gentleman of parts and civility. Dulany, he believed, had now left himself considerably embarrassed with the governor because of his disregard of such advice. Unwilling to bear the brunt of the attack against the fee proclamation, Dulany was shunting responsibility back on the governor when he rejected Carroll's dictum that the king could do no wrong. At a deeper level than this strategy, Carroll was provided in a new letter a chance to enlarge his ideas on reform of the assembly as the representatives of the people. In all of these respects, he had the support of a growing number of the first gentlemen of the colony as well as the people at large. What finally urged him to publish a new "First Citizen" letter was the forthcoming election of May 30. He was intent upon seeing Paca, Chase, Johnson, and a growing number of other liberals returned to the lower house. His message was ready for the May 8 issue of the *Maryland Gazette*.[9]

Carroll proceeded immediately to blunt Dulany's charge that he was the author of crude notions about political theory. Blackstone and Montesquieu were not crude authors, and together with the writer of the pamphlet on Jamaica, they had given him his understanding about the implications of the fee proclamation. "The will to ordain, and the power to enforce," Carroll said quoting Montesquieu to condemn Dulany's scheme for Maryland, "will be lodged in the same person." This was not to say that the governor had been tyrannical. "But the true liberty of the subject (as Blackstone justly observes) consists, not so much in the gracious behavior, as in the limited power of the sovereign." In the unprotected institutional structure in Maryland "the latent designs of our crafty minister [Dulany]" were dangerous and augur destruction of the people's liberty. "Our constitution is founded on jealousy, and suspicion," he wrote of the system's checks and balances. "Its true spirit, and full vigour cannot be preserved without the most watchful care, and strictest vigilance of the representatives over the conduct of administration." By Dulany's preoccupation with precedent to the point of distortion, he would subvert this constitutional edifice of freedom; for "to justify oppression and outrages by instances of their commission" was folly. "Thus the despotism of the east may be supported, and the natural rights of mankind trampled under foot. The question of right therefore does not depend upon precedents, but on the principles of the constitution. . . ." This was the judgment of the best constitutional theorists and Dulany needed to be called back to what he certainly had once known. It was this political tradition which had guided Dulany's own defense of the colonies against the Stamp Act. The active mind of the scholar Carroll uncovered, possibly with Johnson's assistance, new veins of evidence to support his case. The unjust tax in Ireland, drawn from Mollyneux's history, served as an example of what might happen in Maryland. Hawkins, Littleton, and Mansfield were used by way of commentary on Blackstone. Carroll had consulted his friend Daines Barrington, author of the historical study of English statutes, on the limitations of Hume's history, which Carroll had used so much in his first two letters. Hume's full narrative was sound, Carroll explains, even if his interpretations had varied from those of a critical reader such as Carroll. Simply because Hume did not follow the stereotyped diatribes against Stuart divine right theory and practice, it could not be assumed that he and Carroll were less devoted to the contrary principles of freedom which Carroll now defended and Dulany opposed in practice.[10]

While Carroll was a critic of Stuart absolutism, by principle, he was also an enemy of the Glorious Revolution of William and Mary by his connections with the Catholic counter-revolutionary society, because so far it had overturned Maryland freedom. Dulany had sought to embarrass him by the integrity he knew Carroll would maintain in adjusting an explanation to these charges. It was this revolution which ended the pluralism of seventeenth-century Maryland and brought about establishment of the Church of England. Dulany had steered Carroll into this area of controversy, in order to embroil him in Paca's attack on the project for a bishop. Quoting Blackstone, Carroll notes that establishment originated with the years of the reign of Henry VIII, which "were times of the greatest despotism, that have been known in this land, since the death of William the Norman." The condition of law improved, in spite of the obstructions of the Stuarts, and ultimately was helped by the Glorious Revolution. The meaning was clear to his readers, for the Bill of Rights coming from this revolution of 1688 protected dissenter Protestants within the Church of England, although Catholics were excluded from its benefits. What followed for Catholics in Maryland as a result of this revolution "we remember, and forgive," Carroll said. The charter and toleration acts no longer protected them. He would not review that sequence of events which had fallen so hard on his father; but he would deny that the lot of Dulany and his sympathizers resembled that of Catholics penalized by legislation in the lower house. He admitted that he had differed on these and related questions with some of his fellow Marylanders, many of whom now supported his attack on the fee proclamation. He would leave these honest differences regarding interpretation of freedom for Catholics under existing law. A growing number, however, were now brought to see the organic connection between civil and religious liberty in the natural right scheme of English constitutional thought. Carroll brushed aside Dulany's claim that the devices of debate learned at St. Omers disguised his real disaffection from non-Romanists who currently support him. Unwittingly, Dulany was overshooting his objective with this malicious sally, and it fell as much on the other Independent Whigs and their friends as on Carroll.[11]

As it turned out, Dulany's religious asides and Carroll's temperate retorts only leave "Antilon" again more open to attack on the central issue of the minister's role in the fee controversy. Not the governor, Carroll continued to contend, but a corrupt minister must be saddled with the odium of the fee proclamation. That such men should be, but especially that there should be a powerful role provided them by the Maryland government, was indeed a major calamity. The election was imminent, and those who won must act on this constitutional question. "What will the delegates of the people at their next meeting say to *our* minister, this 'Antilon,' *this enemy to his country. . . .?*" He could not escape, but it was clear how he would try. "The whole tenor of Antilon's conduct," Carroll observed, "makes good the old observation, 'that when ministers are pinched in matter of proceeding against law, they throw it upon the king.' " The experience of corrupt England was repeated here in Dulany's conduct. The flame of political vengeance thus flickered here and there throughout Carroll's letter, but he tried to temper it in this case by appeal to historical examples of his opponent's vices. Carroll turned to Tacitus where he described a minister of those days: "A mind dark and unsearchable, prone to blacken others, fawning and imperious." "Antilon" had ridiculed "First Citizen" as a boy guided by a possessive father, a puny weakling, and silly puppy; perhaps these were more annoying than insulting. On the other hand, he would have preferred being called "dark and unsearchable," that is, provided the words were Dulany's, and not those of Tacitus. For Tacitus pointed to a man trusted with the good of his society. Fulfilment of such a rôle was a matter of the highest honor for Carroll. Dulany, not Carroll, was in the office of trusted minister to which Carroll could not aspire. Still the young patriot wondered at what heights of influence this "First Citizen" had arrived in his zeal for freedom.[12]

"Publick gratitude, Sire, for public service is the patriot's due," wrote Paca and Matthias Hammond to Carroll in the *Gazette* published on election day. "We are proud to observe the generous feelings of our fellow-Citizens towards an advocate of liberty." This was typical of the general response from the candidates who stood for election on May 30. Major Ridgely, who was in Philadelphia at the time of "First Citizen's" Third Letter, reported the popular reception which it received there. "Boucher on reading y[ou]r last Paper sayed [said] th[a]t you was [*sic*] an author w[i]th whome it was an honor to Contend." Unexpected praise indeed! And from his old companion of the Homony Club where politics were not to be discussed! Daniel Carroll and his daughter went to Doughoregan Manor to share in the excitement of "First Citizen's" triumph. There was clear evidence that Carroll was esteemed as one who had played the highest role of gentility with both courage and civility. His popularity was not from any demagoguery, and it was therefore important to "seem not to affect Popularity," which attendance at political party meetings at this time might imply. Carroll continued his studious ways and habit of business.[13]

Wary of Dulany, the possibility of another encounter was not ignored in the mood of optimism that prevailed. There was reason to suspect Dulany's recent cordiality toward Chase. Offices of profit and trust were a greater lure for him than for Carroll and the other Whigs. It was also a sign that Dulany might be mounting cannon in a new position. At the beginning of June, Carroll did not like the prospect of again launching a new shelling any more than receiving Dulany's fire. As he acknowledged compliments for his defense of the constitution, he called attention to the controversy as now being protracted beyond a point of enlightenment. The low level of attack that would inevitably develop would be "incompatible with the general good." The people and their cause would suffer. The controversy continued to branch out into other writings in the *Gazette*. Particularly unsettling was the further tangling of the fee question with Boucher's clergy case. The highly complimentary letter of "Protestant Planter" was not an unmixed benefit to Carroll. The writer made explicit a religious issue which Carroll wanted beneath the surface and confined to innuendo in "Antilon." "They have endeavoured to alienate the affections of the people from him," Protestant Planter wrote with naïveté, "by representing him, as a 'political parricide,' as the worst of evils, as a man attempting to subvert both church and state." Carroll's gauche patron needlessly created a distinct church-state question. The public, on the other hand, already knew that Carroll was "no less elevated by nature than fortune, and that his mind, enriched with knowledge, bears the true stamp of honour and dignity." Now they might wonder. These matters ought to be discussed, some would say.[14]

Carroll may not have seen this danger at the moment, but in a few weeks he would. Jonathan Boucher returned from Philadelphia and sensed the changing atmosphere. May 27, he again published a plea for a bishop, but now he based his reasoning on the case of the Catholic bishop of Quebec. Following England's conquest of New France in 1763, Bishop Briand was granted all of the privileges of his office as they were held under the Catholic French monarchy as a conciliatory gesture. Boucher noted one of the traditional duties of his office: "Romish casuists are charged with maintaining that no faith is to be kept with heretics." England was so indulgent toward papists with no hope of reciprocation from them because of their principle of suppressing heretical Protestantism. Marylanders, on the contrary, would not have indulged an Anglican clergyman his own bishop on the same terms, and they were Protestants. In Quebec, the civil and religious liberties of Protestants were in danger from a Catholic bishop bound by such a hostile doctrine on heretics. "We petition only to be put on an equal footing with every other society," Boucher cleverly argued. "Dissenters, quakers, catholicks, all are completely tolerated: the Church of England only wants toleration." Carroll was thus saddled with a doctrine he did not actually hold, and which was attributed to the bishop of Quebec: that a Catholic majority when in power will not tolerate other faiths. There were other items to confuse further the climate of discussion. "Brutus," another *Gazette* correspondent at this time, portrayed Carroll as a contemporary example of the classical type of demagogue defined in ancient times. Another writer made an obtuse presentation of the "First Citizen-Second Citizen" form of dialogue, while attempting to promote free trade.[15]

Sniffing such a change of wind, Dulany gained new vigor to pursue the developing religious ramification of the debate. In the wake of the Whigs' victory at the election, he composed his fourth letter of "Antilon." By again stigmatizing Carroll as a Romanist, he might deter the lower house from a militant stand on the fee question, which Carroll led, before the house convened on June 15. The June 4 issue of the *Gazette* carried much of the previous reasoning of the author. Carroll in his treatment of the Glorious Revolution, it was claimed, appeared to side with James against the Church of England. What did he now have against its bishops? Was he corrupting his factional allies, who sailed under the color of the Independent Whigs? There was a more fundamental question, Dulany believed. What insolence was this that a Romanist should enter into a public controversy about a policy of state? Carroll presumed too much on the indulgence of the Crown and the province toward that religion, which in official English and provincial statutes was regarded as a danger to public order. Dulany's whole attack was thus a calculated risk in the face of his own declining cause. It remained to be seen how extensively the liberal view of Paca, Chase, and Johnson on civil and religious liberty had infected Maryland society. Perhaps Dulany's notion of Maryland's toleration might prove narrower than the view of the ordinary citizen, even though he was not unversed in the popular Enlightenment literature of Carroll's Independent Whigs.[16]

Dulany made only a token effort at further developing the lines of thought in his previous letters. He tried to shift the discussion of precedent to the need for such discretionary power as would justify the settling of fees by proclamation under circumstances similar to present ones. Dulany quibbled over seventeenth-century history and continued to annoy Carroll with ridicule of his person. "First Citizen" had indicated his own variety of ridicule when he took up this weapon himself. He had taken considerable trouble to find authentic evidence that Dulany's father had been an indentured servant, which in Dulany's eyes was nearly as repugnant as being called a papist. Carroll shrewdly saw that it would also appear so in the eyes of the Maryland gentry at large. He himself sustained lesser wounds to his vanity, as when Dulany alluded to his humiliation at owning a shaved head beneath his wig.[17]

The Whigs held the usual round of caucuses where appraisals were made of the latest damage from "Antilon's" fire. All of his power was gone as far as the elder Carroll could determine. On the other hand, the salvo required a response, principally on the religious question. The task Carroll faced was frankly burdensome. How could he deal with it without offense to Protestant citizens? It was heartening to see the crowd gather for a formal burning in effigy of the fee proclamation on June 14. As the assembly convened the next day, he could clearly read the popular support which his leadership had won for the cause of the lower house. Chase and Ridgely had been active in instigating a similar symbolic burning in Baltimore, while Dulany was present in the city. It did not pass without strong charges of demagoguery from Dulany, which won a favorable hearing among some more important gentlemen of both sides of the controversy. Carroll himself had protested against such antics by Chase at the time of the Stamp Act.

He was now warned by this fresh incident to avert any similar charges of demagoguery, particularly at the hands of Protestants who thought as Boucher spoke about men of Carroll's religious persuasion. The Gunpowder Plot, Titus Oates, and other now legendary claims of proneness to violence in English Catholics were woven into the texture of Protestant culture. Carroll never lost sight of the fact, especially at this time. Indeed he himself, without reason, appeared in the eyes of the governor to be implicated in the public disorders. Therefore, it was not a good time to visit the governor and Carroll would wait until those fears proved groundless. At the same time, some relief did come to him on this question when five hundred signed a petition objecting to the attack made on Ridgely for his conduct in the Baltimore protest. Carroll thus found himself in the crucible of his aspiration to play the public-spirited man. If the discipline of his gentility made him master of his thoughts and expression, he might well sum up in his Fourth Letter the whole perspective which he now possessed of both civil and religious liberty in Maryland. His own style of gentility in pursuing these goals would play no small part in winning public acceptance of his idealism.[18]

Carroll did not disappoint the Whigs, nor fall short of his social ideal. "Antilon admitted that he concurred with the rest of the council in advising the proclamation as *expedient* and *legal*," Carroll charged in the Fourth Letter of "First Citizen." "He has since justified it—as a *necessary unavoidable act*." Small wonder that Dulany had resorted first to precedent, and now to justification of discretionary power. "It is not the first time that expediency has discovered itself under the appearance of necessity. "Wretched is the lot of the citizen where the law is vague," the Romans once said. "A free constitution will not endure discretionary powers," he again concluded. The case rested on the ministers, and not the governor. Carroll thus skillfully tied together the delicate threads that ran through the fabric of his four letters. While he summoned fresh erudition to refute precedent, just as Dickinson, Pope, and Dulany (in his pamphlet of 1765) did, the climax of his legal *tour de force* was found where the discretionary power advocated by Dulany nakedly stands as arbitrary power. His beauty of treatment derived to a great extent from the magnificent unfolding of a cyclical interpretation of English constitutional history in which the arbitrary power passage was set. With Gallican clarity and synthesis, he placed his generalizations, and with the restraint of Greek simplicity and great economy, he selected illustrations and conclusions. Clarification of nettling points made by Dulany on Hume and Montesquieu did not clutter this central purpose as occasionally happened in earlier letters. Like a composer, he sensed that he was in the last movement of a grand four-part work.[19]

Discretionary power as discussed in the Fourth Letter was but a variation on an earlier theme. The emphasis which enriched these lines was not civil liberty but religious liberty. Dulany unwittingly had been drawing Carroll to the triumphant entry of this variation on the theme of freedom at this last scene of the controversy. He had twisted Carroll's discussion of the Stuart monarchy to make him appear a partisan of those who attacked the Established Church of England. Not succeeding too well in these efforts, he had challenged the propriety and even the right of Carroll as a Catholic to draw the journalist's pen. The dramatic setting was inescapable: Dulany's malevolent forces were defeated, and civil and religious liberty saved. The Puritans had traditionally moved to a case of civil liberty from religion as a starting point. Carroll reversed the sequence of freedom's story; from a contest over civil liberty, he had come to a defense of religious liberty. Before his fellow citizens, he now unfolded a garment of freedom that was really made of but a single fabric.

He began by further clarifying his condemnation of James II for his treatment of the Church of England. "The National religion was in danger under James 2'd, from his bigotry and a despotic temper," Carroll said to the surprise of Dulany. He had infringed the liberty of Protestants. Carroll therefore resented the implication that he was a partisan of James against the Church. "I bear not the least dislike to the church of England," he continued, "though I am not within her pale. . . ." However, he said, addressing himself to the real issue of the moment, "knaves, and bigots of all sects and denominations I hate, and I dispise." With genteel restraint he made no tedious mention of discrimination against himself (the overthrow of the Stuarts had opened the door to other knaves and bigots in Maryland who are responsible for this). Although he was deprived by law of a seat in the assembly and in a public house of worship in his own faith, he would not cite these instances against Boucher and others who claimed that Maryland was now fair to gentlemen of Carroll's persuasion. "But do these disabilities," Carroll asked, "extend so far, as to preclude them [Catholics] from thinking and writing on matters merely of a political nature?" In being honest about this question and other instances of tolerance, he was, however, inevitably raising the more fundamental one about the effect of establishment of religion; about the whole justification of union of church and state. One not of the establishment was always under threat, for where the law was vague regarding the dissenter he would always be in a wretched condition. Maryland had an atmosphere of duress because of establishment. It was as bad for religion as it was for the dissenting citizen. "I am as averse to having religion crammed down people's throat as a proclamation," Carroll stated quite simply. He was not ashamed of the assumptions behind these honest statements about religion: political questions had their own autonomy as did religious life. He chose to discuss the one in public in the hope that Maryland with its somewhat mild establishment would not choke off the free speech and thought of a religious dissenter speaking on a purely political question. His own tradition, stemming from the founding of the colony, had given him this understanding and hope. Dulany, however, was weakening the case of Boucher for the mildness of establishment and the benefits of tolerance. He presented, according to Carroll, a spectacle of bigotry that appeared from time to time on the Maryland scene. "Antilon would make a most excellent inquisitor," he says by way of commentary on the liabilities of establishment; "he has given some striking specimens of an arbitrary temper; the first requisite."[20]

And so in Carroll's central vision of Maryland political life, civil and religious liberty proved branches of the same stock. It was embarrassing to live out the implications of this reality in response to the aspiration for freedom found in the present controversy. Dulany had needlessly involved religion in the fee controversy. With those who shared his own insight into liberty, Carroll need not belabor by explicit reference the existing disabilities to which Dulany now threatened to add abridgment of free speech on a political question. At this moment, there undoubtedly burned in the bright spirit of Carroll the hope that the current surge for freedom would sweep away every confinement, including those which had kept him from a seat in the assembly and from a public house of worship in his own faith. With as much moral suasion as artistry, he created an effect worthy of his noble cause; far more was suggested than what was said. And so he refused to retell his father's story of the 1750's and the burden of added penal legislation. Resentment had subsided in the Carroll household, and Dulany could not stir it up. "I choose not to meddle with a subject," Carroll said with restraint, "the discussion of which may rekindle extinguished animosities."[21]

This somber brooding indeed held pathos without being pathetic in treatment. The literary high seriousness of the classics is found here, and so too the reason for the great influence of "First Citizen" upon the Independent Whigs together with a public increasingly awakened to the challenges of freedom. Carroll made all aware that veneration and defense of freedom held many ramifications touching each citizen in a particular way, as had been the case with himself. Reading these passages, one thinks of the warm solemnity of *Finlandia* and its air of a struggle which might well be endless. The Fourth Letter of "First Citizen" was held as a melodic theme for the times that inspired it, especially if it proved to be his last composition. The day would come three years to the very month hence when Charles Carroll of Carrollton would enter into the joint authorship of the Declaration of Independence.

On July 3, 1773, the assembly convened and the lower house again protested against the principle of fixing fees by proclamation. Had Carroll held a seat in that chamber, his letter would have served the house as its formal remonstrance to the governor. His great service had been, however, that in the "First Citizen" letters the views of both houses were kept from the obscurity of official proceedings and his principles of freedom became the possession of all the people of Maryland in the pages of the *Gazette*. This, rather than the victory in the fee question, proved historically important. To the chagrin of Dulany as well as Boucher, the clergy per poll tax was defeated. This reassured Carroll that their attack had not stirred up any bigotry in the assembly or among the public in general.[22]

As the government moved toward some kind of adjustment on the fee bill, however, further demands would be made on Carroll and the Whigs. A compromise would have to be reached with the governor and the offended clergy, whose considerable body of sympathizers required mollification. The volatile political climate reflected in the press made it difficult to determine how all of this could be accomplished. There were rumors that the governor was inclined to bring in troops to prevent any further demagoguery as seen in the burning of his proclamations. "Should this be true," Carroll's father said of such rumors, "He may Perhaps meet with greater mortification than the Burning of His proclamation." Carroll himself now put little stock in the prudence of Eden. He regarded him "a very silly idle dissipated man." The memory of his offense to Molly and Carroll's own honor no doubt made it hard to estimate Eden otherwise. Carroll was not very tolerant of these defects, and others of a political nature in men of high office. He was, at the same time, obliged to traffic with the governor; but the occasions of his visits had to be well chosen, with foreknowledge of the young official's mood. In addition to these unsettling circumstances, some were reporting that "Antilon" was still popular and possessed active defenders. Very likely the hostility for Carroll for provoking the elder proprietary official led to compassion among those opposed to Carroll's position on the fee case.[23]

There were other uncharted reverberations. John Hammond lumped Carroll, Johnson, Paca, and Chase into one bundle of demagoguery that would "blind or mislead the understandings, and irritate and inflame the minds of the people." He was annoyed that he was considered to have had some connection with them. The trio of Johnson, Paca, and Chase soon flew to the defense of Carroll for "he was a friend to publik liberty." Leadership of the lower house had once been in the hands of the Hammonds; but it was no longer so, as Carroll pointed the direction of new winds of liberal thought. One writer gave him extravagant praise in this rôle, attributing all progressive writings to his authorship and making him the originator of the ideas that came from the Independent Whigs.[24]

If such praise was flattering, it was also unsettling; and at times it was clearly harmful. "Consistent Protestant," writing in the *Gazette,* would allow for a clergy bill, provided it was drawn up in the spirit found in "First Citizen." The taxed citizen, its author believed, should be free to choose the beneficiary of the levy. This was much like an earlier letter by "A Protestant Planter," which vindicated the place of Carroll even as a Catholic in the discussion of public questions. He expressed satisfaction at Carroll's treatment of the question of established religion. Carroll, of course, was not the author of either of these writings, but his father warned him all the same against defending "Protestant Planter" in the event the latter should be attacked by Dulany. The "Consistent Protestant's" attack, however, bore witness to the way in which even Carroll's restrained discussion of established religion had stirred up radical thought about freedom in Maryland.

"Consistent Protestant" wrongly assumed Carroll to be "Planter," who had recommended broad tolerance. The author restated Dulany's contention that a papist should not be allowed to enter into such controversies. In Catholic countries, he reasoned, this freedom was not allowed to Protestants. Since Maryland was a dominantly Protestant society, Catholics must accept the lot of Protestants as it is found in Catholic countries. If Carroll denied Catholic practices of established religion, he was not a good Catholic; his church upheld the theory of the confessional state, just as Protestantism did. "There has hardly ever been a period," the writer continued, "since this country has been under a protestant government, when a conduct, like his, wou'd have met with such a reception, as it now has. What this may forebode, I care not to enquire—the real friends of their country will think of it." Indeed they had thought of it, but not as men with the ideas of this writer, who confessed himself "so tinctured with the old spirit of our constitution, as to think we go rather too far. . . ." The Whigs and the public as well had heard Carroll deny the theory of "Consistent Protestant." Carroll and the Whigs had indeed gone rather far from the confessional state notions of "Consistent Protestant."[25]

It was understandable that Carroll's father was disturbed and wanted him to write no more. "Attention to y[ou]r own affairs," he advised, "will not admit you to spend y[ou]r time in Political squabbles or Party Writings. . . ." Carroll was not out of sympathy with this advice, and was fortunately able to carry it out. He now sought to give perspective to his debate and by his prudent conduct to prevent any distortion of his single purpose in the public eye. He surprised his critics when he advocated a shilling tax arrangement for the clergy, rather than tobacco, thus taking their income out of a fluctuating medium for a projected twenty-one year period. This promised some satisfaction to the clergy as well as the public. It was in this mood that the lower house arrived at a compromise on the clergy question with the governor and the upper house. Thus, under difficult circumstances Carroll had averted an involvement in the clergy question which his enemies had hoped would discredit him in the potentially effective role he had in the fee proclamation controversy.[26]

As for this question, an impasse had developed in July following the "Fourth Letter" of Carroll. The hostility of the lower house to the measure was now met by the unveiled intransigence of the governor and the upper house. Carroll awaited new attempts at conciliation in the fall and early winter. He continued his Whig collaboration, benefiting from the month of August at the Doughoregan retreat, where study could go on as well as meetings with Johnson, Paca, and Chase. In September, this Whig trio attacked John Hammond's view of the fee question, particularly regarding proclamations as a legal privilege of office. Their discussion largely centered in an explication of John Locke's commentary on this feature of the British Constitution. Proclamation was an act, not a power belonging to a prerogative of office. For the good of the people, in lieu of any other institutional instrument, a power of office might be used to decree a salutary and urgent measure. The Whigs then return to Carroll's line of reasoning where it had been established that the assembly was the appropriate instrument for settling fees, or the courts until such remedial action should have been brought about by the assembly. Finally, the letter identified the fees by proclamation action with the passage of the Stamp Act by Parliament, seeing them as part of the same piece of arbitrary exercise of power. This was a familiar thought and conviction with Carroll.[27]

Sufficient evidence was available to support the belief that in October and November Carroll went into print himself, or directly influenced a writer or writers under the name of "Voter." The revolutionary characteristic of his approach to the whole discussion of fees as related to freedom under the constitution was evident. As a reformer, he wanted to remedy the defects in the upper house and in the judiciary, which make the fee proclamation so mischievous. He passed beyond the general application of Montesquieu's theory to the assembly. "I wish to see the c_____l [council and upper house] of this province," "Voter" recommended, "composed of gentlemen unconnected with the offices of government, then might they become guardians of the people, and from principle (they having no interest but the general interest) be induced to join in such measures as most assuredly would center, in the happiness of the people, of whom they are a part." Maryland, then, had a purified version of the House of Lords in Parliament. The creation of a body which aspired to the idealization found in the *Senatus Populusque Romanus*, so cherished by Carroll, the classicist, was envisaged. He then proceeded to relate this institutional reform to a practical and urgent case, the tobacco inspection legislation. Those who were empowered to act in this rôle, and who controlled the price and production of tobacco, should have their own fees of office clearly fixed by assembly legislation. Fairness in the prices resulting from inspection practices could be maintained by recourse to the courts as another legal source of protection for the people. The confusion prevailing in the two branches of government, if continued, would work great harm.[28]

Before the year was concluded, the adjustment of the fee and inspection controversies came about, even though the reforms which Carroll envisioned for the upper house had not. He had planted the seeds of change and created the climate which, if maintained, would bring them to maturity. The implications of the change he advocated were indeed revolutionary. The thoughts behind them had followed a straight line from those he had uttered upon leaving England in 1765—"America must become Independent." As 1773 came to a close, Charles Carroll of Carrollton was already entering upon a stirring rôle on a broader stage, which would soon be filled with even more heroic action. His revolutionary thought and highly fashioned gentility now possessed the subtlety and polish needed for this new and larger drama.

"The union of All America," Carroll wrote of Daniel Dulany a year later, "has swallowed him up in the great vortex, he follows its motion, but not daring to be the first mover, nor possessing a temper sufficiently intrepid to guide its course: he is carried away with the Whirlwind, he does not ride on it, nor direct the storm."[29] Dulany could not do so, because Carroll had seized for himself that rôle at this decisive moment in history.

DOCUMENTARY NOTES

[N.B. Where studies have already been referred to in chapter footnotes, only the author is noted here.]

Chapter 1

The Revolution of 1688 is viewed here primarily as it affected Catholics. They believed that they had clear legal rights of which the event and its sequel deprived them. This gave moral suasion to their rebellious attitude toward that event of 1688. In *Their Rights and Liberties: The Beginnings of Religious and Political Freedom in Maryland* (Westminster, Md., 1959), the author has given the historical development of the legal rights which were embodied in a tradition among Catholics. The Carroll manuscripts and other sources used in this study are consistent with this limited interpretation of the Revolution of 1688. The larger question as discussed by Francis X. Curran and by Michael G. Kamerer, *et al.* (eds.), *The Glorious Revolution in America: Documents on the Colonial Crisis of 1689* (Chapel Hill, N. C., 1964), pp. 143-211, in their interpretations are not directly affected by what I have established in a more limited area.

Political maneuver in the Hart-Carroll controversy has been studied by the writer in "His Excellency's Council: Maryland 1714-1720," *American Catholic Historical Society of Philadelphia Records*, LXXIV (1963), 137-150. To what extent individual Catholics were experiencing political advantage in voting and other areas, by the Indulgence of Queen Anne, has not been studied. Hart's fears and the Catholic hopes are reflected in material on this conflict.

The Carroll manuscripts have suggested "Catholic Counter-Revolutionary Society" by their references to "the late Revolution." Such a theme does not demand that these partisans had a formulated plan the logic of which depended upon a careful historical analysis of the event of 1688. The harshest measures had already been counteracted not merely by the efforts of Catholics but by others in Maryland and England. Nor should the regime in power be regarded as a target of the Catholic rebels, since some of these members were viewed as friends. The Revolution of 1688 in Maryland embodied certain hostile policies together with supporting ideas. Maryland Catholics were trying to counteract these and replace them with those of their own tradition, which in this sense made them a counter-revolutionary society. The dynamics of the political collaboration by the Catholic and Anglican gentry were discussed by me at the annual convention of the Organization of American Historians in 1968, an account of which has since been published in *The Magazine of the Protestant Episcopal Church*, XXXVIII (June, 1969), pp. 143-51, entitled, "The Catholic and Anglican Gentry in Maryland Politics."

Chapters 2-3

Carroll admitted the great influence of a Jesuit education upon his republican ideas; his opponents had made such an accusation at the time of the "First Citizen" controversy in 1773. The intellectual influence of these forces was historically important only in the way they were moulded to the experience of Carroll in his English continental and provincial environment. The author has described this process in greater detail in "Young Mr. Carroll Meets Montesquieu," *MHM*, 62 (Dec., 1967), 394-418. Professor Bernard Bailyn described this process to the writer with the phrase "French Whig influence." This suggests further meaning in the light of Carroll's later alliance with the Independent Whigs discussed below in the notes to chapters 13 and 14.

On one occasion, however, Carroll took exception to the Jesuit intellectual tradition in connection with the Order's often attacked rule of "blind obedience" as popularly understood in England. (See letter to father, Oct. 11, 1761). His educators had exalted reason in the spirit of the Enlightenment, and he was scandalized for the moment at the discussion of the Jesuit Constitutions by its critics who gave no room for Ignatius of Loyola's own exaltation of reason and personal initiative as seen in many of his directives. Carroll would have found congenial thought here and in Father General Pedro Arrupe's writings during the times of Vatican Council II. Ultimately Charles' judgment stood on what he had personally observed of the men in the Order for so many years. As an institution, however, it came under the scrutiny of his reform mentality.

Chapter 4

The American Enlightenment in the era of the American Revolution has been shown to possess a cult of classical antiquity as a chief ingredient. The formal study of Roman civil law by Carroll intensified this element of influence. He also had a highly developed formation in the classical literature of Antiquity. The mark of these studies would become historically significant in the republican spirit in which he worked for reform of Maryland's Upper House in 1773. (See notes below for chapters 13 and 14.)

Charles' letter in French to his father of Aug. 10, 1758, is the source of my disagreement with Smith's interpretation of Charles' relationship to Mademoiselle Alcock. Here an elaboration of Willoughby's involvement was presented in humorous fashion.

Chapters 5-6

The letter of Charles' father of Oct. 6, 1759, gives his plans for the legal studies of his son. It indicates that there was no obstacle to Charles' enrollment at the Temple; but it does say that the universities, such as Oxford and Cambridge, would be closed to him except for a specific program of lectures in common law, for which a Catholic student could obtain permission without great difficulty. In his own letter of Sept. 16, 1970, Charles confirms this interpretation as he specifically discusses the Temple, Gray's and Westminster inns of law. In his studies, therefore, the pattern was one of his own choosing rather than one forced by penal legislation. Access to a law office, however, may have had other explanations which are found only implicitly in his letters. A Roman Catholic, being excluded by law from the role of barrister in court, was probably not so welcome in the sole function of apprentice counsellor in a law office. Even this deficiency was later remedied, for upon his return to Maryland he collaborated as a counsellor with the eminent lawyer and First Governor of Maryland, Thomas Johnson.

Chapter 7

I have made a radical revision of Smith's chronology of Charles' courtship, which probably began during his first meeting with Louisa in late 1761. Smith believes that Charles mistakenly dated this letter to his father as October 11, 1761, instead of the same day of 1763. I do not believe this to be accurate. The clearest evidence for my judgment is in this same letter a reference is made to his anticipated departure from England the following spring, which he designates as 1762 but which would constitute a second, and unlikely, error in dates. If the courtship began with a meeting in October of 1763, as Smith says, then Charles' presence in Paris must have followed his trip of that year which began with the definite date of departure from London in July of 1763. The period of four to five months for such an absence from London was highly unlikely. His letter to his father of October 13, 1761, also is not explained in the Smith version; this letter refers to the courtship and appears a second letter to cover the possibility of the October 11 one not reaching his father. A letter of March 12, 1761, which Smith uses in connection with the courtship because it speaks of the possibilities of the Paris visit toward fostering the marriage, complicates the matter likewise. There were, therefore, two visits to Paris: one in the fall of 1761 and another in the summer of 1763.

Whether Charles was clearly in love is as problematical as I have found it in Charles' letters. An important consideration regarding the rejection by the Bakers has not been given the importance heretofore which I have indicated. I refer to the hostility of Mrs. Baker and Louisa's older half-sister toward Charles and his response to it, which tended to alienate him from Louisa.

Chapter 8

The independence for America, which Carroll foresaw and to which he aspired, was considerably more than what Benjamin Franklin and other colonials recommended in the "Albany" and other plans of union of the 1750's. By a kind of cyclical determinism, the motion toward independence would terminate, according to Carroll, in a very loose dominion status bound only by fealty to the king. His thoughts on this matter were unfolded in his writings from 1765-70 in the wake of the Stamp Act, as discussed in subsequent chapters below. He therefore stands on very radical grounds for one speaking in 1765, when the germ of this thought was definitely expressed.

Chapter 9

Carl Bridenbaugh in *Myths and Realities: Societies of the Colonial South* (Baton Rouge, La., 1952) has given a portrait of a planter culture in the Chesapeake colonies with which my Carroll social profile and commentary conflicts. As a man of books and culture, Carroll indeed was eminent among the few hundred gentlemen Bridenbaugh singles out as faithful to the seventeenth-century William Byrd-type of gentry. But it would be more accurate to say that such men were a magnification of such traits as well as a bright source from which intelligence and culture radiated to the masses of the gentry whom Bridenbaugh finds crassly absorbed in concern with crops and commerce. Furthermore, he has not seen the implication of his own studies of the rise of the towns as a confirmation of my more favorable estimate of Chesapeake culture, which was something more than the inspiration of a rural planter society characteristic of the seventeenth but not of the eighteenth-century Maryland gentry. Carroll consciously harmonized the life of culture with reasonable concern for his commerce.

Chapter 10

The Carroll and Darnall family histories have their own ambiguities. To my knowledge, the execution of Henry Darnall, father-in-law of Charles Carroll of Carrollton, is not noted in these as I have found the fact stated in the Carroll manuscripts. Another item, a marriage license for Charles' parents dated 1752 and kept at the MHS, has given rise of some unpublished discussion. The common law status of the marriage before that date is possibly best explained as protection against the Carroll family estate's passing into the family of Charles' mother in lieu of her failure to make a settlement regarding dowry and jointure until that date. Nothing in all of this prevented the marriage from being sacramentally valid in the eyes of the Church. The legal justification was acceptable to people in general as they viewed families of fortune and seemed to cause no dismay.

Chapter 11

C. Vann Woodward, in his "The Southern Ethic in a Puritan World," *William and Mary Quarterly*, XXV (Jul., 1968), 343-70, effectively challenges two interpretations of southern culture. David Bertelson's *The Lazy South* (New York, 1967) contends that its debility as a contrast to New England Puritan culture derives from a condition brought from England. A moral vacuum accounted for the limitation, not slavery or any other institutional force. Edmund S. Morgan, on the contrary, contends in "The Puritan Ethic and the American Revolution" (*ibid.*, XXIV [Jan., 1967], 3-43) that there were expressions of the Puritan ethic in the South, but it came from a broad American influence created by Puritanism rather than the region. Woodward in the face of a currently amorphous condition of research on this topic does well to refute in large measure these two interpretations.

I believe that Carroll as examined here gives a more constructive set of evidence toward an understanding of Southern culture and particularly the Chesapeake provincial phase. Acquaintance with Marylanders and other Southerners of the period suggests that his gentility envisioned a unified moral force in his society, which was functionally similar to the Puritan inspiration of a Wilderness Zion. All three authors omit the gentry class of the eighteenth century as a central point of reference, and their assumptions are similar to those of Bridenbaugh as discussed in the note for Chapter 9 above.

Chapter 12

James Otis is perhaps correctly considered the foremost of *avant-garde* radicals of the Revolution. Carroll was clearly among these ranks by the cast of his thought. The precise measure of his adherence to this group is his early conviction which equated regulation of trade in any form, as a tax by the mother country and therefore a violation of the Maryland constitution with its destiny to one day become "free and independent." Even more unique in his position beyond this advanced element, was his reasoning by reference to the Glorious Revolution of 1688. Furthermore, Carroll provides an example of a well-rounded radical position similar to what is seen in Edmund S. and Helen M. Morgan's view of Otis in their study, *The Stamp Act Crisis: Prologue to Revolution* (Chapel Hill, N. C., 1953).

Chapter 13

Carroll's theory of the upper house and his idealization of it as a form of the *Senatus Populusque Romani* become increasingly important in the light of Jackson Turner Main's recent study, *The Upper House in Revolutionary America, 1763-1788* (Madison, 1967). Except for Maryland and South Carolina, the upper house progressively passed from control by the "upper class" or from an aristocratic to a democratic organ in the hands of the "lower class." Main's distinctions, however, are alien not only to Carroll's mentality but that of the people in viewing that body in Maryland. This probably explains why Maryland is not in the author's pattern as found elsewhere. The senate was a republican form and a possession of the people *(res publica)* apart from class divisiveness, Carroll told Marylanders. He and the Independent Whigs sought to bring the will and interests of the people to the upper house in a more substantial, even if subtler, form than it existed in the lower house. The voters disregarded class identification and voted for these spokesmen.

Chapter 14

The ideological leadership of Carroll clearly emerges from the implications of the notes of the foregoing two chapters and their texts. In the revolutionary political developments, his position in the controversies of 1773 was most strategic. In the context of the culture of politics, these questions and his leadership crystallized the sources of social unity in Maryland. Clearly these sources were Maryland's aspirations for political and religious freedom in secular terms. I suggest that we find here a polarization of southern culture similar to the Puritan vision of society as a functional process. Because this moral impetus to Maryland society is clothed in secular garb and the language of "the good of our country," it is no less forceful as evidence against a contrary view of southern culture discussed in the note for Chapter 11 above.

Corroboration of the picture of Carroll, the Independent Whigs, and their compatriots as liberal and tolerant is found in their consistent conduct a few years later when they held power in the revolutionary government. I have explored this matter in "The State and Dissenters in the Revolution," *Maryland Historical Magazine,* LVIII (1963), 325-32; and more broadly in the "Impact of the American Revolution on Religion in Maryland" (Ph.D. dissertation, Georgetown Univ., Dept. of History, 1961). A fuller study in this area is in the process of completion for publication by The Catholic University of America Press.

NOTES

Abbreviations for Frequently Used References

Manuscript numbers of collections indicate deposits at the Maryland Historical Society, Baltimore, Md. Where no collection reference is given, the Carroll Papers, 1702-1782 (MS No. 206) are indicated.

203.1	Letterbook of Charles Carroll of Carrollton, 1765-68.
203.2	Charles Carroll of Carrollton Letterbook, 1770-1774.
216	Carroll Papers, 1750-1854.
220	Carroll McTavish Papers, 1652-1850.
1225	Carroll-Harper Papers, 1749/50-c. 1896.
LC	Charles Carroll Papers, 1768-1828; Library of Congress, Washington, D.C.
MHS	Maryland Historical Society.
AM	*Archives of Maryland*, William H. Browne, *et al.*, eds. (68 vols.; Baltimore, 1883—).
MHM	*Maryland Historical Magazine.*
Field	Thomas M. Field, *Unpublished Letters of Charles Carroll of Carrollton, and of his Father, Charles Carroll of Doughoregan* (New York, 1902).
First Citizen	Elihu S. Riley, *Correspondence of "First Citizen"—Charles Carroll of Carrollton, and "Antilon"—Daniel Dulany Jr., 1773, With a History of Governor Eden's Administration in Maryland 1769-1776* (Baltimore, 1902).
Rowland	Kate M. Rowland, *The Life and Correspondence of Charles Carroll of Carrollton* (2 vols.; New York, 1898).
Smith	Ellen Hart Smith, *Charles Carroll of Carrollton* (Cambridge, Mass., 1942).

Chapter 1

1 Rowland, I, 3, 8-11; Field, pp. 11-14.

2 Francis X. Curran, *Catholics in Colonial Law* (Chicago, 1963), Introduction.

3 Founder to Governor Copley, Apr., 1693, *AM*, VIII, 508; Field, p. 10; Founder to Lord Baltimore, Sept. 1689, *AM*, VIII, 124.

4 Rowland, I, 11; Thomas Hughes, *The History of the Society of Jesus in North America, Text and Documents* (4 vols., New York, 1917), *Text*, II.

5 Rowland, I, 6; Founder to Charles' father and Uncle Daniel, July 7, 1719 (220).

6 *Ibid.*

7 Father to Sir Daniel O'Carroll, Sept. 9, 1748, in Field, p. 15.

8 Rowland, I, 11, 14, 17; Smith, p. 22; father to Clement Hill, 1761.

9 John M. Hammond, *Colonial Mansions of Maryland and Delaware* (Philadelphia, 1914), pp. 110-130.

10 Smith, pp. 21-22; Rowland, I, 15, 2.

11 Rowland, I, 7-8, 5; II, 12; Hughes, *Text*, I, 500; *AM*, XXX, 468-70.

12 *AM*, XXX, 372-74.

13 Thomas O'Brien Hanley, *Their Rights and Liberties: The Beginnings of Religious Liberty in Maryland* (Westminster, Md., 1959).

14 *AM*, XXXV, 557; Rowland, I, 14.

15 Hughes, *Text*, II, 526-30.

16 *Ibid;* Rowland, II, 437.

17 Rowland, II, 380; Aubrey C. Land, *The Dulanys of Maryland* (Baltimore, 1955), pp. 107-113.

18 Charles A. Barker, *Background of the Revolution in Maryland* (Cambridge, Mass., 1940), pp. 107-108.

19 Henry Darnall, *A Just and Impartial Account of the Transactions of the Merchants in London for the Advancement of the Price of Tobacco* (Annapolis, 1729); Barker, pp. 70 ff.; Rowland, II, 373-80.

20 Indenture Paper, July 30, 1737 (220), and Aug. 25, 1735 (LC: #593, #588-89); Charles Daniel to Charles' father, July 29, 1734 (LC).

21 Rowland, I, 17; Land, p. 109.

22 Father to Clement Hill, 1761; Rowland, I, 9, 16; Daniel Carroll to James Carroll, Dec. 20, 1762, in Peter Guilday, *The Life and Times of John Carroll, Archbishop of Baltimore (1735-1815)* (New York, 1922), pp. 3-4.

23 Robert Brooke Document for Plaintiff (220); Rowland, II, 447; G. Rodney Crowther, "Lowe of Denby, County Derby, England and Maryland," *National Genealogical Society Quarterly,* 51 (Mar., 1963), p. 40.

24 Rowland, I, 14; Deering Davis, *Annapolis Houses, 1700-1755* (New York, 1957), pp. 11, 22, 106-107.

25 Rowland, I, 18.

26 William T. Russell, *Maryland, Land and Sanctuary* (Baltimore, 1907), ch. xix; pp. 412-14.

27 Hughes, *Documents*, I, 136-37; William C. Davis, "Catholic Schools in Colonial Maryland," *Woodstock Letters,* 81 (May, 1952), 123-34; Guilday, pp. 13-15; James Burns, "Bohemia Manor School," *American Catholic Historical Society of Philadelphia Records,* XXII (June, 1913), 105.

28 George Hunter, S.J., "Religious History of Maryland," unpublished MS, n.d. [1750's] (Md. Province Archives of the Society of Jesus, 5 R 4) substantially reflects the Catholic Marylander's view of his freedom heritage very much as published studies in recent times establish it. See Documentary Notes ch. 1. The remainder of this chapter sums up the literature on this topic as related to the study here.

Chapter 2

1 To father, Mar. 22, 1750, and Sept. 4, 1749; from father, Sept. 17, 1750; to father, Mar. [?] 1749, and May [?], 1749; to the Countess Auzoüer, Sept. 20. 1771 (203.2). The foregoing references are for chronology. From mother, 1756 [?] (1225); Hughes, *Text*, II, 521; from father, Oct. 10, 1753 (1225), and July 26, 1756; Guilday, p. 14.

2 George Guggan and Joseph Keating, *Stonyhurst: Its Past History and Life in the Present* (London, 1901), p. 26.

3 Beales, Arthur, *Education Under Penalty; English Catholic Education from the Reformation to the Fall of James II, 1547-1689* (London, 1963), pp. 261, 158-73.

4 Hughes, *Text*, II, 521; Hubert Chadwick, *St. Omers to Stonyhurst* (London, 1962), pp. 404-405, 261-64.

5 Pierre DeLattre (ed.), *Les Establissements des Jésuites en France depuis quatre siècles* (5 vols., Enghien, Belgium, 1956), IV, 908.

6 Guilday, p. 22; to father, Dec. 16, 1761; from father, July 26, 1756 (220).

7 DeLattre, IV, 868, 908.

8 To parents, Sept. 4, 1749; to father, Mar., 1750.

9 *Ibid.;* from father, Oct. 10, 1753 (1225); Guggan, pp. 20-21.

10 To father, Mar. 23, 1751; Transcribed Booklets (MHS, 1225 [?]).

11 Chadwick, p. 270; Henry Foley, *Records of the English Province of the Society of Jesus* (7 vols., London, 1875-83), III, Ser. vii, 541-43.

12 Pierre Pourrat, *Christian Spirituality: Later Developments: Part II: From Jansenism to Modern Times*, trans. by Donald Attwater (4 vols., Westminster, Md., 1955) IV, 3, 251-55, 271-84, 338-41; André Schimberg, *L'Education morale dans les collèges de la Compagnie de Jésus en France sous l'Ancien Régime (XVIe, XVIIe, XVIIIe siècles)* (Paris, 1913), pp. 251-55.

13 Schimberg, *loc. cit.*

14 Hughes, *Text*, II, 521; Anthony Carroll to Charles's father, Feb. 10, 1758.

15 Anthony Carroll to Charles's father, Feb. 26, 1751, and Mar. 2, 1750; from father, Oct. 12, 1751 (216); to father, May [?] and Mar. 22, 1750.

16 To father, Dec. 19, 1761; Chadwick, pp. 245-48; from father, Oct. 10, 1753 (1225); Anthony Carroll to Charles's father, Feb. 26, 1751.

17 Chadwick, pp. 265-67.

18 To father, Mar. 22, 1750; from father, Sept. 17, 1750 (216) and Oct. 10, 1753 (1225).

19 *Ibid.;* George Oliver, *Collection towards Illustrating the Biographies of the Scotch, English, and Irish Members of the Society of Jesus* (London, 1845 [Exeter, 1838]), pp. 88, 150.

20 Guilday, p. 22; from father, Oct. 10, 1753 (1225); to father, Sept. 30, 1754 (220).

21 From father, Oct. 10, 1753 (1225).

22 *Ibid.*

23 *Ibid.*

24 To Countess Auzoüer, Sept. 20, 1771 (203.2); from father, Sept. 30, 1754 (220); Anthony Carroll to Charles' father, Jan. 6, 1757.

25 DeLattre, I, 279-307.

26 From father, Sept. 30 and 25, 1754 (220); from mother, Oct. 30, 1754 (in Field, pp. 23-4); to Countess of Auzoüer, Sept. 20, 1771 (203.2).

27 From father, Sept. 30 and Sept. 25, 1754 (220).

28 Schimberg, pp. 18, 95-112; Walter Dorn, *Competition for Empire* (New York, 1940), p. 181.

29 Schimberg, pp. 256-80, 291.

30 *Ibid.*, pp. 112-15; from father, Nov. 15, 1756 (220).

31 From father, Sept. 14, 1756 (216); Oliver, pp. 18, 98; from father, Apr. 16, 1759 (220); to father, Mar. 28, 1761; Oliver, p. 18; Joseph Gillow, *A Literary and*

Biographical History or Biographical Dictionary of the English Catholics from the Breach with Rome in 1534, to the Present Time (5 vols., New York, 1885), V, 294-95; from mother, 1756 (216); to parents, Aug. 10, 1758.

32 Rozolina to Charles' father, Sept. 25, 1757; from father, Sept. 12, 1755 (Pa. Hist. Soc., Phila., Pa., in Rowland, I, 23); Anthony Carroll to Charles' father, June 6, 1757; to father, Sept. 30, 1754 (220).

Chapter 3

1 From father, Oct. 10, 1753 (220), and July 26, 1756 (220).

2 *Ibid.*

3 *Ibid;* Sister Mary Augustina Ray, *American Opinion of Roman Catholicism in the Eighteenth Century* (New York, 1936), p. 236: John T. Ellis, *Catholics in Colonial America* (Baltimore, 1965), p. 356.

4 From father, July 26, 1756 (220); Charles' father to Rideout, May 13, 1756 (Md. Province Archives of the Society of Jesus, 5 T 5) and Digges to Charles' father, May 13, 1756 *(ibid.).*

5 *Ibid.;* Ellis, pp. 261-64; Anthony Carroll to Charles' father, Feb. 11, 1758.

6 From father, July 26, 1756 (220); to father, Aug. 31, 1756 (220); from father, Sept. 10, 1756.

7 From father, July 26, 1756 (220).

8 To father, Aug. 23, 1756 (220).

9 Anthony Carroll to Charles' father, June 6-7, 1757; Journal of Voyage to England, June 2-July 18, 1757 (216); from father, Nov. 15, 1756 (220).

10 From father, Oct. 10, 1753 (220); Russell, chs. xxii, xix; *AM*, XIV, 507.

11 *Ibid.;* Barker, ch. viii, 241, 254; *Maryland Gazette*, Nov. 24, 1754, and March 6, 1755; *AM*, XIX, 315-18; Russell, pp. 424-30.

12 Russell, pp. 570-577, Appendix T, pp. 582-83; *AM*, VI, 208; Land, p. 241.

13 Thesis Sheet at Doughoregan; from father, Sept. 9, 1761.

14 Anthony Carroll to Charles' father, June 7, 1757.

15 From father, July 26, 1756 (220); *AM*, VI, 240, 297; Russell, ch. xix.

16 From father, Sept. 14, 1756; to father, Jan. 1, 1758; Russell, ch. xix.

17 From father, July 26, 1756 (220).

18 *Ibid.*, Sept. 9, 1761 and Apr. 16, 1759 (220); to parents, Aug. 10, 1758; Oliver, p. 18; Rozolino to Charles' father, Nov. 17, 1757, and Jan. 12, 1758; to Countess Auzoüer, Sept. 20, 1771 (203.2).

19 From father, June 21, 1758 (220) and Sept. 14, 1756 (216); to father, Jan. 1, 1758.

20 Power to Charles' father, Sept. 23, 1757.

21 Oliver, p. 264; Power to Charles' father, Sept. 23, 1757; from father, July 17, 1757 and Feb. 8, 1758 (220).

22 To father, Jan. 1, 1758 and Dec. 26, 1757; from father, Jan. 1, 1758 (220).

Chapter 4

1 From father, Jan. 1, 1758 (220).

2 To father, Jan. 1, 1758: from father, July 25, 1758.

3 *Ibid.;* DeLattre, I, 879-87; Power to Charles' father, Sept. 23, 1757; to father, Jan. 1 and Feb. 11, 1758; Crookshanks to Charles' father, Feb. 13, 1758; from father, Jan., 1758 (1225).

4 To father, Jan. 1, 1758.

5 *Ibid.,* Feb. 4 and Feb. 11, 1758.

6 To parents, Aug. 10, 1758; to father, Feb. 19, 1763.

7 To father, Aug. 10, 1758; to parents, Aug. 10, 1758.

8 From father, Aug. 10, 1758; to parents, Aug. 10, 1758; to father, Aug. 10, 1758.

9 From father, July 14, 1760; from father to L'Isle Dieu, 1758; from father, Jan. 1, 1758 (220); Anthony Carroll to Charles' father, Feb. 10, 1758.

10 *Ibid.;* from father, Jan., 1758 (1225).

11 *Ibid.,* July 25 and Aug. 30, 1758 (220).

12 *Ibid.*

13 To parents, June 14, 1758.

14 *Ibid.,* Aug. 10, 1758.

15 From father, Jan. 1, 1758.

16 Oliver, p. 67; to parents, Nov. 7 and Aug. 10, 1758; Preserved Smith, *The Enlightenment* (New York, 1962), p. 497.

17 To parents, Nov. 7, 1758; from father, July 25, 1758 (220).

18 *Ibid.*

19 F. L. Cross, *Oxford Dictionary of the Christian Church* (London, 1958), p. 1428; to parents, Nov. 7, 1758; Buckner B. Trawick, *World Literature* (2 vols., New York, 1955), I, 81-5; to father, Jan. 17, 1759.

20 To father, Jan. 17, 1759.

21 To parents, Nov. 7, 1758.

22 *Ibid.;* Trawick, pp. 67-8.

23 To father, Jan., 1758 (1225).

24 Anthony Carroll to Charles' father, Feb. 10, 1758, and Feb. 8, 1759.

25 Abbé de l'Isle Dieu to Charles' father, Dec .26, 1757; Abbé's Account of the Acadians, 1758; Abbé to Charles' father, Feb. 14, 1758; Charles' father to Abbé, 1758; from father, Aug 13, 1759 (220).

26 Rozolino to Charles' father, Jan. 12, 1758; from father, July 25, 1758 (220), and Aug. 10, 1758.

27 To parents, Nov. 7, 1758; from father, Aug. 13, 1759 (220).

28 To father, Jan. 17 and 22, 1759; from father, Apr. 16, 1759 (220); to parents, Nov. 7, 1758.

29 From father, Apr. 16, 1759 (220).

30 *Ibid.;* to father, Sept. 14, 1759.

31 *Ibid.,* Dec. 19, 1759.

32 From father, Apr. 16, 1759 (220); to father, Sept. 14, 1759; to father, June 22, 1759; from father, June 26 and Feb. 9, 1759 (220).

33 *Ibid.*

34 *Ibid.*

Chapter 5

1 To parents, Sept. 27, 1759; from father, Oct. 6, 1759 (220), and July 14, 1760.

2 To father, Jan. 29 and May 16, 1760; to parents, Sept. 27, 1759.

3 *Ibid.*, Jan. 29, 1760.

4 From father, Sept. 9, 1761.

5 R. W. Linker, "English Catholics in the Eighteenth Century," *Church History*, XXXV (September, 1966), pp. 288-310; to father, Mar. 28, 1761, and Nov. 13, 1759.

6 Wallace Notestein, *The English People on the Eve of Colonization, The New American Nation Series*, ed. by Henry S. Commager, *et al.* (New York, 1954), pp. 86-95; to father, July 15, 1761, and Jan. 5, 1762. The letter from his father, Jan. [?], 1763 (Field, pp. 79-81 [Philadelphia, Pa., The Historical Society of Pennsylvania]), indicates that Charles made no formal enrollment in the Temple, which I interpret as in the inns rather than in all lectures. This may also have meant enrollment for that particular year, allowing for the possibility of some kind of enrollment previously. Charles Carroll the Barrister is sometimes confused with Charles of Carrollton in this question. The former was clearly enrolled at the inns.

7 To father, Sept. 16, 1760.

8 *Ibid.*, May 16, 1760, and Mar. 28, 1761.

9 Leslie Stephens, *et al.* (eds.), *Dictionary of National Biography* (22 vols., London, 1917 [1960 Reprint]), XIII, 1231-34. Hereafter cited as *DNB*.

10 To father, Feb. 13 and July 15, 1761; *DNB*, XIII, 1231-34; Bonamy Dobrée, *English Literature in the Early Eighteenth Century, Oxford History of English Literature* (12 vols., Oxford, 1949), VII, 230-232.

11 To father, May 15, Dec. 16, 1761, and May 14, 1761; "An Inventory of Goods in ye House at Doohoregan [*sic*]," to father, Sept. 16, 1760.

12 To father, Dec. 16, 1761; from father, Sept. 9, 1761.

13 To father, Apr. 10 and Sept. 16, 1760 and Mar. 3 and May 14, 1761; from father, Sept. 9, 1761.

14 To father, Dec. 19, 1759, and Feb. 13, 1761.

15 From father, July 14, 1760; to father, Sept. 16, 1760.

16 *Ibid.*

17 *Ibid.*, Jan. 22, 1759, and Sept. 16, 1760.

18 *Ibid.*, and July 20, and Feb. 13, 1761.

19 To father, Mar. 28 and Feb. 13, 1761.

20 From father, Nov. 10, 1761; to father, Sept. 16, 1760.

21 *Ibid.*, Feb. 13, Mar. 28, July 20 and 23, 1761; from father, Nov. 10, 1761 and Oct. [?] 6, 1760 (1225).

22 To father, May 15, Mar. 3, and Dec. 16, 1761; from father, Apr. 17 and Sept. 9, 1761.

23 To father, Feb. 13, Dec. 16 and 19, 1761.

24 *Ibid.* and [?], 1762.

25 To father, Sept. 16, 1760 and July 15 and 20, and Mar. 28, 1761; from father, July 14 and Oct. 13, 1760.

26 Deed from John Gittings, Esq., to Charles Carroll's father, 1753; deed of Mar. 11, 1750; Statement to Company, Nov. 3, 1759; land titles, Feb. 5, 1754, and Apr. 1781; to father, Feb. 13, Mar 28, 1761.

27 *Ibid.*, Aug. 13, 1759 (220) and Feb. 13, Mar. 3, May 16 and Dec. 19, 1761.

28 To father, Mar. 28, May 14, 15, [?] Oct. 3, 1761 and Apr. 15, 1760; Certificates of Death of Frenchman held by the Carrolls, 1761.

29 To father, Oct. 3 and Mar. 28, 1761.

Chapter 6

1 To father, Sept. 16, 1760; Apr. 15, Nov. 27, and May 22, 1760 and Mar. 3, 1761; father to Clement Hill, n.d. (1761? Rowland, I, 41).

2 Michael Macnemara to Charles' father, Feb. 10, 1761; to father, Mar. 28, July 15, 1761; to Bradshaw, Nov. 21, 1765; from father, Sept. 9, 1761 (216).

3 *DNB*, I, 613; Gillow, I, 68-70; to father, May 16, 1760, and Sept. 16, 1760, and May 14, 1761, and May 22, 1760.

4 *Ibid.*, Dec. 16, July 15 and Aug. 8, 1761 (1763? [206 I, 101]).

5 *DNB*, I, 1206-07; to father, July 15, 1761, and Jan. 14, 1770; to Graves, Aug. 15, 1774; to Jennings, Nov. 3, 1765; Hart, pp. 54, 57, 122-23, *et passim*.

6 From father, July 14, 1760; to father, Apr. 15, 1760 and July 15, 1761.

7 *Ibid.*

8 *Ibid.*, Sept. 16, 1760, and Mar. 3, 1761.

9 *Ibid.*, Jan. 29, 1760.

10 From father, Oct. 5 and 6, 1759 (220), and Mar. 22, 1761; to father, Mar. 28, 1761.

11 From father, Sept. 9, 1761 (216); to father, Dec. 25 [26?], 1759, and Feb. 13, 1761.

12 From father, Mar. 22, 1761; to father, Dec. 26 [25?], 1759 and Nov. 10, 1761.

13 To father, May 16, Sept. 16, 1760 and Mar. 28, May 14-15, 1761.

14 From father, Mar. 22, 1761.

15 To father, July 23, 1761.

16 From father, Mar. 22, 1761; to father, Dec. 16, 1761.

Chapter 7

1 To father, Oct. 11, and 13, 1761.

2 *Ibid.*, Oct. 11, 1761, and Oct. 3, 1761 [1763?] (206, I, 102).

3 To father, Oct. 11, 1761.

4 *Ibid.*, and June 14, 1763.

5 *Ibid.*, Mar. 21 [23?], 1764 and June 14, July 2, Nov. 12, Mar. 22, 1763, and Nov. 14, 1762.

6 *Ibid.*, May 14-15, 1763.

7 *Ibid.*, May 14, 1764, and Nov. 12, 1763.

8 *Ibid.*

9 *Ibid.*, Jan. 8, 1762; from father, Sept. 1, 1762, and Feb. 28, 1764.

10 *Ibid.*

11 To father, Feb. 19, 1763.

12 *Ibid.;* from Thomas [Joseph?] Baker, Dec. 15, 1763.

13 To father, Aug. 8, 1763; from father, June 22, 1763.

14 To father, Aug. 8, 1763.
15 *Ibid.,* Jan. 9, 1764, and Nov. 21, 1763.
16 *Ibid.,* Jan. 27, 1764.
17 *Ibid.*
18 From Baker, Dec. 15, 1763.
19 From father, Jan. 9, 1764.
20 *Ibid.,* Jan. 27, 1764.
21 *Ibid.,* Jan. 9, 1764.
22 *Ibid.,* Apr. 10, 1764.
23 *Ibid.,* Feb. 27-28, 1764.
24 *Ibid.,* Feb. 18 and Apr. 10, 1764.
25 *Ibid.,* and to father, Apr. 19, 1764.
26 *Ibid.,* and Mar. 21 [23?] and May 1 and 30, 1764.
27 *Ibid.,* May 10, Mar. 21 [23?], 1764.
28 To Esther Bird Browne, Oct. 6, 1766.
29 To father, July 26, 1764.
30 *Ibid.,* Apr. 19, 1764.
31 *Ibid.*
32 *Ibid.,* and May 1, 1764.

Chapter 8

1 To father, July 4, 1762.
2 *Ibid.,* Nov. 14, 1762 and Feb. 17, May 1, 1764.
3 From father, July 24, 1762; to father, Jan. 5, 1762.
4 From father, Dec. 24, 1762; to father, July 4, 1762.
5 *Ibid.*
6 To father, July 2, 1763.
7 *Ibid.*
8 To father, Mar. 21 [23?], May 30, and July 26, 1764, and Aug. 8, 1763.
9 To father, Jan. 5, 1762; from father, May 11, 1762.
10 To father, Apr. 26, Nov. 14, 1762, and Mar. 22, May 14, 1763.
11 *Ibid.,* Jan. 5, 1762.
12 To father, July 4, Apr. 26, 1762 and May 14, July 2, 1763, and Feb. 27-28, 1764.
13 To father, Feb. 5, Mar. 22, July 2, 1763 and Mar. 21 [23?], 1764 and Nov. 14, 1762; from Edward Whitten, May 28, 1763.
14 To parents, Nov. 7, 1758; to father, Jan. 8 and July 4, 1762, and Aug. 8, 1763; Rozolino to Charles' father, Mar. 3, 1758.
15 To father, Aug. 8, 1763.
16 *Ibid.,* Feb. 5, 1763.
17 *Ibid.,* Oct. 11, 1761, and June 14 and Feb. 5, 1763.
18 *Ibid.;* and June 14 and Aug. 8, 1763.
19 *Ibid.;* and July 26, 1764.
20 *Ibid.,* Jan. 27, 1764.
21 Robert Shackleton, *Montesquieu; A Critical Biography* (London, 1961), pp. 19-20, 54.

22 To father, Apr. 10, 1760; J. Steven Watson, *The Reign of George III: 1760-1815* (Oxford, 1960), pp. 4-5.

23 To father, July 26, 1764.

24 Dorothy Marshall, *Eighteenth Century England*, (New York, 1962), p. 348.

25 To father, Jan. 27, 1764.

26 *Ibid.* and Feb. 27, 1764.

27 *Ibid.*, Jan. 31, and Nov. 12, 1763, and Mar. 21 [23?], May 1, Apr. 19, and Feb. 28, 1764.

28 *Ibid.*, Apr. 19, 1764.

29 *Ibid.*, July 26, 1764.

Chapter 9

1 To father, Oct. 8 and Dec. 20, 1764.

2 To mother, Aug. 12, 1760 (431: Harper-Pennington Papers); from mother Sept. 10, 1760 (*ibid*); to father, Sept. 1, 1762, and Jan. 29, 1765.

3 To Graves, Sept. 15, 1765 (203.1); to Jennings, Nov. 23, 1765 (203.1); Carrollton Manor deeds noted 1743 and 1761 (220).

4 Contract of May 30, 1768; to Philpot, Oct. 1, 1767; to Graves, Sept. 15, 1765 (203.1).

5 To Daniel Carroll, Sept. 5, 1765, and May 26, 1766 (203.1). On his collaboration in the Baltimore Iron Works, see memorandum of company, Mar. 10, 1768 (San Francisco, Calif., Univ. of San Francisco Library). A typical operation of Charles' father as a financier is seen in his letter [to ?], Dec. 14, 1754 (*ibid.*).

6 To Bradshaw, Nov. 21, 1765 (203.1); Directive to Croxall, 1768 [?] (LC, 1684-1771, #673).

7 To Graves, Apr. 16, 1768 (203.1).

8 To Charles Carroll, Barrister, Dec. 3, 1771 (203.2); to Graves, Aug. 2, 1772 (203.2).

9 From father, Apr. 15, Nov. 8, and Nov. 30, 1771; to Graves, Mar. 7, 1772 (203.2); to Countess of Auzoüer, Sept. 20, 1771 (203.2).

18 To Charles Digges, Dec. 2, 1766 (203.1); to Bradshaw, Nov. 21, 1765 (220).

11 To Daniel Carroll, May 29, 1766 (203.1); to Gordon, July 8, 1766 (203.1); to Graves, Nov. 27, 1766 (203.1); from father, June 19, 1772, and Aug. 4, 1760 (1225) and Aug. 30, 1771; to gentlemen, July 23, 1766 (203.1), and Mar. 13, 1767 (203.1); to Philpot, Oct. 1, 1767 (203.1); to Bird, Oct. 13, 1766 (203.1); to Daniel Carroll, Aug. 9, 1771 (203.2).

12 From father, July 20, 1773; to Graves, Sept. 15, 1765 (203.1), Aug. 14, 1772 (203.2) and Nov. 7, 1767 (203.1); to Jennings, Aug. 13, 1767, and Oct. 14, 1766 (203.1); to Bird, Sept. 28, 1765 (203.1); to Richard Corbin and Robert C. Nicholas, Nov. 8, 1767 (Worcester, Mass., American Antiquarian Society).

13 To Graves, Aug. 2, 1772 (203.2), Mar. 7, 1772 (203.1), Feb. 7, 1768 (203.1 and 203.2); from father, Nov. 11 and Oct. 11, 1770.

14 To Esther Bird Browne, Oct. 6, 1766 (203.1); from father, Mar. 20, 1772; to Graves, Sept. 15, 1765 (203.1), and August 2, 1772 (203.2); Land, p. 299.

15 Hart, pp. 87-8.

16 To father, June 14, 1763; to Graves, Sept. 15, 1765 (203.1).

17 To Daniel Carroll, Sept. 5, 1765, and May 29, 1766 (203.1); from father, Sept. 10, 1772; to Graves, Apr. 16, 1768 (203.1).

18 From father, Dec. 3, Nov. 18, and Apr. 8, 1773; and Aug. 1, 1770; to Graves, Sept. 15, 1765 (203.1).

19 To Graves, *ibid.*

20 To Bradshaw, Aug. 26, 1766 (203.1); to Frances Browne, Oct. 6, 1766 (203.1); to Daniel Barrington, May 29, 1766 (203.1); to Harrison, Oct. 19, 1767 (203.1); to Bird, July 22, 1766 (203.1).

21 To Bird, Sept. 10, 1767 (203.1); to Graves, Aug. 27, 1767 (203.1).

22 To Daniel Carroll, Aug. 9, 1771 (203.1); Deards to Charles's father, Sept. 30, 1769.

23 To Jennings, Nov. 23, 1765 (203.1).

24 From father, Aug. 16, 1771; to Countess of Auzoüer, Sept. 20, 1771 (203.1).

25 To Bradshaw, Aug. 26, 1766 (203.1).

26 To Graves, Feb. 7, 1768, and Nov. 7, 1767 (203.1); from father, Jan. 9, 1764 and to father, Oct. 3, 1769; to Jennings, Oct. 14, 1766 (203.1).

27 From father, July 2, Sept. 10, Oct. 28, Mar. 11, and June 5, 1772; and July 30 and Dec. 3, 1773; and Oct. 18, 1770; Charles' father to Bishop Challoner, July 16, 1765 (Md. Province Arch. of Society of Jesus, 202 K 6).

Chapter 10

1 To Graves, Sept. 15, 1765 (203.1).

2 To Bird, Mar. 8, 1767 (203.1).

3 To Graves, Sept. 15, 1765 (203.1); to Bird, Sept. 28 and Dec. [?], 1765 (203.1); to Bradshaw, Aug. 26, 1766, and Nov. 21, 1765 (203.1).

4 To Jennings, Apr. 14, 1768 (203.1), and May 29, 1766 (in Field, p. 120); to Graves, Apr. 16, 1768 (203.1); to Esther Browne, Oct. 6, 1766 (203.1).

5 *Ibid.;* to Bradshaw, Aug. 26, 1766 (203.1); to Bird, Sept. 17, 1766 (203.1).

6 To Daniel Carroll, May 29, 1766 (203.1); to Bird, July 22, 1766 (203.1); to Graves, July 16, 1766 (203.1); to father, Aug. 14, 1759.

7 To Bird, July 22, 1766, and Sept. 17, 1766 (203.1); to Bradshaw, Aug. 26, 1766 (203.1); to gentlemen, Aug. 27, 1766 (203.1); to Esther Browne, Oct. 20 and [Frances Browne (?)], Oct. 6, 1766.

8 Marriage documents, Oct. 14, 1766 (220); to Jennings, Oct. 14, 1766, and Mar. 9, 1767 (203.1); to Graves, Nov. 27, 1766 (203.1).

9 To Jennings, Mar. 9, 1767 (203.1).

10 *Ibid.*

11 To Bird, Mar. 8, 1767 (203.1).

12 To father, Oct. 13, 1761.

13 Charles expressed his affection for Molly in gifts before his courtship. See letter to Bird, Sept. 10, 1767 (203.1).

14 Charles' father to Graves, Dec. 23, 1768; to Graves, Jan. 16, 1768 (203.1).

15 Charles' father to Graves, Dec. 23, 1768.

16 To Graves, Jan. 16, 1768, and Aug. 27, 1767 (203.1); to Jennings, Apr. 14, 1768 (203.1).

17 To Graves, Jan. 16, 1768 (203.1).

18 *Ibid.*, and Nov. 7, 1767; Jan. 22, Apr. 16, and Dec. 23, 1768 (203.1); Charles' father to Graves, Dec. 23, 1768; to gentlemen, Oct. 23, 1767, and Jan. 17, 1768 (203.1); to Thomas Digges, June 3, 1768 (216); to William Browne, Oct. 17, 1767 (203.1); to Harrison, Oct. 9, 1767 (203.1).

19 To Graves, Nov. 7, 1767, and Dec. 23, 1768 (203.1); Charles's father to Graves, Dec. 23, 1768.

20 *Ibid.;* from father, Apr. 20, 1770, and Nov. 2 and Oct. 28, 1772.

21 *Ibid.*

22 To Countess of Auzoüer, Sept. 20, 1771 (203.1); from father, May 4, Sept. 4, Apr. 26, and Aug. 27-8, 1770, and Mar. 28, 1771; to father, Apr. 27 and May 22, 1770.

23 From father, Aug. 23, 1771; to father, Nov. 8, 1771; to Charles Carroll, Barrister, Dec. 3, 1771 (203.1); Hart, pp. 90-91.

24 To Graves, Mar. 7 and Aug. 2, 1772 (203.1).

25 *Ibid.*, Aug. 15, 1774; from father, Nov. 19, 1772.

26 *Ibid.*, Sept. 6, 1772.

27 *Ibid.*, Mar. 11, 1772, and Apr. 8 and Mar. 12, 1773, and Oct. 14, 1772.

28 *Ibid.*

Chapter 11

1 From father, May 4, July 31 and Aug. 17 and 12, 1770; and Aug. 14, Sept. 22, 1772; and Apr. 8 and Nov. 26, 1773.

2 *Ibid.*, Dec. 3, 1773.

3 *Ibid.*, Apr. 25, 26, May 4, and Aug. 28, 1770; Oct. 19 and Nov. 23, 1772.

4 *Ibid.*, Sept. 15, 1771; Oct. 23, 1772; Apr. 30, 1773. On slaves working in the Baltimore Iron Works and his interest in them, see letter to secretary of province [?], June 19, 1771 (San Francisco, Calif., Univ. of San Francisco Library).

5 *Ibid.*, Apr. 25, May 4, and Aug. 27, 1770.

6 *Ibid.*, May 15 and Sept. 2, 1771; Apr. 10, 14, June 5, and Oct. 28, 1772.

7 *Ibid.*, May 7, July 16, and 31, 1770; June 23 and 26, July 2, Sept. 2 and Oct. 1772; July 20 and 23, 1773.

8 *Ibid.*, Aug. 31, 1770, and Oct. 23, 1772; Barker, p. 342.

9 From father, July 10 and Mar. 26, 1772; and Apr. 8, 1773; Company Report, Mar. 26, 1773 (LC); Land, p. 293. On loans to Catholics, see to William Brent and Agent, Mar. 25, 1769 (Cambridge, Mass., Harvard Univ. Library). As an example of his activity with the iron works, see memorandum for April 23, 1773 (*ibid.*). Charles with others provided bond for John Ridout in the position of Naval Officer; see document, Sept. 1, 1769 (Boston, Mass., Mass. Historical Society).

10 To father, May 22, 1770; from father, June 30, Oct. 14 and 19, 1772; and Apr. 30 [?], Oct. 21, 1773.

11 From Graves, Dec. 23, 1768; from father, Nov. 18, 1773; to father, Oct. 3, 1769; Shipley to Charles' father, Nov. 18, 1773.

12 *Ibid.;* to father, Oct. 3, 1769.

13 *Ibid.,* Oct. 3, 1769, Apr. 30, 1773; Incorporation Petition, Aug. 29, 1771 (220, I); from father, Aug. 9, 1770.

14 From Lloyd Dulany, Sept. 24, 1769.

15 To Lloyd Dulany, Sept. 29, 1769.

16 *Ibid.*

17 *Ibid.*

18 *Ibid.;* Deards to Charles' father, Sept. 29, 1769.

19 From Lloyd Dulany, Sept. 29, 1769. Charles wrote to Walter Dulany after this episode Aug. 11, 1772 (New York, N. Y., New York Public Library).

20 To father, Sept. 29 [-30?], 1769.

21 *Ibid.,* and Sept. 30, Oct. 2, 1769; Charles's father to Deards, Sept. 30, 1769.

22 To father, Oct. 3, 1769.

23 *Ibid.*

24 *Ibid.;* from father, Nov. 13, 1769.

25 To father, Apr. 17, 1771; to Countess of Auzoüer, Sept. 20, 1771 (203.2); from father, Apr. 13, 1770.

26 *Ibid.,* Apr. 5, 15, 1771; to father, Apr. 17, 1771.

27 *Ibid.,* May 4, 1771 and Apr. 30, 1773; from father, May 4, 6-8, 10, 1771, and Sept. 22, 28, and Oct. 28, 1772, and Apr. 8, 1773; Carroll-Digegs Account, Mar. 16, 1773 (220, I); Land, pp. 293-94.

28 From father, May 30, Aug. 8-9, Sept. 15, 1771 and July 17, 1772.

29 *Ibid.,* Nov. 30, 1770, and Aug. 16, 1771; and June 1 and Oct. 1772; to Countess of Auzoüer, Sept. 20, 1771 (203.2).

30 From father, Sept. 4, 1771, and May 27 and June 1, 1772; to William Browne, Oct. 17, 1767 (203.1); to Graves, Jan. 16, 1768 (203.1), and Aug. 9, 1771 (203.1).

31 From father, Aug. 27, Sept. 5, 1770, Aug. 26, 1771, and Mar. 17, 1772, Oct. 21 and Nov. 18, 1773; Graves to Charles' father, Jan. 14, 1770; to Daniel Carroll, Sept. 5, 1765 (203.1).

32 To Jennings, Apr. 8, 1771 (203.2).

33 To Bradshaw, Nov. 21, 1765 (203.1); to Bird, July 22, 1766 (203.1); to Daniel Barrington, May 29, 1766 (203.1); to Graves, Aug. 27, 1767 (203.1); to Jennings, Oct. 10, 1766 (203.1) and Apr. 8, 1771 (203.2). On Colonel Ludwell's bequest to Charles, see letter to executors of Ludwell's estate, Nov. 8, 1767 (Boston, Mass., Mass. Historical Society).

34 To Graves, *ibid.*

Chapter 12

1 To Graves, Aug. 2 and 14, 1772 (203.1). A listing of books chosen by Charles in November, 1767 (New York, N.Y., New York Public Library), indicates his great interest and taste in books.

2 *Ibid.,* Aug. 14, 1774 (203.2).

3 To Jennings, Oct. 14, 1766 (203.1); to Graves, Mar. 7 and Aug. 2 and 14, 1772 (203.2); from father, Mar. 27 and Nov. 8, 1771.

4 To Graves, July 16, 1766 (203.1) and Aug. 15, 1774 (203.2); to Jennings, Aug. 9, 1771 (203.1).

5 To Graves, Feb. 7, 1768 (203.1) and Aug. 14, 1772 (203.2); to Jennings, Aug. 13, 1767 (203.1).

6 To Graves, Aug. 12, 1766 (203.1) and Aug. 27, 1767 (203.1).

7 To Jennings, Oct. 14, 1766 (203.1), and Aug. 13 and 18, 1767 (203.1).

8 To Graves, Nov. 7, 1767 (203.1), and Aug. 15, 1774 (203.2).

9 *Ibid.*, Aug. 2, 1772 (203.2).

10 *Ibid.*, Apr. 5, 1771, and Aug. 15, 1774 (203.2).

11 To Daines Barrington, Aug. 29, 1767 (203.1); Stowe Persons, "The Cyclical Theory of History in Eighteenth Century America," *American Quarterly*, VI (Summer, 1954), 163.

12 *Ibid.*; to Graves, Dec. 23, 1768 (203.1) and Jan. 14, 1770 (203.2); Duncan Forbes review of *David Hume politico e storico* (1962) by G. Giarrizzo in *The Historical Journal*, VI: 2 (1962), 289 and 280-295; Peter Gay, *The Enlightenment: An Interpretation: the Rise of Modern Paganism* (New York, 1967), p. 121.

13 To Bradshaw, Nov. 21, 1765 (203.1); Peter Gay, *Voltaire's Politics: The Poet as Realist* (Princeton, 1959), pp. 167-69; J. H. Brumfitt, *Voltaire: Historian* (London, 1958), pp. 111-21.

14 To Graves, Aug. 12, 1766 (203.1) and Mar. 7 and Aug. 14, 1772 (203.2); to Jennings, Oct. 14, 1766 (203.1), and Apr. 8 and Aug. 9, 1771 (203.2); Sir William Blackstone, *Commentaries on the Laws of England*, ed. by William D. Lewis (4 vols., Philadelphia, 1902), III, 1231-3.

15 From father, Nov. 5 and Oct. 30, 1769; to Countess of Auzoüer, Sept. 20, 1771 (203.2); to Graves, Jan. 22 and Dec. 23, 1768 (203.1).

16 *Ibid.*, Aug. 27, 1767 (203.1); Barker, p. 313.

17 *Ibid.*; to Graves, Aug. 27, 1767 (203.1), and Apr. 5, 1771 (203.2); to Jennings, Mar. 9, 1767 (203.1); to Countess of Auzoüer, Sept. 20, 1771 (203.2); to Daniel Barrington, Mar. 17, 1766 (203.1).

18 *The Privileges of the Island of Jamaica Vindicated; with an Impartial Narrative of the Late Dispute between the Governor and House of Representatives upon the Case of Mr. Oliphant a Member of that House* (London, 1766 [LC]), pp. 27-8, 46-50, 64-5, 32-3; to Countess of Auzoüer, Sept. 20, 1771 (203.2).

19 To Jennings, Aug. 13, 1767 (203.1); Dec. 8, 1770 (203.2), and Apr. 8, 1771 (203.2).

20 *Ibid.*, Nov. 23, 1765 (203.1); to Daniel Barrington, Mar. 17, 1766, in Field, pp. 109-110.

21 To Graves, Aug. 12, 1766 (203.1).

22 To Jennings, Nov. 23, 1765 (203.1); to Daniel Carroll, May 29, 1766 (203.1) and Sept. 5, 1765 (203.1); Hart, p. 73.

23 To Jennings, Nov. 23, 1765 (in Field, p. 100); and May 29, 1766 (203.1); to gentleman, Oct. 5, 1765 (203.1).

24 To Jennings, Nov. 23, 1765 (203.1); to Bradshaw, Dec. 8, 1765 (in Field, pp. 101-103); to Daniel Barrington, Dec. 22, 1765, and Mar. 17, 1766 (in Field, pp. 103-106, 108-114); Barker, ch. 3.

25 To Graves, Sept. 15, 1765 (203.1); to Bird, Sept. 28, 1765 (203.1); to Bradshaw, Nov. 21, 1765 (203.1); Hart, p. 73.

26 To Jennings, Mar. 9, 1767 (203.1); to Daniel Carroll, May 29, 1766 (203.1).

27 To Jennings, May 29, 1766 (203.1).

28 *Ibid.*

29 To Graves, July 16, 1766 (203.1) and Nov. 7, 1767 (203.1); to Jennings, Mar. 9, 1767 (203.1).

30 To Graves, Nov. 1767 (203.1); Charles' father to Graves, Dec. 23, 1768; to father, Oct. 3, 1769.

31 To Bird, July 22, 1766 (203.1); to Graves, Sept. 15, 1765 (203.1); to Daniel Barrington, Mar. 17 (in Field, p. 109), and May 29, 1766 (203.1).

32 To Bird, Dec. [?], 1765 (in Field, p. 107); to Bradshaw, Nov. 21, 1765 (203.1).

33 To Graves, Apr. 16, 1768 (203.1); to Daniel Barrington, Mar. 17, 1766 (in Field, pp. 108-109); to Bird, Oct. 5, 1765 (203.1).

34 To Graves, Sept. 15, 1765 (203.1); to Daniel Barrington, Dec. 22, 1765 (in Field, pp. 105-106).

35 From father, May, 1770; Charles' father to Graves, Dec. 23, 1768; Graves to Charles' father, Jan. 14, 1770.

36 To Graves, Jan. 16, 1768 (203.1); to Daniel Barrington, Mar. 17, 1766 (in Field, pp. 112-113); from father, May 4, 1770; Barker, pp. 315-316, 320-328.

37 To Daniel Barrington, Mar. 17, 1766 (in Field, p. 110); to Jennings, Dec. 8, 1770 (203.2).

Chapter 13

1 Edward S. Delaplaine, "The Life of Thomas Johnson," *Maryland Historical Magazine,* XIV (Mar., 1919), 37-46, 53, 185-186; from father, May 7, 1771.

2 Delaplaine, *MHM,* XIV, 196-198.

3 *Ibid.,* XIV, 177; *Maryland Gazette,* Sept. 23, 1773.

4 "William Paca," *Dictionary of American Biography* (22 vols., New York, 1928-58), XIV, 123-124.

5 "Samuel Chase," *ibid.,* IV, 34-37; *Maryland Gazette,* Sept. 23, 1773.

6 Barker, p. 359.

7 *Ibid.,* pp. 360-361.

8 *Ibid.,* pp. 361-362; from father, Nov. 8, 1771.

9 To Charles Carroll, Barrister, Dec. 3, 1771 (203.2); Daniel Carroll to Charles' father, Apr. 14, 1771.

10 From father, Dec. 5, 1770, and Apr. 12, 1771 and June 30 and Sept. 11, 1772; *Maryland Gazette,* Sept. 23, 1773.

11 Daniel Dulany, *The Right to the Tonnage, the Duty of Twelve Pence per Hogshead on all Exported Tobacco, and the Fines and Forfeitures in the Province of Maryland, State; in a Letter from a Gentleman in Annapolis to his Friend in the Country* (Annapolis, 1766), p. 276.

12 From father, May 22, 1770, Sept. 4 and 13, 1771, and Aug. 14, 1772; to Daniel Carroll, Aug. 9, 1771 (203.2).

13 To Charles Carroll, Barrister, Dec. 3, 1771 (203.2); from father, Oct. 28, 1772.

14 To Countess of Auzoüer, Sept. 20, 1771 (203.2); Barker, pp. 347-348; from father, Oct. 11, 18, 30, and Nov. 10 and 30, 1770.

15 From father, Oct. 18 and 30, Nov. 2 and 30, 1770 and Apr. 12, 1771 and Sept. 22, 1772.

16 From father, Nov. 30, 1770, and Apr. 2, 5 and 15, 1771.

17 *Ibid.*, Apr. 12 and Nov. 6, 1771; Barker, p. 349.

18 *Ibid.*, Nov. 6 and 13, 1771; and Sept. 17 and Nov. 23, 1772.

19 *Maryland Gazette*, Jan. 21, 1773.

20 *Ibid.*, Jan. 28 and Feb. 4, 1773.

21 *First Citizen*, pp. 44-52.

22 *Maryland Gazette*, Feb. 11 and 15, 1773.

23 *First Citizen*, pp. 54-68, 59.

24 *Maryland Gazette*, Mar. 11, 1773.

25 *Ibid.*, and Feb. 11, 1773.

26 *First Citizen*, pp. 76, 72-94.

27 *On Privileges of the Island of Jamaica Vindicated. . .*, see above ch. 12, footnote 18, and related text.

Chapter 14

1 From father, Mar. 17 and 20 and Apr. 1, 1773.

2 *Ibid.; Maryland Gazette*, Mar. 18 and 25, 1773.

3 *Ibid.*, Mar. 18 and 25, and Apr. 1 and 29, 1773; from father, Mar. 12, 17 and 25, and Apr. 1 and 8, 1773.

4 Jennifer to Charles's father, Mar. 28, 1773; Charles's father to Jennifer, Apr. 2, 1773.

5 To father, Mar. 17, 1773; from father, Mar. 17, 20 and 25, and Apr. 8, 1773.

6 To father, Apr. 3-4, 1773.

7 *First Citizen*, pp. 96-119.

8 *Maryland Gazette*, Apr. 8, 1773.

9 To father, Apr. 3 [30?], 1773; from father, Apr. 13 and 16, and May 6, 1773.

10 *First Citizen*, pp. 142-143, 123, 132, 140, 136, 129, 124.

11 *Ibid.*, pp. 125-126, 139, 146.

12 *Ibid.*, pp. 138, 120-122, 146.

13 *Maryland Gazette*, May 20 and 27, 1773; from father, May 14, and 20, 1773.

14 *Ibid.*, May 15, 1773; *Maryland Gazette*, May 13 and June 3, 1773.

15 *Ibid.*, May 13 and 27, 1773; from father, May 15, 1773.

16 *Maryland Gazette*, June 4, 1773.

17 *Ibid.*

18 From father, June 4, 13, 18, and 24, 1773.

19 *First Citizen*, pp. 220-222, 223, 227, 232.

20 *Ibid.*, pp. 230-231.

21 *Ibid.*

22 Barker, pp. 354-355.

23 From father, July 20 and 30, and Aug. 26, 1773.

24 *Maryland Gazette*, July 29, Sept. 23, and Oct. 7, 1773; Land, p. 305.

25 *Maryland Gazette*, Aug. 19 and Oct. 21, 1773; from father, July 20, 1773.

26 From father, July 30, and Dec. 3, 1773; Barker, pp. 368-369.

27 *Maryland Gazette*, Sept. 9, 1773.

28 *Ibid.*, Oct. 7 and 21, 1773; Barker, p. 358; from father, Nov. 18, 1773.

29 To father, Oct. 27, 1774.

INDEX

1

HQ ADULT
241430
CARROLL HAN
Hanley, Thomas O'Brien.
Charles Carroll of Carrollton: